IMPLEMENTATION GUIDE

LEVELED
Book room

SCHOLASTIC

Table of Contents

Table of Contents

USING YOUR
LEVELED BOOKROOMS

All children need to be surrounded by a full and rich range of books in order to become fully engaged readers. Becoming literate means being able to read and write for many different purposes. And once students have started on this path, teachers need to keep assisting students to expand their learning, explore their curiosities, extend their questions, and deepen their understandings. According to many current educators, such as Clay (1991) and Fountas and Pinnell (1996), the teacher's role involves setting students "on a self-expanding system" that enables them to keep learning.

Similarly, Wilhelm (2004) believes this process of ongoing learning is based on *inquiry*. He states, "The criteria of good inquiry are the same as the criteria of good questioning and good discussion, because effective questioning and conversation are forms of inquiry into specific texts or ideas." Wilhelm often cites Wiggins and McTighe (1998) for their classic approach to learning through *understanding by design*. Instead of "instruction by mentioning" (Wiggins and McTighe in Wilhelm, 2004), research shows how important it is to teach for *understanding*. Such a process involves unpacking for students the story behind the facts and presenting them as *useful* and "worth understanding" (17).

What makes something useful to students? As Robb (2004) suggests, teachers improvise as do jazz musicians. Teachers' "improvisations are sensitive to the needs of their students within the context of the lesson." Robb finds that responsive teaching includes scaffolding strategies within lessons that engage students—especially through think-alouds and talking. "When students talk, they are thinking out loud, . . . making connections and deepening their understanding" (5).

In guided reading, the teacher's starting goal should be to provide the most effective instruction and strategic activities for engaging students, followed by matching resources to the students' needs and interests (Iaquinta, 2006). Then, teachers need to gather students in flexible, supportive groups, ensuring that students feel a part of a "community of readers" (414). Continually changing the composition of the group, according to the needs of different students, keeps small group reading fresh for students.

Fountas and Pinnell (2006, 329) suggest that providing children with a real foundation for a literate life does not just happen. Rather, it is a conscious thing. They suggest setting up early experiences having characteristics where:

- **reading is seen as a valued activity**
- **people close to children talk about reading**
- **wide varieties of books are available**
- **people own books and often read them many times**

One way of participating in constructing such valuable settings for students is through guided reading and its implementation through leveled bookrooms. Pages 18–22 of this Guide focus on these issues.

RESEARCH
FOUNDATION

Background on Book Leveling

Prior to Fountas and Pinnell's leveling work, Peterson (1991) developed a system for selecting books, beginning at level 1, involving books with one-sentence patterns, and proceeding through ever more complex books to end at level 20, involving material usually found at the end of first grade.

Later, researchers such as Short, Kane, Peeling (2000) found the characteristics Fountas and Pinnell used to create a text gradient were broad and most apt: "diversity, interest to children, breadth of genre, curriculum links, content, length, format, and quality of illustrations" (286). The Short et. al (2000) research project focused on a Title 1 group of students, grades 1-3, in a small town in Virginia. They based their work on using a small group approach to reading and, not wanting to "re-create the wheel," Short used the Fountas and Pinnell book list to guide the text selection.

Cornwell's (2009-1996) research indicates that an "appropriate match can mean the difference between a student becoming a confident, skilled reader or a frustrated, struggling reader." Leveled books offers teachers, Cornwell says, the precision of fitting instruction to student needs and supporting them with a system that moves away from "one size fits all." Instead of readability formulas "that focus on units of measures," Cornwell finds that "leveling systems focus on such factors as complexity of concepts, syntax, ... length of text on a page, ... and amount of contextual supports." In this way, leveling systems are built on qualitative and descriptive norms rather than quantitative ones.

While there is excellent research behind most leveling systems, no matching system takes the place of the teachers' knowledge of students and the instructional way in which teachers connect the reader with information about the text. This kind of matching is a balancing act. Similarly, Dzaldov and Peterson (2005) assert the importance of the reader-text interactions. They cite Fountas and Pinnell's (1999, 3) caution about using descriptors such as "easy" or "hard" in broad ways. "A text that is 'just right' is termed that way because it 'provides the context for successful reading work and enables readers to strengthen their processing power'" (223). The leveling Fountas and Pinnell established goes from A to Z, beginning with a reader's ability to read one line that repeats and continues to highly complex, multi-plot texts at level Z.

Dzaldov and Peterson reiterate how much the success of selecting leveled books that match students rests on teachers' willingness to take time to survey students' self-interest and background. In so doing, they gain valuable information about the students (227). Dzaldov and Peterson concluded their study by finding that "teachers 'familiarity with their students' backgrounds, interests, and sociocultural identities is at least as important in identifying appropriate books for students as are lists based on book, print, language, and literary uniformity" (228).

As Rosenblatt (1991) points out, what is at stake is "each child's total school experience—in speech, reading, and writing. ... No one episode ... will be decisive. But [each experience] will either reinforce or weaken the student's sense of the diverse possibilities of texts—and of the world" (448). Thus, many teachers believe, with Vygotsky, that to scaffold instruction for students with tasks in their zone of proximal development, states Robb (2004), will mean that "children learn new skills and strategies . . . that they can accomplish with the help of the teacher or peer" (5).

What Are Leveled Bookrooms?

The environment that builds this sense of success in students, and in the group as "a community of readers," contributes to the important place of the leveled bookroom in the big picture of literacy. In Keene's (2008) in-depth analysis of what it means to understand, she describes the climate necessary for literacy learning. In so doing, she often divides the tasks between teacher and students— both of whom need to be actively engaged in the leveled bookroom process. Her optimal literacy environment includes one that looks like it shares the foundation and goal of leveled bookrooms:

Teacher	Students
Create a culture conducive to in-depth study of a variety of books, genres, topics, authors, writer's tools, and comprehension strategies	Select books, topics, and authors appropriate for level, challenge, interest; engage in book discussions; share recommendations and insights with other readers; seek to understand the insights of others (p 32)

Leveled bookrooms are a tool, and a place. They are not teaching, but the bookrooms require teacher instruction. The leveled bookroom is based on gathering books and organizing them by level to support an ongoing process for reading, thinking, talking, and writing—so that all contribute to building ever-deeper understandings. The bookroom is a thing or a tool, based on significant concepts. It relies on guided reading and leads to independent reading.

Independent reading, according to Fountas and Pinnell (2006) is not "free reading." On the contrary, at all levels, independent reading is "surrounded by a strong instructional frame" (334). The structure of the guided reading approach always leads toward what matters most in developing competent readers—quantity, time, variety, choice, fluency, and conversation (335-336). The teachers' role is to help students consistently choose books that they can read "with understanding and fluency and to have a conversation about those books." This kind of reading allows students to come away from books with "a satisfying feeling of having enjoyed a text" (336).

Gradient

Fountas and Pinnell, having created a gradient for moving through leveled readers from easy to more complex, define the purpose of a gradient this way:

Creating a text gradient means classifying books along a continuum based on the combination of variables that support and confirm readers' strategic actions and offer the problem-solving opportunities that build the reading process (Fountas and Pinnell 1996, 113).

What may sound like an overly organized style or a "housekeeping detail" is far from the reality of making use of leveled books along a continuum (Fountas and Pinnell, 2006). Having leveled books for students has "everything to do with successful processing" (152) as students read and engage in all the activities surrounding comprehending—thinking, talking, writing.

Obviously, then, the levels of books are not organized so that students simply want to "move up a level" (Fountas and Pinnell, 2006). Rather, the purpose of the teacher support and instruction is to ensure that students are reading "widely and thoughtfully" (153) and with ease at one level before reading texts at a more difficult level. Then students choose books—not by the letter of the alphabet—but for the high interest or compelling cover of a title.

FROM **A LEVELED BOOKROOM TO CLASSROOM**: THE HOW-TO OF LEVELED BOOKROOMS

"Reading is the new civil right."
Phyllis C. Hunter

Leveled reading instruction enables teachers to tailor reading instruction to meet individual students' needs. Here are some leveled reading instruction characteristics that highlight its advantages:

Match readers to "just right" text.	Educational psychologist Lev Vygotsky (1978) suggests that effective learning takes place in the "zone of proximal development." This "zone" is when you use skills that you haven't quite mastered but are on the verge of grasping.
Provide a wide variety of texts that are interesting, appropriate, and personally relevant.	Students are naturally motivated to read about something that is important in his or her life. Hunter et. al (2005) show how the right connection between a student's interest and the right book can change a reluctant reader to an enthusiastic reader. This includes books of various levels of difficulty as well as different content areas, genres, and formats.
Group students who are similar in their development at a particular point in time.	Forming small groups of students with similar needs and interests is one way for reading teachers and coaches to match books to readers. As readers grow in proficiency in their own way and develop new interests, the groups change.
Provide small group instruction/guided reading options for small groups of students at similar levels.	Once a text is selected, the teacher or reading coach introduces it and "sets the scene" for reading and supporting comprehension. Then members of the group read it to themselves as the teacher monitors. Afterward, the teacher can make several teaching points based on observation. Members of the group can also engage in literature discussions, independent reading, lessons on words and word usage, and writing.
Measure and monitor student progress.	Leveled reading instruction provides a measurable means of monitoring student progress. Research (Braunger & Lewis, 1998) has shown that teachers must engage in frequent assessment as they encourage students to monitor their own reading progress through charts or reading logs, keeping track of books they've read, words they've learned, or time they've spent reading. Studies conducted by the Center for the Improvement of Early Reading Achievement (Taylor & Pearson, 2004) have shown that high performance in elementary schools has been linked to frequent, consistent student assessment and high levels of student engagement.

Advantages of a Leveled Book Collection

Organizing a leveled bookroom can begin with:

- Colleagues collecting a large set of books, with multiple copies, gathered from various classrooms.
- Gradually, categories evolve and a continuum of difficulty emerges.

Leveled bookrooms are highly cost-effective.	Leveled bookrooms offer an opportunity for schools and districts to invest funds in resources that will benefit multiple classrooms and grade levels. When numerous instructors have access to the same material, monies can be stretched further and still allow for individual classroom needs.
Leveled bookrooms promote a shared vision about learning among teachers across all grade levels.	Creating a bookroom encourages people to pool resources in a central location, which becomes a gathering place for teachers and associates. All teachers become familiar with books being used across the grade levels and can see visible evidence of a reading continuum. Fountas and Pinnell (2006) recommend pooling resources, because this practice encourages administrators and community members to all work together to promote success for students in the school environment.
A well organized, user-friendly bookroom encourages frequent use.	While this is an exciting opportunity, the prospect of creating a leveled bookroom can also be a challenging one. It is extremely important that the leveled bookroom be well organized and user-friendly. A little planning may make the difference in whether or not teachers and students use the room as often and as efficiently as possible. Pages 13–21 in this Guide are a blueprint for organizing and managing a leveled-bookroom. The following suggestions come from interviews with teachers and staff members who have created these rooms in their schools and districts and have compiled the information to make the process easier.

HOW TO GET
STARTED

Gathering your collection

A school bookroom, says Hunter (2004), like a good classroom library, should support, enhance, and elevate all students. It is imperative to find a wide variety of books to meet an enormous range of interests and curriculum needs. The books should match varying reading levels of students at each grade level at different points in time.

The International Reading Association, in partnership with various groups such as the Children's Book Council, the National Science Teacher's Association, and the National Council for Social Studies, produce yearly lists of best books for students: Kids' Choice, Teacher's Choice, and Notable Science and Social Studies Trade Books. In addition, Scholastic offers an excellent resource to begin a leveled reading collection:

Scholastic Teacher Book Wizard

A searchable database of book titles Teacher Book Wizard saves time and enables educators to quickly identify the levels of all of the books in their collection. Users can search for titles by interest level and by Lexile® Levels, guided reading levels, or by grade-equivalent levels. Teacher Book Wizard can locate titles to support the various themes and topics being explored in class, or one can search by genre, award winners, series/programs, and more!

Scholastic Leveled Reading Bookroom Collections

To ensure that a leveled bookroom is as useful as possible as soon as possible, Scholastic Leveled Bookroom collections offer three large bundles of captivating leveled books. Each of the Scholastic Leveled Bookroom collections, for either K–3, 4-6 or K–6 bookrooms, provide a strong start with titles that include a variety of genres, topics, and content area knowledge to expand the reading experiences of each student at the "just-right" level. All the Scholastic Leveled Bookroom collections include carefully leveled, high quality, engaging titles. In addition, each book is accompanied by a teaching card that contains skills and strategies to help educators differentiate instruction for each student. The collections also offer corresponding quizzes to match each title. Scholastic guarantees that there will be no title overlap within the collection.

Scholastic Guided Reading: 6-Book Sets

Each leveled set contains six copies of a best-selling fiction or nonfiction title and is accompanied by guided-reading suggestions. This makes it easy to add to and update the bookroom with high-interest books for grades K–6.

Building your collection

It is often easy to supplement and expand an established leveled book collection. The following steps can be helpful for educators who wish to supplement their bookroom collections:

Inventory the books in the school's classrooms.	This process uses existing resources to support the bookroom initiative, and it enables all the teachers and reading coaches in the school to participate in the effort. Classroom teachers can evaluate and update classroom libraries and determine which books can best be pooled for use in the bookroom. As it introduces the leveled reading concept, this process also reinforces ways in which the project benefits the entire school community. Scholastic provides an online tool for an initial evaluation of classroom libraries for titles, duplicates, book sets, fiction and nonfiction genres, etc. To access Evaluation Protocol Questions, go to **www.scholastic.com/classroombooks**
Level the books added to the existing inventory.	There are a number of book leveling systems available. When reviewing leveling systems, be sure to check with the district to determine whether the state has leveling guidelines that must be followed. The three most commonly used book-leveling systems are: Fountas & Pinnell's Guided Reading Levels, Developmental Reading Assessment (DRA), and Lexile Levels: • **Fountas & Pinnell's Guided Reading Levels: Created by Irene Fountas and Gay Su Pinnell (2006), these levels range from A to Z.** • **Developmental Reading Assessment (DRA): Created by Pearson Education, Inc., DRA levels range from 1 to 44.** • **Lexile Levels: Created by Metametrics, Inc., Lexile levels range from 200L to 1700L. This scale is based upon sentence length and word frequency and is one of the most commonly used scales in leveled reading instruction. It is not necessary to select just one system. The Scholastic Leveling Chart pictured on page 101 of this Guide shows how easy it is to use all three.**

Regardless of which system chosen, it is important to accomplish two objectives:

Train users on the book-leveling system you select.	It is important that bookroom users understand the system and know how to use it. Familiarity with the system enables instructors to be more effective in the classroom; teachers and reading specialists can also more easily identify the levels of books that have not already been leveled. It is useful to organize book-leveling training sessions or workshops during the summer or on staff development days. Contact a Scholastic representative to locate a training session nearby.
Prominently display Scholastic's "Reading Level Correlations" chart (on page 99 of this Guide) in a bookroom and familiarize users with the chart.	The colorful, easy-to-read chart saves time and allows users to align Scholastic's leveling system, based on Fountas & Pinnell's guided-reading system, with the DRA and Lexile systems. The levels on the chart have been broadly aligned with grades K–6 according to the recommendations of Scholastic's reading experts and professional educators. The "Meeting Your Leveling Needs" chart is an easy, effective tool for busy educators who strive to help every child become a successful reader by matching each student with the right material at the right time.

SET PROCEDURES

Evaluating Needs

Establishing a bookroom will take time and will naturally involve additions, deletions, and other changes. Once the existing collection is inventoried, compare the collection with school or district mandates and other actual needs.

Assess current leveled bookroom needs.	The needs will depend in part on the number of students and classrooms in the school. While this may vary, it is helpful to have at least six copies of each book title in your collection—one book for each student to use during small-group reading instruction. Also, having extra classroom copies available is a powerful tool for reinforcement. Once a child has read and mastered a book in his or her reading center, he or she may wish to return to it during free or independent reading periods.
Create and maintain separate collections for classroom and reading specialist instruction.	Building different collections for each instructional environment prevents repetition for students who are working with reading specialists. It also allows students to practice reading independently with titles that are at or even slightly below their reading levels. 

Establishing the leveled bookroom location

The leveled bookroom is an important support to leveled reading and small-group instruction. Choose a location that is convenient, useful and comfortable for all users.

Closet, Cloakroom, or Vacant Office	Many schools place their collection in a large supply closet. This closet may be used exclusively for the book collection, or it may also house supplies and lesson plans that can be used with each title. This is a useful location because it is quiet, out of the way, and because students will not be able to access it.
Teacher's Lounge	If the school has a large teacher's lounge, teachers may browse through the collection. This location may help to integrate the collection into the faculty's everyday thinking and activities.

Library	Several reasons make this an appropriate location: the school librarian can help manage the collection; the leveled bookroom check-out procedures can tie into the existing library system; and teachers are more likely to remember to return their books to the library than to a separate room.
Reading Specialist's Office/ Classroom	This location allows the reading specialist easy and convenient access to the collection.
Classroom	A lightly used classroom is a good location because teachers visit it regularly.

Working Together

Regardless of the location of the collection, it's always helpful for colleagues to work together to select an optimal and central location so that leveled classroom libraries support the bookroom. This way, teachers have their own easily accessible collections to supplement the titles in the leveled reading collection. Here are some additional issues to consider:

Is the collection conveniently located?	Will all teachers and associates know where it is and be able to access it at different times during the day?
Will students have access to the collection?	To ensure that the collection remains intact, we suggest that access to the collection be restricted to teachers and staff.
Is the space sufficient to accommodate a growing collection?	It is preferable to start in a larger space and aspire to grow into it, rather than coping with clutter and resulting disorganization as your collection outgrows the space allocated for its storage.
Is the room well lit, comfortable, and easy?	It is important to design an area where teachers want to spend time browsing.
Is there space to post bookroom policies and Scholastic's "Reading Level Correlations" chart?	Conspicuously posting policies and leveling charts in the bookroom ensures that all users are aware of the procedures for borrowing and returning books, and it enables them to select the best books for their students.

Organize the Leveled Bookroom

Organizing the leveled bookroom may be the most important task of all. A well-organized room will ensure that users are able to optimize the benefits of having a leveled bookroom because they will be able to use it efficiently and will actually enjoy using it. A well-organized room will also enable collection managers to keep track of the collection and may reduce the wear and tear sustained by the collection. There are two commonly used storage options for your bookroom:

Hanging bags and Storage boxes

Hanging bags　Rather than using bookshelves, use plastic hanging bags for the books. This is a useful way to separate the books, make it easy for teachers to transport the books to and from the classroom, and may protect the books from wear and tear. If using hanging bags, they should be labeled. In addition to labeling the storage boxes or bags, it is important to label each individual book. When labeling books, place the label in a place where it will not fall off, such as the front or back cover.

Do not place labels on or around the book spine because they tend to fall off more quickly. Include the following information in the labels:

- **Title**
- **Level (some prefer to use color coding to indicate levels)**
- **Fiction/nonfiction designation**
- **Running word count**
- **Number of copies in the set**
- **Publisher (if a book in the set is lost, it will be easier to replace it if the publisher's information is readily available)**

Storage boxes　Use magazine boxes, shoeboxes, cut cereal boxes, or plastic tubs to store the books. Depending on the size of the boxes, it is possible to store one or multiple titles in each box. For example, if using magazine boxes, store one title in each box. If using plastic tubs, designate one tub per level and put all of that level's titles in the one tub. Each box should be clearly labeled, and the label should be easy to read when the box is on the shelf. If storing one title per box, the label should have the same information listed above.

Check-out procedures

Schools have identified a number of methods to keep track of their collections, and it is important to select a system that works for the school. Some common practices include the following:

Clothespin system	This system is most effective for bookrooms with separate boxes for each book. Gather a set of clothespins, set aside 8–10 clothespins per teacher, and label each with the teacher's name. Teachers can store their own clothespins, or they can all be stored in the bookroom. When teachers borrow a set of books, they clip a clothespin to the box indicating who has taken the collection.
Card system	This system is most effective for bookrooms with collections bundled together in bags or with rubber bands. Within each collection, include a card labeled with the title, level, and number of books. Place a bulletin board on the bookroom wall, listing each teacher's name and a corresponding bag or pocket. When teachers borrow a collection, they remove the card from the collection and place it in their own bag or pocket.
Notebook system	This may be the simplest of all check-out systems. Simply provide a notebook in which teachers sign out the title of the book and the number of copies borrowed. When they return the book, they cross their name off the list.
Other systems	Here are some suggestions for other check-out systems: • **Use the existing library check-out system, particularly if the collection is stored in the library.** • **Assign one staff person to the bookroom. Teachers place their bookroom orders with this person, who checks the books in and out. This staff person may want to create and maintain a computer spreadsheet with all of the relevant information.**

Book return procedures

There are two common book return procedures:

Individual returns	Each borrower returns his or her books and places them back on the shelves. In this case, the teacher is responsible for correctly reshelving the books and removing the clothespin or card from the book box or bulletin board.

Centralized returns	Borrowers return their books to a central location and designated staff reshelf the books. Depending on the size of the collection, there maybe multiple bins for returned books; for instance, bins for levels A–D, E–H, etc. If it's a smaller collection, one bin may be sufficient. In addition to the return bins, it's helpful to use a separate bin for incomplete collections. This ensures that an incomplete set of books is not reshelved and enables you to set the collection aside until a lost book is found or replaced.

Bookroom staffing

Some schools may be able to designate a staff member (usually a reading specialist) to manage the leveled bookroom. Here are two other options.

Rotate teachers	Set a schedule for bookroom staffing. Designate a month of bookroom management for each grade, and the team of teachers in that grade level is responsible for reshelving books and monitoring the room's cleanliness and organization during a given month.
Volunteers or aides	Bookroom management offers an outstanding opportunity for an older student, a dedicated parent volunteer, or a classroom aide. This arrangement gives more mature students, parents, and aides the opportunity to get involved in the school and also helps them to better understand the importance of leveled guided reading.

Plan for the Future

After you complete your existing inventory, consider your school's future needs and identify the gaps in your collection. For instance, if you are in a rapidly growing, younger community, it may be useful to focus on lower-level book acquisition first. If your school cannot afford to purchase a collection all at once, strive to fill the collection's most pressing gaps first. Set realistic objectives for this process. It is useful to think of your leveled-bookroom project as one that will span several years, rather than something to be accomplished in a short period of time. A great leveled bookroom continues to grow year after year. Here are some useful suggestions for building your collection and ensuring that it will be sustainable well into the future.

Be sure to include funds for book replacement in the budget.	A leveled reading program works best when teachers are able to send books home with students, encouraging reading both in the classroom and at home. As such, some of the books will be damaged or lost. It will be important to replace these books.

Strive for variety in the collection.	Students are more likely to develop a lifelong love of reading when they are interested in the books they are reading. Offer fiction and nonfiction as well as content area titles, ensuring that the collection covers many topics, appealing to students with all types of interests.
Match the books in the collection with the curriculum.	Review the curriculum and select expository texts at various levels that coordinate with the curriculum. For example, if your kindergarten curriculum includes a section focused on animals, reinforce your students' learning during leveled reading sessions by including such titles as the following:

- **My Cats, Level A**
- **Animal Homes, Level B**
- **Mice Squeak, We Speak, Level C**
- **Where Is Max?, Level D**

This method enables teachers to reinforce their subject lessons during small-group reading instruction.

CONCLUSION

Taking efforts in establishing a leveled bookroom today will impact hundreds, if not thousands, of children in the future. This resource will not only support education professionals to inspire their students to learn to read, but also help accelerate students academic achievement through school and into adulthood.

Establishing a leveled bookroom is a large task. Make the leveled bookroom user-friendly and easily accessible to maximize the benefit of this invaluable instructional tool. Creating a well organized, forward-thinking leveled bookroom will set up everyone for success for years to come.

As educational consultant Phyllis C. Hunter reminds us, "Reading is the new civil right." The International Reading Association also declares, "Children have a right to reading instruction that builds both the skill and the desire to read increasingly complex materials." And in the wise words of the educator, Louise Rosenblatt, "We need to make sure that students are cumulatively developing, in their transactions with texts, the ability to adopt the stance on the continuum appropriate to their particular personal purposes and to the situation" (448).

In that spirit, Scholastic has developed an engaging, comprehensive leveled-reading collection to partner with you in the effort to cultivate in all children a lifelong love of reading.

USING YOUR
GUIDED READING PROGRAM

The *Scholastic Guided Reading Program* is a varied collection of books that are categorized by the kind and level of challenge they offer children as they are learning to read. The Guided Reading Program consists of 260 books organized into 26 levels of difficulty—Levels A–Z. Many different characteristics of the texts are considered in determining the level of challenge and support a particular book or shorter story presents.

Advantages of a Leveled Book Collection

A leveled book set has many advantages, including the following:

- **It provides experience with a wide variety of texts within a level.**
- **It makes it easier to select books for groups of children.**
- **It lends itself to flexible grouping.**
- **It provides a way to assess children's progress.**
- **It provides a basic book collection that can be expanded over time.**

Multiple Copies of Books	Six copies of each book are provided so that children in small groups will have access to their own copies. Having a collection of books on various levels, with multiple copies of each book, allows you to consider individual strengths when grouping and selecting books. To help you identify a book's level quickly, you may place a Guided Reading Program sticker for the level on the front or back of each book cover.
Flexibility of Use	With a gradient of text, grouping can be more flexible. Children might read only some of the books in a level, and not necessarily in the same sequence. In addition, children may change groups based on individual needs. The **Characteristics of Text** and **Behaviors to Notice and Support**, on pages 100–125, will assist you in placing children in the appropriate levels.
	If you note that some students need extra support for a particular text or that the selection is too difficult for most of the group, you can abandon guided reading and instead use shared reading to experience the book. Then you can select an easier book the next day. As students progress, have them reread books on a lower level for enjoyment. Students will become more confident readers as they reread a book for meaning with no need for problem solving.
Adding to the Guided Reading Program	The Guided Reading Program has been designed with adaptability in mind, so you may add copies of children's and your own favorite books to the library. You may place a Guided Reading Program sticker for the suggested level on each book you add.

Variety Within Levels in the Collection

When working with groups in classroom reading, a broad base of text is needed. The Guided Reading Program provides this broad base. Readers who experience only one kind of book may develop a narrow range of strategies for processing text. With a leveled set, difficulty is controlled because all text characteristics have been factored in. Yet the level of text is not artificially controlled because the variety of text characteristics occurs within natural story language.

The early levels of the Guided Reading Program introduce students to reading print. While reading at these beginning levels, students apply phonics skills, develop a core of high-frequency words, work with print in a variety of layouts, and engage with a variety of high-interest texts.

Books at later levels (Levels J and beyond) include a wider range of text. Within each level, literary texts are included. Essentially, there are three kinds of books at these levels, although there is variety within each category.

- **First, there are picture books at a more sophisticated level than before. These picture books provide an opportunity to expand vocabulary, to interpret stories, and to recognize how illustrations contribute to the story. Like the short story, picture books provide the advanced reader with complex reading material that does not take several days to complete.**

- **Second, there are informational books that are generally shorter. These present complex ideas and some technical language. They challenge students to acquire and discuss ideas and information and to go beyond the text to research topics of interest to them.**

- **Third, there are longer stories and chapter books. These longer selections provide an opportunity for readers to sustain reading over time, remembering details and getting to know characters as they develop.**

FACTORS CONSIDERED IN
LEVELING BOOKS

In placing a book, short story, or article along a gradient of text, multiple characteristics of text are considered. Here is a sample list.

Book and Print Features
Refers to the physical aspects of the text—what readers cope with in terms of length, size, print layout, and font size. It also refers to the interpretation of illustrations and the relationships between information in graphics and the body of the text.

- How many words are in the book?
- How many lines of text are on each page?
- How many pages are in the book?
- What size is the print?
- How much space is there between words and lines?
- How easy is it to find information?
- What is the relationship between print and illustrations?
- Are there graphics (photos, diagrams, maps) that provide essential information and how easy are the graphics to interpret?
- What are the features of print layout? (For example, do sentences begin on the left or do they "wrap around" so that end punctuation must be relied upon?)
- Is print placed in standard, predictable places on the pages or is it used in creative ways that require the reader's flexibility?
- Do the size and shape of book, binding, and layout play a role in text interpretation?

Genre
Means the "type" or "kind" and refers to a classification system formed to provide a way of talking about what texts are like (fiction—including realistic fiction, fantasy, traditional literature; and nonfiction—including biography, autobiography, and informational texts).

- What is the "genre" or "kind" of book?
- What special demands does this genre make on readers?
- Is this an easy or more difficult example of the genre?

Content
Refers to the subject matter that readers are required to understand as they read both fiction and nonfiction texts.

- What background information is essential for understanding this text?
- What new information will readers need to grasp to read the text?
- How accessible is the content to the readers?

Themes and Ideas
Refers to the "big picture," the universality of the problem in the text and its relevance to people's lives.

- What is the theme of the text?
- Are there multiple themes that the reader must understand and be able to talk about?
- How accessible are the "big ideas" to the reader?

Language and Literary Features

Refers to the writer's style and use of literary devices. Literary features are those elements typically used in literature to capture imagination, stir emotions, create empathy or suspense, give readers a sense that the characters and story are real, and make readers care about the outcome of the plot. Nonfiction books may incorporate some literary features.

- From what perspective is the story or informational text written?
- Does the book include devices such as headings, labels, and captions?
- Are graphical elements such as diagrams, tables, charts, and maps included?
- To what degree does the writer use literary language, such as metaphor?
- How easy is it to understand the characters and their motivations and development?
- Is character development essential to the story?
- Is dialogue assigned (using he said) or unassigned with longer stretches of interchange that the reader must follow and attribute to one character or another?
- How are characters revealed through what they say or think and what others say or think about them?
- How essential to the story are understandings about setting and plot?

Vocabulary and Words

Refers to the words and their accessibility to readers. Vocabulary generally refers to the meaning of words that readers may decode but not understand. Word solving refers to both decoding and to understanding meaning.

- What is the frequency of multisyllabic words in the text?
- How complex are word meanings? (For example, are readers required to understand multiple meanings or subtle shades of meaning of words?)
- What prior knowledge is needed to understand the vocabulary of the text?
- How many content or technical words are included in the text? How complex are these words?
- Does informational text utilize timeless verb constructions? (Ants carry sand as opposed to carried.)
- Are generic noun constructions used in informational and/or nonfiction text?

Sentence Complexity

Refers to the syntactic patterns readers will encounter in the text; sentences may be simple (short, with one subject and predicate) or complex (longer, with embedded clauses).

- What is the average length of sentences in the text?
- To what degree do sentences contain embedded clauses?
- What is the sentence style of the writer?
- Are there complex sentences joined by and, but, or other conjunctions?
- Are paragraphs organized so that readers can recognize lead sentences and main ideas?

Punctuation

Refers to the graphic symbols that signal the way text should be read to reflect the author's meaning.

- What punctuation symbols are used in the text?
- What do readers need to notice about punctuation in order to fully understand the text?
- What punctuation is essential for readers to notice to read with fluency and phrasing?

Using Leveled Books With Readers

The success of guided reading depends on many factors other than text characteristics. These, of course, have to do with the young readers using the texts as well as teacher-student interactions and include:

- **The reader's prior knowledge of the topic, including vocabulary and concepts.**
- **The reader's prior experience with texts that have similar features.**
- **The way the teacher introduces the text.**
- **The supportive interactions between the teacher and students before, during, and after reading.**
- **The level of interest teachers help students build.**

Level-by-Level Descriptions

Characteristics of text for each level in the Guided Reading Program are listed on pages 100–125. These descriptions are general: not every book included in a level will have every characteristic noted. Also listed are some important behaviors to notice and support at each level. As you use these books with students, you will notice how they support and challenge readers.

Other Resources

You may want to refer to the following resources for descriptions of guided reading as well as additional books for each level:

- **Duke, Nell K., and Bennett-Armistead, V. Susan, 2003.** *Reading & Writing Informational Text in the Primary Grades.* **New York, NY: Scholastic Inc.**
- **Fountas, I. C., and Pinnell, G. S., 2008.** *Benchmark Assessment System 1 and 2.* **Portsmouth, NH: Heinemann.**
- **Fountas, I. C., and Pinnell, G. S., 1996.** *Guided Reading: Good First Teaching for All Children.* **Portsmouth, NH: Heinemann.**
- **Fountas, I. C., and Pinnell, G. S., 2001.** *Guiding Readers and Writers, Grades 3–6: Teaching Comprehension, Genre, and Content Literacy.* **Portsmouth, NH: Heinemann.**
- **Fountas, I. C., and Pinnell, G. S., 2005.** *Leveled Books, K–8: Matching Texts to Readers for Effective Teaching.* **Portsmouth, NH: Heinemann.**
- **Fountas, I. C., and Pinnell, G. S., 1999.** *Voices on Word Matters.* **Portsmouth, NH: Heinemann.**
- **Pinnell, G. S., and Fountas, I. C., 2007.** *The Continuum of Literacy Learning, Grades K–8: Behaviors and Understandings to Notice, Teach, and Support.* **Portsmouth, NH: Heinemann.**
- **Pinnell, G. S., and Fountas, I. C., 1998.** *Word Matters: Teaching Phonics and Spelling in the Reading/Writing Classroom.* **Portsmouth, NH: Heinemann.**
- **Fountas, I. C., and Pinnell, G. S., 2006.** *Teaching for Comprehending and Fluency: Thinking, Talking, and Writing About Reading, K–8.* **Portsmouth, NH: Heinemann.**

WHAT IS
GUIDED READING?

Guided reading is an instructional approach that involves a teacher working with a small group of students who demonstrate similar reading behaviors and can all read similar levels of texts. The text is easy enough for students to read with your skillful support. The text offers challenges and opportunities for problem solving, but is easy enough for students to read with some fluency. You choose selections that help students expand their strategies.

What is the purpose of guided reading?

You select books that students can read with about 90 percent accuracy. Students can understand and enjoy the story because it's accessible to them through their own strategies, supported by your introduction. They focus on meaning but use problem-solving strategies to figure out words they don't know, deal with difficult sentence structure, and understand concepts or ideas they have never before encountered in print.

Why is guided reading important?

Guided reading gives students the chance to apply the strategies they already know to new text. You provide support, but the ultimate goal is independent reading.

When are children ready for guided reading?

Developing readers have already gained important understandings about how print works. These students know how to monitor their own reading. They have the ability to check on themselves or search for possibilities and alternatives if they encounter a problem when reading. For these readers, the guided reading experience is a powerful way to support the development of reading strategies.

The ultimate goal of guided reading is reading a variety of texts with ease and deep understanding. Silent reading means rapid processing of texts with most attention on meaning, which is achieved as readers move past beginning levels (H, I, J). At all levels, students read orally with fluency and phrasing.

Matching Books to Readers

The teacher selects a text for a small group of students who are similar in their reading behaviors at a particular point in time. In general, the text is about right for students in the group. It is not too easy, yet not too hard, and offers a variety of challenges to help readers become flexible problem solvers. You should choose Guided Reading Program books for students that:

- match their knowledge base.
- help them take the next step in learning to read.
- are interesting to them.
- offer just enough challenge to support problem solving while still supporting fluency and meaning.

Supporting Students' Reading

In working with students in guided reading, you constantly balance the difficulty of the text with support for students reading the text. You introduce the story to the group, support individuals through brief interactions while they read, and guide them to talk together afterwards about the words and ideas in the text. In this way, you refine text selection and help individual readers move forward in developing a reading process.

Good readers employ a wide range of word-solving strategies, including analysis of sound-letter relationships and word parts. They must figure out words that are embedded in different kinds of texts. Reading a variety of books enables them to go beyond reading individual words to interpreting language and its subtle meanings.

For more specific teaching suggestions, see individual cards for each book title.

Procedure for Guided Reading	

Procedure for Guided Reading

- The teacher works with a small group of students with similar needs.
- The teacher provides introductions to the text that support students' later attempts at problem solving.
- Each student reads the whole text or a unified part of the text.
- Readers figure out new words while reading for meaning.
- The teacher prompts, encourages, and confirms students' attempts at problem solving.
- The teacher and student engage in meaningful conversations about what they are reading.
- The teacher and student revisit the text to demonstrate and use a range of comprehension strategies.

ORGANIZING YOUR CLASSROOM FOR GUIDED READING

adapted from *Guided Reading: Making It Work* (Schulman and Payne, 2000)

Good management begins with a thoughtful room arrangement and careful selection of materials; the way you organize furniture and supplies will support the learning that takes place within your classroom. For guided reading to be effective, the rest of the class must be engaged in other literacy activities that do not require direct teacher involvement. For most classes, this means literacy centers that accommodate small groups of students. So, a strategically arranged classroom for guided reading would have a class library, inviting spots for individual work, spaces for whole-class gatherings and small-group meetings, and several literacy centers.

Arranging the room and organizing materials for effective reading and writing workshops takes thought and planning. So before the school year even begins, consider the activities you're planning for your class and the physical layout of your room. With a little ingenuity, you can provide an environment that will support learning all year long.

Scheduling for Guided Reading

To determine the time you'll need for guided reading, consider the number of students in your class and the range of reading abilities they possess. Then create your initial groupings; the ideal group size is four to six, though guided reading groups might range from three to eight. Place below-grade or struggling readers in smaller groups. Keep in mind that sessions are short—often 10–15 minutes for emergent readers, and 15–30 minutes for more advanced readers. You will want to meet with at-risk groups every day; five meetings over a two-week period for more advanced groups is typical. You'll also want to allow yourself some time for assessment—taking a running record, jotting anecdotal notes, or conducting oral interviews, for example. Finally, allow a few minutes between groups to check in with the rest of the class.

THE SCHOLASTIC
GUIDED READING CLASSROOM

Scholastic Guided Reading Programs support a comprehensive reading program by integrating guided instruction, assessment, and independent practice into your classroom. Here's what the Guided Reading classroom looks like:

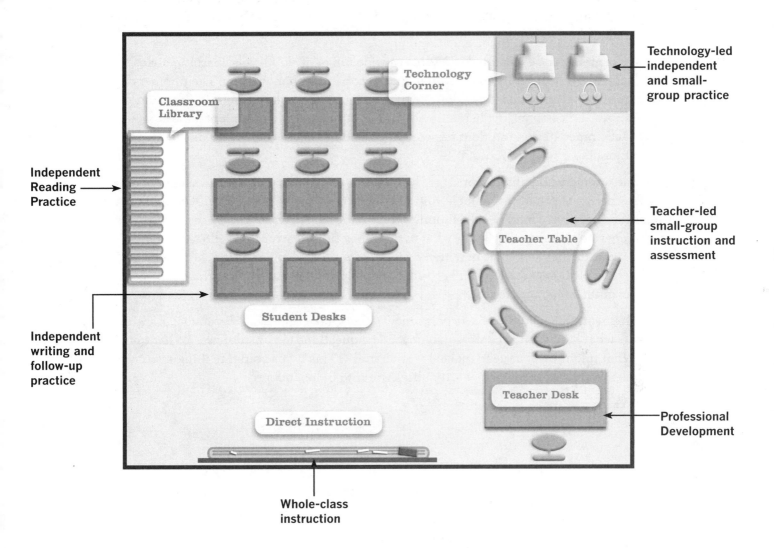

Technology-led independent and small-group practice

Teacher-led small-group instruction and assessment

Professional Development

Independent Reading Practice

Independent writing and follow-up practice

Whole-class instruction

Technology Corner

Classroom Library

Teacher Table

Teacher Desk

Student Desks

Direct Instruction

SETTING UP
LITERACY CENTERS

adapted from *Guided Reading: Making It Work* (Schulman and Payne, 2000)

As a way of managing the time to meet with small groups of students, teachers often use literacy centers. At literacy centers, students continue to participate in purposeful and authentic literacy activities. These centers provide many opportunities to practice the skills real readers and writers use. They take the place of traditional worksheets and are not meant to be graded.

Literacy centers can be designed to address a wide range of skill levels, learning styles, and interests. Students work in heterogeneous groups that change often. The number of students at each center depends upon the type of center and the space for it. For example, in one first-grade classroom, the listening center has stations for four students, the computer center accommodates one student per computer, and the library center holds up to three students.

When arranging your centers, consider the number of students you want to accommodate at once, the space you have available, and the topics that you want to cover. Also think about transitions between centers—will students work at the same center during the whole guided reading period? If so, do they know what to do if they finish early? If not, do they know how to move to another center or activity without disturbing you or other class members? Establishing clear expectations and routines will help centers run smoothly, so you can focus on guided reading groups.

When first setting up students' use of literacy centers, take time each day to discuss with students what happened at centers that day. Some questions to consider are, "What went well? What might we change to make it work better?" This helps students think about ways to problem-solve when they meet difficulties working independently.

Things to Consider When Setting Up Literacy Centers

- Establish a manageable number of centers that can be changed easily and routinely.

- Plan time to introduce and demonstrate how each center operates. Some teachers do this during scheduled shared reading/writing time.

- Consider the physical arrangement of the centers to permit movement and a balance of quiet and noisy areas.

- Design centers to meet the range of all learners, addressing a variety of interests and learning styles.

- Have supplies accessible and labeled for independent student use.

- Create signs or charts that communicate functional information and directions, such as "How to Use the Audiocassette Player."

- Develop a plan for the rotation of students through centers and a way to keep track of centers.

- Provide an opportunity for students to select centers.

- Develop a signal or a problem-solving technique for students to use while they are at centers and you are working with other students.

- Periodically review what's working and not working at centers.

Managing and Organizing Literacy Centers

There are a variety of ways to organize and manage centers. Some teachers have students select literacy centers, while others choose the centers for the students to ensure they regularly rotate through them. No matter which approach you take, it is important to have a record-keeping system in place to monitor student participation in various centers.

Alternatives to Centers

Instead of centers, some teachers prefer to involve students in productive reading and writing work at their tables or desks. For Kindergarten and Grade 1, remember that children will need a chance to stretch and move periodically.

For students in Grades 3 and above, you will want to phase out most work at centers. For independent work, students can:

- Read silently a book of their choice at their independent level

- Write or draw in response to reading

- Engage in longer projects that involve research, reading, and writing.

GROUPING
STUDENTS

Your job is to take each student from his or her present level to a more advanced one. Therefore, there must be assessment of individual students. With class sizes ranging from 20 to 35, grouping for instruction makes sense. As teachers, we want to make learning manageable, while avoiding any negative aspects of grouping.

Fundamentals of Grouping

Assessment of Students' Knowledge Base

Students' knowledge base is the key element in selecting texts and planning instruction for groups so that they can read with 90 percent accuracy and use the skills that assure understanding. Other aspects to consider when selecting the best level for a group include:

- **how well developing readers can control a strategy, such as analyzing a new word.**
- **the kinds of language students find understandable and which they find challenging.**
- **what concepts they know or what concepts they don't understand.**
- **the kinds of texts and genres they have experienced. For example, if they have handled only narrative texts, then informational texts may be difficult.**

See pages 100–125 for help in assessing which level is best for a group.

Dynamic Grouping

Because students' individual needs change so often, ongoing observation of behavior and assessment of their knowledge and experience are essential to the guided reading process. Students progress at different rates, so regrouping is also ongoing. By grouping in different ways for different purposes, you can avoid labeling students with group names that are symbols of a static achievement level.

As you informally assess students' reading on a daily basis, you may wish to use the descriptions of **Behaviors to Notice and Support** on pages 100–125 for the level of book you are using. A quick, informal observation of students' reading will help you determine if the book was at the appropriate level.

- **Was this book too hard for this student? If the student can't read it independently with 85–95 percent accuracy and isn't using strategies as he or she reads, then the book is too hard.**
- **If the student reads with such fluency that there is no need for problem-solving behaviors, then the student should be reading a higher-level text for guided reading. Of course, the lower-level text will be useful for fluency practice.**

RUNNING
GUIDED READING GROUPS

Step 1   **Select a Book**

With students' needs in mind, select a book for a group of two to six. Use the **Characteristics of Text** to determine general level appropriateness and the description of **Behaviors to Notice and Support** to determine if students' reading ability matches that level. (See pages 100–125)

Depending on available time, each group of readers at Levels A–J might read fewer books but must sustain attention and memory over several days or a week of reading. For readers in Grades 3–6, the goal of independent and guided reading instruction is to enable students to read one chapter book a week or several shorter selections. No two groups will read exactly the same sequence of books, and groups will change as the assessment system helps track progress.

Step 2   **Introduce the Book**

Introducing the story is probably the most important and most difficult part of guided reading, and it is your opportunity to provide most of the support to the reader. A brief introduction helps a group to read successfully with minimal teacher support. You may tailor the introduction based on the group and the particular text. Depending on the level of difficulty and students' reading abilities, the introduction includes any combination of these elements:

- **a short conversation about the main idea of the text.**
- **a briefing on the author's purpose for writing and some important features of the plot or informational text.**
- **a description of the main characters, facts, or ideas in the book.**
- **a presentation of any unusual or unique language, such as a repetitive refrain or content words.**
- **a discussion of the concepts needed for an understanding of the text by activating prior knowledge.**
- **drawing attention to any aspects of print that you consider important such as captions, headings, charts and/or tables.**
- **instructions on how much to read and what to do when finished.**

Without actually reading the text to students, frame it in a meaningful way. Using oral language in a way that familiarizes students with some words they will meet in print helps prepare them to read. It isn't necessary to introduce every page, preteach words, or give a purpose for reading. The idea is to help students to be able to move through the text on their own. Any brief intervention should not interfere with the momentum of independent reading.

Step 3 Read the Book

Once the book has been introduced, students are ready to read. Unlike round-robin reading, in which each student reads a page or sentence, each student using guided reading reads the entire text.

- **Each student reads independently and problem-solves on his or her own.**
- **Reading may be oral or silent, depending on level and skill.**

As students read, you are nearby to observe them, providing support when necessary. As they read, note reading behaviors and offer praise when students use a strategy successfully. Students reading in Levels A through J will be reading in a soft whisper. More advanced students will be reading silently. You can sample their oral reading by asking them to lift their voices to an audible level for a page or two. All students continue reading silently at their own rates as you sample oral reading from several of them.

If students have been placed in the appropriate level, they will problem-solve independently. However, if the whole group seems stuck, you may want to stop the group to assist in problem solving. You might also make teaching points, such as pointing out inflectional endings or consonant digraphs. Detours should be brief, not interrupting the momentum of students' reading.

Try to choose one student in the group daily to observe and interact with, helping him or her develop reading strategies, and encouraging the independent use of those strategies.

Step 4 Respond to the Book and Learn about Reading

After students read, first invite them to discuss the meaning of the text. Then select one or two teaching points to bring to their attention. What you select to teach depends on students' needs. You might focus on the meaning of a portion of text, on character interpretation, on information or facts, or on some aspect of word solving, such as multisyllabic words. For example, you might:

- **promote fluency and phrasing by asking students to read aloud a favorite part of the story.**
- **help students focus on key ideas and language by having them find a turning point in the story, an informational part, or a description.**
- **help students figure out new, longer words by having them focus on word parts or known words.**
- **engage students in actively exploring how words work—building words, changing words, and noticing their features.**
- **help students interpret information provided in nonfiction features such as maps, charts, graphs, etc.**

By following up the reading of a text in this way, you are helping students develop strategies that they can apply to the reading of other books. You are helping them learn the "how to" of reading and to move forward toward the goal of developing a reading process.

Step 5 Assess Behavior

The day after a new text is read, record the ability level of one child and note any progress. The **Behaviors to Notice and Support** can help you assess.

GUIDED READING AND THE
STRUGGLING READER

Guided reading groups shift as students' reading abilities and interests change. As you work with your guided reading groups, you will be able to identify students who need extra help. Guided reading provides many advantages in helping these students. After assessing their reading levels and pinpointing what skills and strategies they need help with, you can move struggling readers to groups that provide support. Within these groups, struggling readers will be able to read more with greater accuracy and fluency, as they will be working with text at their level. You will also be able to work with them on word skills that other students may already know.

Select books that match your students' reading levels.	Any group of struggling readers will likely vary widely in their abilities. Because of this, you will need to be careful in selecting texts that are interesting, yet not too difficult. Struggling readers are usually slow readers because they have been trying to read texts that are too challenging. Slow reading interferes with comprehension, but with appropriate texts, students will be able to increase their speed and improve their comprehension. Gradually, students should be able to take on more challenging texts as their reading abilities and confidence improve.
Involve students in reading every day.	Struggling readers need to spend more time actually reading than doing activities related to reading. Plan daily guided reading time for these students to increase the amount of time they read with support.
Plan additional time to introduce and discuss texts.	Extra time may be needed for introductions and discussions before and after reading to guide students in anticipating what they will read and then thinking about and understanding the text. This extra time will help students learn how to approach text as they prepare to read. It will also give them opportunities to discuss what they have learned and to hear others' ideas. Encourage students to ask questions, and teach them how to find answers in the text.
Include working with words in guided reading lessons.	At the end of each guided reading lesson, spend a few minutes showing students the principles of how words work. Have them apply the principles to selected examples. To make this work more interesting, create word games.
Allow time for silent reading.	As students' reading abilities improve, give them time to read silently as well as orally. Silent reading is beneficial in that it is faster than oral reading and text is easier to comprehend.

USING RESPONSE TO INTERVENTION

One tool educators can use to identify and help struggling readers is the Response to Intervention (RTI) framework. Many states have used RTI to identify students with specific learning disabilities as part of the Individuals with Disabilities Education Improvement Act (IDEA), implemented in 2004.

RTI provides for frequent, short tests to indicate a student's skill level relative to other students or established benchmarks. These short tests can be used to determine the success or failure of interventions and to determine how much additional support and instruction will be needed. The advantage of using RTI is that students who are at risk of having reading difficulties are identified early. Early identification can prevent some students from being placed in special education when all they need is a short period of intense intervention. With RTI, student progress is carefully monitored so that the intervention can be adjusted as needed. If students continue to have difficulty, then special education may be considered.

Implementing and using RTI requires a commitment on the part of teachers and administrators and may result in restructuring daily schedules and tasks. In practice, RTI can look very different from school to school, as it is tailored to fit specific situations and students. However, RTI programs do have common elements:

- **Instruction is based on individual students' needs.**
- **The program is preventive and proactive.**
- **All students are assessed.**
- **Assessments used must be reliable and valid.**
- **Response to assessment results is rapid and efficient.**
- **At-risk students are provided with various levels of intense intervention.**
- **Student progress is closely monitored.**
- **Professional development is a critical part of the program.**
- **Strong administrative support ensures commitment and resources.**

PROMPTS TO SUPPORT
PROBLEM-SOLVING STRATEGIES

adapted from *Guided Reading: Good First Teaching for All Children* (Fountas and Pinnell, 1996)

Throughout a guided reading session, the teacher prompts, encourages and confirms students' attempts at problem solving. The teacher helps students apply the in-the-head strategies they already know to new text. The teacher also helps students use a variety of strategies as they read. The key is to prompt with just the right amount of support so that eventually, each student will take over the strategizing for herself.

Prompts to Support Early Readers
• **Read it with your finger.**
• **Try _____. Would that make sense?/Would that sound right?**
• **Do you think it looks like _____?**
• **Can you find _____? (a known or new word)**
• **Did you have enough (or too many) words?**
• **Read that again and start the word.**
• **Did it match?**
• **Did you run out of words?**

Prompts to Support a Reader's Self-Monitoring Strategies
• **Were you right?**
• **Why did you stop?**
• **What letter would you expect to see at the beginning? At the end?**
• **Would _____ fit there?/make sense?**
• **Check it. Does it look and sound right to you?**
• **What did you notice? (after hesitation or stop)**
• **Could it be _____?**
• **It could be _____, but look at _____.**
• **You almost got that. See if you can find what is wrong.**

Prompts to Support a Reader's Use of All Sources of Information

- Check the picture.
- Does that sound right?
- You said (_____). Does that make sense?
- What's wrong with this? (Repeat what the student said.)
- Try that again and think what would make sense.
- What could you try?
- What can you do to help yourself?
- Try that again and think what would sound right.
- Do you know a word like that?

Prompts to Support a Reader's Self-Correction

- Something wasn't quite right.
- I like the way you worked that out.
- You're nearly right. Try that again.

Prompts to Support Phrased, Fluent Reading

- Can you read this quickly?
- Put your words together so it sounds like talking.

THE IMPORTANCE OF READING A
VARIETY OF TEXTS AND GENRES

Creating motivated readers is a challenge for any teacher faced with a class that varies widely in backgrounds, interests, and abilities. For students to become active readers, they must be exposed to a number and variety of texts and genres that are interesting and engaging, informative, accessible, representative of our diverse world, and include content appropriate for each student's age and gender. By selecting and introducing a variety of texts and genres over a period of time and demonstrating the many ways one can experience texts, you can help your students build a flexible reading process that will make any text accessible.

How do texts vary?

When students are exposed to a variety of good-quality texts within many genres, they can compare and connect texts across genres and become familiar with text characteristics. However, variety is more than an assortment of books of different genres. It includes format, special types of text across genres, different media, and a wide range of content and diversity.

Why is format important?

The sizes, shapes, designs, layouts, illustrations, binding, and placement and styles of print constitute some of the different formats in which text is presented. The types of formats students are most likely to encounter include fiction and nonfiction picture books, leveled readers, short stories, chapter books, series books, poems, short stories, short informational texts, magazines targeted to young readers, graphic novels, and comic books. Having available texts in different formats will increase opportunities for all students to find something they want to read. By experiencing texts in a wide range of formats, students also develop the ability to process different kinds of language and visual information.

How do genres vary?

Genre means types of text that are basically prose or poetry. Poetry comes in many forms, including traditional songs and rhymes, free verse, chants, and haiku. Prose can be divided into fiction and nonfiction, which is further divided into many types of text. Fiction can include realistic fiction, historical fiction, fantasy, science fiction, and traditional literature such as fables, folktales, and myths. Nonfiction includes biography; autobiography; memoirs; and informational, narrative, expository, and persuasive texts. Across genres, students will encounter text types with common features, including mysteries and stories of adventure, sports, and survival.

Why is genre important?

Different genres make different demands on readers. Students who are exposed to a wide variety of genres develop analytical-thinking skills and become more flexible in processing text. As their knowledge of genre grows, readers learn what to expect when they begin to read a text and can adjust their reading strategies accordingly. Even more important, they learn how to think within, beyond, and about their reading.

Through prose, students learn how language can be used to explain, describe, persuade, and elaborate. They become a part of the wider world, past and present, in nonfiction and enter imaginary worlds in fiction. They also discover how to think critically about what they read.

Why is diversity important?

Students also should be exposed to texts in both leveled books and books available for independent reading that reflect different cultures, languages, races, geographic regions, religions, and traditions. Through fiction and nonfiction texts that reflect our world, students will identify with characters in books and will learn about diversity, also learning to value it. In addition, they will discover viewpoints and perspectives that are different from their own.

How do different types of media help readers?

Providing variety in types of text is important in stretching students' thinking, but doing so also requires accessibility. Reading aloud varied texts gives all students quick and easy access to a wider range of genres and text levels they might not be ready to read independently. This same access can be provided with audiotapes or CDs and DVD movies based on books or stories. By making texts accessible to all students, you will have a basis for discussion that can involve the whole class.

Creating a Collection

When creating a classroom collection of books that will develop strong readers and writers and demand growth, remember to look for:

- **high-quality texts**
- **a variety of genres in fiction, nonfiction, and poetry**
- **favorite authors and illustrators**
- **enough copies for students' needs and your curriculum**
- **variety to interest students, both male and female**
- **variety in a range of reading levels**

GENRE DESCRIPTIONS AND KEY FEATURES

The *Scholastic Guided Reading Program: Fiction Focus 2nd Edition* provides a wide variety of genres, including fictional prose, poetry, graphic novels, and some nonfiction text.

FICTION

Poetry	Poetry is difficult to describe because it is a personal and emotional expression of the poet. Poetry's language can create an image in a few words and give readers an unexpected and fresh way to see something.
Key Features	• may have rhythms and patterns of language that are best discovered when read aloud • may include rhyme within or at the end of lines • may be free verse, which breaks from fixed stanzas and rhyme, instead setting up a rhythm through the language of the whole poem • often breaks from conventional capitalization and punctuation
Realistic Fiction	Realistic fiction tells a story that could possibly happen to real people. The characters appear to have problems and goals that real people have, and attempt to solve these problems or reach goals with plausible actions. Readers often experience realistic fiction as truthful and can identify with and see themselves in the characters.
Key Features	• believable characters with human problems and desires • setting that reflects real places and time • character-driven events • reasonable outcomes that reflect real life • humor may be an element
Historical Fiction	Realistic fiction that takes place in the past is considered historical fiction. The story combines imagination and fact with characters as part of a fictional plot placed in a real historical setting. The setting is often integral to the plot as it affects how characters live and act as well as the events they are a part of.
Key Features	• believable characters • setting that reflects a historical time and place • details of how people live and work fit the time and place • real historical people may appear as characters although what they do and say may be fictional unless historically documented
Fantasy	Fantasy includes stories that are not possible in real life. Characters or settings may be imaginary, or the events and characters' actions or abilities are not realistic. Once readers willingly accept the fantasy, the characters may be plausible with realistic problems, and the outcome may be reasonable.

Key Features	• characters may be imaginary, have magical abilities, and/or include personified animals
	• settings may be imaginary and change as characters travel through time or move into alternate worlds
	• plot may involve a conflict between good and evil

Science Fiction

Science fiction is a type of fantasy that tells about events that have not happened yet or that could not happen in real life as it is known today. The imaginary elements are technology-driven instead of magical. The science established in a science fiction story may not be explained, but it must remain consistent to be believable.

Key Features

• stories may take place in outer space, on other worlds, or in alternate dimensions

• science and technology are used to create a world or characters that are not possible in present real life

• the setting is usually important to the story as it affects characters and their actions

Traditional Literature

Traditional literature encompasses stories that have been passed down orally through many generations. Different versions of the same tale often appear in many cultures. Readers expect recurring themes and structures, such as three wishes, journeys or quests, tricksters, or heroes who are often young.

Key Features

• **Folktale:** an often humorous story that comes from a particular culture and is told orally until it is eventually recorded; includes stock characters that fill one function, simple conflicts and goals, fast action, repetitive events often in threes, and a definitive outcome

• **Fable:** a brief story, usually with animal characters, that teaches a moral or a lesson that is stated clearly at the end of the story

• **Fairy Tale:** a short story with magical characters and events; characters are usually all good or all bad; repetition in characters and actions; often begins with "once upon a time" and ends with "and they lived happily ever after"; has a more elaborate structure than a folktale

• **Myth:** a story that explains something in nature; found in many cultures; often includes ancient gods who interact with humans; characters may also be personifications of natural forces such as the wind

• **Legend:** a story that tells about the great deeds of a hero who may have been a real person in history, such as Davy Crockett; often mixed with mythical elements; may once have been based on fact, but is fictional in detail

• **Trickster Tale:** a particular type of folktale in which a character, usually an animal, attempts to trick other characters into doing or giving something that will benefit the trickster; common tricksters include Anansi the Spider

Mystery	A mystery is a special type of fiction that centers on a problem that needs to be solved. The problem can be missing or stolen objects, puzzles, criminals to be identified and caught, and strange behavior that needs to be explained. Suspense and sometimes danger and fear play an important part in the action.
Key Features	• characters involved in solving a problem such as a puzzle or a crime • setting may be mysterious or ordinary • plot carries the story as characters follow clues to solve the mystery • mood is suspenseful • familiar forms are detective stories, strange adventures, and tales of espionage and crime
Play	A play is a story that is intended to be performed. Plays are character-driven, as they are told through what the characters say and do.
Key Features	• written in dialogue form with character names identifying the speaker • includes character actions and expressions briefly indicated, usually parenthetically • may include one or more acts with a clearly identified setting • usually includes in the beginning a list of characters and their characteristics such as name, age, and identity or profession
Novel	A novel is a longer work of fiction that contains all story elements, including characters, setting, plot, and theme. Because of its longer length, a novel can more fully develop characters over time and place. The length of a novel requires readers to develop reading stamina and the ability to follow plots and characters over an extended period of time and several reading sessions.
Key Features	• story is usually divided into chapters • may include several major and minor characters that are fully developed • may include story background in the beginning or as the story unfolds • may include several subplots • plot may include many events as action rises and falls • may include a resolution and events after the climax or turning point
Graphic Novel	Graphic novels are similar to comic books, but they tell a more complete story with a beginning, middle, and end. A graphic novel often resembles a novel in length and narrative. The term *graphic* refers to the pictorial nature of the novel.
Key Features	• story told through pictures • dialogue included in speech balloons • narrative may be within story frames or at the top of a page • characters developed through dialogue and illustration

NONFICTION

Informational Text	Informational text provides factual information. Content may be scientific or social, exploring the natural and physical world or people and places in the past or present. Informational text can be presented in a variety of formats including reference books, books on specific subjects or processes, magazines, CDs, or filmed documentaries.
Key Features	• provides information on a whole class of things, places, or people • describes and explains • compares and contrasts • includes technical vocabulary • often includes headings and subheadings to divide text • presents information through graphics such as photographs, charts, diagrams, and maps as well as text • includes labels and captions • includes a table of contents and an index • may include a bibliography
Narrative	Narrative nonfiction tells the story of an event or series of events that occur in the present or past. Background to the event is often provided along with specific details about what happened and who was involved.
Key Features	• describes an event or series of events, including dates, time, places, and the people involved • may include graphics such as photographs, illustrations, and charts • may include a table of contents, an index, and a bibliography
Biography/Autobiography	A biography or an autobiography is about a single historical or current person. It may cover the person's whole life or a significant period. An autobiography is written by the person who is the subject of the story. An autobiography may take the form of a memoir in which the person relates his or her experiences during a meaningful time. A biography is written by an author about a person who is the subject of the book.
Key Features	• covers one person's life or a significant period of that person's life • usually written about an important person • may include photographs and illustrations • may include a table of contents, an index, and/or a bibliography

INCLUDING NONFICTION AND INFORMATIONAL TEXT IN PRIMARY CLASSROOMS

adapted from *Reading & Writing Informational Text in the Primary Grades* (Duke and Bennett-Armistead, 2003)

Guided *Reading: Fiction Focus, 2nd Edition* includes a variety of nonfiction and informational texts as part of its genre array. Often the terms "informational text" and "nonfiction" are used interchangeably, but they are not the same. Informational text is a type of nonfiction—a very important type. Nonfiction includes any text that is factual. (Or, by some definitions, any type of literature that is factual, which would exclude text such as menus and street signs.) Informational text differs from other types of nonfiction in that its primary purpose is to convey information about the natural or social world, and typically includes particular linguistic features such as headings and technical vocabulary.

It is important to note that within informational text, there are several different types of text that might be considered informational text genres or subgenres including:

- **reference books such as encyclopedias, field guides, and so on**
- **"all about" books, on topics such as spiders or dinosaurs**
- **process-informational books including books about how an animal develops from conception to adulthood or about how some substance is created or transformed**
- **magazines, newspapers, posters, pamphlets, Web sites, CD-ROMs, and so on**

Why focus on informational and nonfiction texts in primary classrooms? There are a number of arguments for doing so. Some of these arguments have a more solid research base than others, and some may be more compelling than others. But the research available to this point is clear. Students need to encounter more informational text because:

Informational Text Is Key to Success in Later Schooling

We have all heard that from around fourth grade on, "reading to learn" is a major focus in school (Chall, 1983). Students encounter more textbooks and other forms of informational text as they move through the grades. The tests they take contain increasingly more difficult informational texts. If teachers include more informational text in early schooling, they put students in a better position to handle the reading and writing demands of their later schooling.

Informational Text Is Ubiquitous in Society

Several studies have looked at the kinds of things people write *outside* of school—what students and adults read and write in their workplaces, homes, and communities. Again and again these studies have shown that adults read a great deal of nonfiction, including informational text (e.g., Venezky, 1982; Smith, 2000). This is not likely to change and, in fact, in our increasingly information-based economy, it may only increase. According to one study (Kamil & Lane, 1998), 96 percent of the text on the World Wide Web is expository.

Informational Text Is Preferred Reading Material for Many Students

When researchers investigate the kinds of texts students like to read, they've found that different students have different reading preferences. Some students seem to prefer informational text, some seem to prefer narrative text, and many don't seem to have preferences for any particular genre. For those students who prefer informational text—students Ron Jobe and Mary Dayton-Sakari (2002) call "Info-Kids"—including more informational text in classrooms may improve attitudes toward reading and even serve as a catalyst for overall literacy development (Caswell & Duke, 1998).

Informational Text Builds Knowledge of the Natural and Social World

By definition, informational text conveys information about the natural and social world (Duke, 2000). Reading and listening to informational text therefore can develop students' knowledge of that world (e.g., Anderson & Guthrie, 1999; Duke & Kays, 1998). This in turn can promote students' comprehension of subsequent texts they read (e.g., Wilson & Anderson, 1986), because it can build background knowledge.

Young Children Can Handle Informational Text

The research is clear. Young children *can* interact successfully with informational text. (See Dreher, 2000; Duke, 2003; and Duke, Bennett-Armistead, & Roberts, 2002, 2003, for reviews of research on this point.) Studies show that Kindergartners can develop knowledge of information-book language and content from information-book read-alouds and shared readings. Primary-grade students can comprehend informational text that they read themselves. Research also indicates that young children can write informational text. So you needn't worry that informational text is inherently "over the heads" of your students, and you should be able to respond with confidence to colleagues who have doubts.

THINKING WITHIN, BEYOND, AND ABOUT THE TEXT

Adapted from *Teaching for Comprehending and Fluency: Thinking, Talking, and Writing About Reading, K-8* (Irene C. Fountas and Gay Su Pinnell, 2006)

When proficient readers process a text, they simultaneously draw on a wide range of strategic actions that are physical, emotional, cognitive, and linguistic. As students learn the skills and strategies they need to make sense of a text, this process becomes more effective and automatic. Eventually, the reading process becomes unconscious. In order to reach this point, students need to learn how proficient readers think about reading. Teachers may often interpret this as making sure students comprehend what they are reading. However, checking for comprehension by asking endless questions during reading can turn into an interrogation that interferes with the reading process. Having students learn and focus on one reading strategy at a time also can make the reading process less effective. Instead, students need guidance in how to integrate strategic actions and use them effectively with many kinds of texts. For the teacher, this means knowing what readers must be able to do and the information they need to access to process a text.

Readers access a wide range of information that is both visible and invisible. Visible information is what students see as words and art in the text. As they read, readers recognize letters, words, punctuation, format, and text structures, and they attach meaning to what they see. Proficient readers are barely aware of this processing of visual information as they focus on meaning. Invisible information—including the knowledge and experience of language, facts, and the world both past and present—is what readers know and think about as they respond to visual information. Such personal knowledge is different for each student and is shaped by family, culture, and community. As students learn about different cultures and communities, they expand their perspectives and make new connections. Many of the texts they encounter can become the basis for this expansion.

Another form of invisible information is readers' experiences with many kinds of text, including knowledge of genres, text structures, and formats. This knowledge helps readers form expectations and predictions about a new text, access meaning as they read, and respond to the text after reading.

Different kinds of texts make different demands on readers. Texts that students can read independently help them build their knowledge. Texts that students can read with teacher support challenge them to develop new strategic actions for reading. You can help students meet these demands by giving them opportunities to think about their reading within, beyond, and about text.

Thinking Within the Text

When readers think within the text, they gather basic information from the text and determine its basic meaning. To do so, readers must process the text by:

- **decoding words and using word meaning and what they know about language**
- **searching for information, and noting and sorting important details**
- **determining how the text is organized**
- **monitoring themselves for accuracy and understanding**
- **adjusting reading speed and technique according to the type of text**
- **sustaining fluency**

Understanding the basic meaning of a text forms the foundation for higher thinking skills. By thinking within the text, readers can gather important information and summarize what they have read.

Thinking Beyond the Text

When readers think beyond the text, they go more deeply into its meaning beyond their literal understanding of it. They are able to:

- **make predictions**
- **connect their reading to their own experiences**
- **relate the text to similar texts**
- **integrate what they know with new information**
- **infer ideas that are not directly stated**
- **think about the greater meaning of the text**

Thinking beyond the text allows readers to understand character motivations, explore how setting influences the story, and follow more complex plots. They also identify and learn new information that they can incorporate into what they already know and understand.

Thinking About the Text

To think about the text, readers analyze and critique what they read. They examine a text to:

- **note how it is constructed**
- **note how the writer uses language**
- **identify literary devices**
- **determine how the writer has provided information, such as using compare and contrast, description, or cause and effect**
- **identify characteristics of the genre**
- **use their own knowledge to think critically about ideas**
- **evaluate quality and authenticity**

Thinking about the text helps readers move beyond identifying likes and dislikes and helps them learn more about how texts work. It also helps them better appreciate different genres, good-quality writing, and their own writing.

Guiding Students to Think Within, Beyond, and About the Text

Thinking about the text is a complex process that is difficult to teach or demonstrate. Although there is value in directing readers to important aspects of the text, effective reading strategies should be shown as working together in an integrated process. You can talk about the text before reading, at certain points during reading, and after reading to motivate questions and ideas. You can share your own ideas and demonstrate the different kinds of thinking readers do. However, instruction must still allow readers to respond to the text in a way that expands and expresses their own thinking.

In your guided reading groups, you can help your students learn how to think within, beyond, and about the text by being mindful of:

- **the important aspects of processing related to reading the texts you have selected**
- **what you want your students to do**
- **the learning opportunities presented by a particular text**
- **how students might respond to text features that could open opportunities for teaching**

What follows are some tips about how to help students think within, beyond, and about fiction and nonfiction texts.

Fiction

To think within the text, help students to:

- **follow the events of the plot; show how to think about what happens first, then next**
- **gather information about characters and setting by giving examples of what to look for**
- **learn about the characters by noting how they are described, what they say or think, what others say about them, and how they change over the course of the story**
- **identify the conflict or problem, and the solution**
- **solve words by thinking about their meaning in context**

To think beyond the text, help students to:

- **infer character motivations and feelings by looking for evidence in the text and by making connections between themselves and the characters**
- **infer why characters change over time by looking for evidence in the story**
- **connect the text to background knowledge, personal experiences, and other texts by thinking about other stories the text reminds them of, what they already know about the topic, place, or time, and how the plot or characters are similar to another text**
- **predict how the problem is solved by thinking about what has happened, what will happen next, and what is known about the characters**
- **understand the theme or message by thinking about what the writer is trying to say**
- **relate the theme, plot, or characters to their own lives**
- **infer how events are significant**
- **note new ideas, identify how their thinking has changed and what they have learned**

To think about the text, help students to:

- evaluate the importance of the setting by thinking how the text would be different if set in another time or place, or how the story changed when the setting changed
- notice how the writer made the characters realistic
- pay attention to the plot structure by thinking about how the story is organized, how the writer shows the passing of time, and identifying any flashbacks
- note aspects of the writer's craft by looking for language that helped them clarify something
- evaluate the quality or authenticity of the text

Nonfiction

To think within the text, help students to:

- gather and remember important information by deciding what they will learn from the text and what they think is important
- gather and remember information from the illustrations and graphics
- use different tools, such as a table of contents, headings, captions, index, and glossary, to locate and use information

To think beyond the text, help students to:

- identify new information and add it to their existing knowledge by thinking how their ideas might have changed after reading the text
- make connections between the text and background knowledge, personal experience, and other texts by thinking what the text reminds them of and what they already knew about the topic
- infer cause and effect by thinking about what happened and why
- identify the problem and the solution posed by the writer
- notice and understand the sequence of events
- analyze description by examining details and looking for examples in the text

To think about the text, help students to:

- recognize if and how the writer uses cause and effect, problem and solution, description, sequence, and compare and contrast by noticing how the writer constructed the story
- evaluate the authenticity and accuracy of the text by thinking about why the text seems accurate and how facts could be checked
- decide how the writer made the topic interesting by looking for specific examples
- analyze why the writer chose particular information to include in graphics

THE IMPORTANCE OF TALKING ABOUT BOOKS

Discussing books should be a rich part of every student's reading life. When students are encouraged and given opportunities to talk about books with peers and their teachers, they become motivated to share what they liked best about a text—and what they found interesting or surprising. They learn how to ask questions to find out what other students thought about a text and how to recommend a favorite book. They experience having their opinions valued rather than evaluated. They also discover that talking about books is fun.

Getting students to talk about books beyond the usual "I liked it" or "I didn't like it" or short answers to questions about specific texts is often difficult. However, there are a variety of ways you can spark discussion about books in your classroom including book clubs, literature circles, and topic discussions.

Interactive Read-Aloud

Before students can effectively discuss books with others, they need to learn how to talk about books. You can help them learn by conducting interactive read-alouds in which you demonstrate how to talk about books. Begin by selecting a text you know your students will enjoy, or invite them to select a text from several you offer. After you introduce the text, read it aloud and pause occasionally to demonstrate how to talk about the book. Then invite students to join in. Students can share comments or questions or respond to a discussion prompt with the whole group, another student, or a small group. After reading, you can invite students to comment on what the text means, link it to other books, reflect on the writer's craft, and evaluate text quality.

During an interactive read-aloud, students learn how to:

- **focus on the text**
- **use suitable words when talking about a text**
- **listen actively and respect others' ideas**
- **build on others' comments**
- **back up their opinions with evidence from the text**

Through active participation, students learn that they are expected to respond to one another's comments and that everyone should participate.

Literature Discussion Groups

Once students have learned how to talk about books, they can try out their skills in literature discussion groups. These small groups, each consisting of four to six students, operate under many different names including book clubs, literature circles, and topic discussions. They all are organized around students sharing their thinking about texts.

In literature discussion groups, students are in charge of their own thinking, talking, and writing. They have a chance to share what they think within, beyond, and about a text. As a result, interest in their own learning grows.

At first, you will need to be closely involved with book clubs and literature circles to set routines and select books. Choose books that are developmentally appropriate as well as interesting. Have a copy for each student in a group. Be sure that everyone in the class is a part of a discussion group. A group can consist of students who are interested in a particular author, topic, or genre. Some groups might be all girls or all boys.

Designate where and when book clubs will meet. Encourage members to come prepared by having read the selected book and spending some time thinking about it, deciding on information and ideas to share. Have students sit in a circle at a table or on the floor so they can see one another. You may want to post a list of text elements for fiction and nonfiction for the group to refer to as they discuss the book. Book club meetings will normally last about fifteen minutes for younger students and up to thirty minutes for older, more experienced students.

You can participate by helping groups get their discussions started, move beyond a sticking point, or continue when they think they have run out of things to say. Note how group members work with each other, and be sure they give evidence for their opinions from the text or personal experience. Encourage them to ask questions, especially when they don't understand something. As students become more experienced in discussing books, you can move gradually into the role of observer, interacting with groups only as needed.

As you observe book discussions, pay attention to both process and content. Some groups may be proficient at the process of talking about a book but not about the content, so they end up saying little about the deeper meaning of a book. The purpose of a book club is for students to learn how to explore the meaning of a text and express their thinking about that text. Other groups may have many ideas to share, but they don't know how to organize their meeting. You may need to spend some time with these groups to remind them how to lead a discussion, let everyone have a turn, listen when others are speaking, and participate in the discussion.

USING THE TEACHING CARDS:
FICTION FOCUS

Each card provides teachers with a quick and essential analysis of the book students will read.

GUIDED READING PROGRAM
Fiction Focus
2nd Edition

Tangerine

Summary & Standard

Paul Fisher sees more than his thick glasses would allow and tells his diary all that happens when his family moves from Houston to small-town Florida. Students will read to better understand the various cultures of the United States.

Author: Edward Bloor
Genre: Realistic Fiction

Word Count: 250+
Theme/Idea: facing challenges

Meets standards and makes real-world connections.

Making Connections: Text to Self

Students may have prior knowledge about moving to a new home or new town or attending a new school. Discuss what students experienced when making these changes.

Extend the real-world connection by talking about how students would want to be treated at a new school. Ask for suggestions as to how best to welcome a new student. Discuss practical difficulties a student might encounter at a new school during his or her first week.

For additional teaching ideas and resources, see http://www2.scholastic.com/browse/collateral.jsp?id=972.

Builds rich oral and written vocabulary.

Vocabulary

Essential Words: development, eclipse, handicap, majority, minority, portable, regulation, threatening

Related Words for Discussion: admiration, fame, perceive, reputation

Genre

Realistic Fiction Remind students that realistic fiction has characters, settings, and conflicts that may be found in real life.

Supportive Book Features

Text The text is organized as a diary with dated entries. Its strict chronology and first-person narrative create structural simplicity.

Content Students will be familiar with the difficulties and challenges that can arise when trying to fit in with new friends, a new school, or even new siblings or other family members.

Praise students for specific use of "Behaviors to Notice and Support" on page 100 of the *Guided Reading Teacher's Guide*.

Challenging Book Features

Text The book has nearly 300 pages and a great deal of text on each page. Remind students that the dates at the beginning of the diary entry can help them follow the sequence of events in the story.

Vocabulary Students may not be familiar with idioms, colloquialisms, and figurative language used in the book. Read aloud sections where these expressions are used and explain that they make the text more lively and often give it added meaning. Also, these devices give dialogue the quality of natural speech.

Level U

ELL Bridge

To help students understand the organization of the book, talk about keeping a journal. Explain that journal entries are dated and arranged chronologically. A journal can be used to record daily personal experiences in the order in which they happen. Have students keep a log of how they spend one day, complete with the time each event or activity happened. Then have them compare their logs to the diary entries in the book, discussing how the dates/times help the reader understand the sequence of events.

📖 SCHOLASTIC

Easily adapts lessons to meet the needs of English language learners.

Builds the reading skills identified by the **National Reading Panel** and reading experts.

Teaching Options

Developing Comprehension

Helps students think within, beyond, and about each text to enhance comprehension.

Thinking Within the Text
Have students discuss what they learned about Paul. How was he able to cope with the change in schools? Summarize the events that Paul experienced and how he handled each situation.

Thinking Beyond the Text
Ask students to describe Lake Windsor Middle School and Tangerine Middle School. Have students make connections by asking which school is more similar to theirs and why. Have students predict how Paul might have felt if he had transferred to their school. Would he have been just as excited? What if Erik had transferred to their school?

Thinking About the Text
Remind students that figurative language refers to language that means something beyond the dictionary definition of the words. Point to the line *If you think we're slugs . . .* on page 45. Ask: *Is Paul saying that the students are actually slugs? Why does he make this comparison?* Have students notice and point to other examples of how the writer uses figurative language to describe actions, characters, and how people feel.

Compare and Contrast
Remind students that authors often compare and contrast things and people to show how they are alike and different. Point out how the book contrasts Paul's two schools. Have students identify ways in which the schools and the students at each are different.

- Ask: *How does Paul feel about these differences throughout the book? Are there any similarities between the schools?*

- Have students support their answers with sentences or passages from the story.

For more prompts and ideas for teaching problem-solving strategies, see page 22 of the *Guided Reading Teacher's Guide.*

Developing Phonics and Word-Solving Strategies

Varying Words With Prefixes and Suffixes
Explain that prefixes, suffixes, or both can be added to base words to form new words.

- Ask students to identify the base word that can be found in both *undeveloped* and *development* (*develop*). Then have them identify the affixes that have been added (*un-, -ment*). Challenge students to use these words in a sentence. Then have students list other prefixes and suffixes.

- Ask them to add prefixes and suffixes to *pack* to form variations of the word.

Developing Fluency
Model expressive reading of a passage from the book, stressing appropriate pauses. Have students read the passage aloud, paying attention to phrasing and using appropriate expression.

Oral Language/Conversation
Talk About Reputation Lead a discussion about reputation. Have a volunteer look up *reputation* in the dictionary and read the definition aloud. Talk about how a person's reputation may or may not describe his or her character. Discuss Erik's reputation and how people perceived him.

Extending Meaning Through Writing

- Challenge students to write a diary entry from the point of view of another character in the book, such as Theresa, who shows Paul around the school. **(Narrative)**

- Have students write a page explaining why the sinkhole, termites, and muck fires are metaphors for Paul's life. **(Expository)**

Extends meaning through writing and expanded reading lists.

Other Books
Report to the Principal's Office by Jerry Spinelli
The Secret Garden by Frances Hodgson Burnett

GRFF2U10

USING THE TEACHING CARDS: CONTENT AREAS

Each card provides teachers with a quick and essential analysis of the book students will read.

GUIDED READING PROGRAM Content Areas

Thunder and Lightning

by **Wendy Pfeffer**
text type: **Informational**
word count: **250+**
content area: **Earth Science**
topic: **weather**

Level J

Summary & Standard
This fact-filled book takes a close look at thunderstorms—how they develop, and how to stay safe during a violent storm. Children will learn how weather changes from day to day and over the seasons.

Meets standards and makes real world connections.

Making Connections: Text to World

Children will have considerable real-life experience with storms, thunder, and lightning to draw upon as they read this book. Have them share any observations and questions.

Extend the real-world connection by talking about weather broadcasts. Encourage children to watch one and to note the language that the meteorologist uses and how the weather is depicted on the map.

For more information on thunderstorms, see **www.wildwildweather.com**, the Web site for Dan's Wild Wild Weather Page.

Vocabulary

Builds rich content area vocabulary.

Content Words: cloud, lightning, scientist, static electricity, storm, water vapor

Essential Words: billion, join

Related Words for Discussion: systems, water cycle

Nonfiction Text Features: boldface words, captions, glossary

Supportive Features

Text This book is filled with beautiful photographs that clearly illustrate the text. Although some pages contain a lot of text, the text is clearly positioned and difficult words are followed by their phonetic pronunciations.

Content This book presents complex scientific concepts using a topic children know well from their daily life, providing a high-interest entry point and scaffolding.

Praise children for specific use of "Behaviors to Notice and Support" on page 61 of the *Guided Reading Teacher's Guide.*

Challenging Features

Text Some of the long sentences may be challenging for children. A lot of information is sometimes covered in a short space. Pages often have a few paragraphs and topic changes.

Vocabulary There are several specialized words, multiple-meaning words, and science concepts that may require further explanation. These include the water cycle, static electricity, gas, limbs, blue jets, and the causes of thunder.

ESL Bridge

Introduce the topic of the book by showing the cover and by clarifying the meanings of the words *thunder* and *lightning*. Lead children to discover the word *light* embedded in *lightning*, and brainstorm together other words that contain *light*. Next, page through the book, pointing out and naming images of content-related words represented in the pictures: *cloud, lightning, water, storm,* and so on. Encourage children to understand that captions underneath pictures are great places to learn the names of content-related words.

Easily adapts lessons to meet the needs of English-Language Learners.

■SCHOLASTIC

Builds the reading skills required by *No Child Left Behind.*

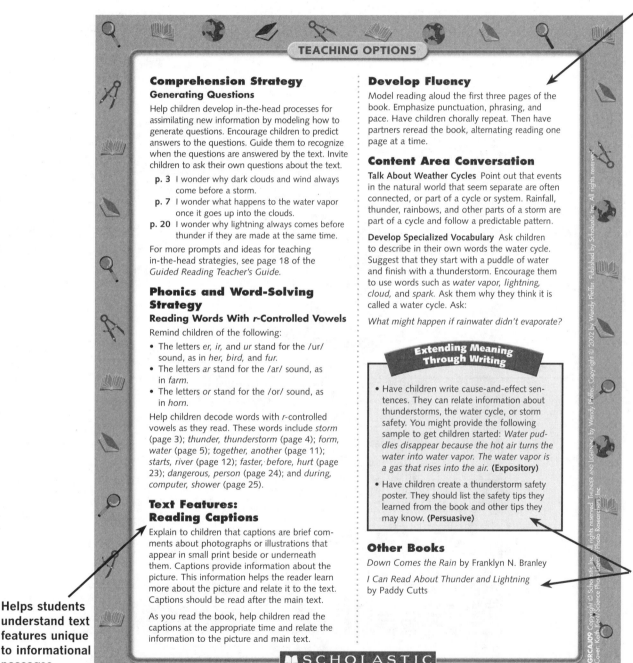

Comprehension Strategy
Generating Questions

Help children develop in-the-head processes for assimilating new information by modeling how to generate questions. Encourage children to predict answers to the questions. Guide them to recognize when the questions are answered by the text. Invite children to ask their own questions about the text.

p. 3 I wonder why dark clouds and wind always come before a storm.

p. 7 I wonder what happens to the water vapor once it goes up into the clouds.

p. 20 I wonder why lightning always comes before thunder if they are made at the same time.

For more prompts and ideas for teaching in-the-head strategies, see page 18 of the *Guided Reading Teacher's Guide.*

Phonics and Word-Solving Strategy
Reading Words With *r*-Controlled Vowels

Remind children of the following:

- The letters *er, ir,* and *ur* stand for the /ur/ sound, as in *her, bird,* and *fur.*
- The letters *ar* stand for the /ar/ sound, as in *farm.*
- The letters *or* stand for the /or/ sound, as in *horn.*

Help children decode words with *r*-controlled vowels as they read. These words include *storm* (page 3); *thunder, thunderstorm* (page 4); *form, water* (page 5); *together, another* (page 11); *starts, river* (page 12); *faster, before, hurt* (page 23); *dangerous, person* (page 24); and *during, computer, shower* (page 25).

Text Features: Reading Captions

Explain to children that captions are brief comments about photographs or illustrations that appear in small print beside or underneath them. Captions provide information about the picture. This information helps the reader learn more about the picture and relate it to the text. Captions should be read after the main text.

As you read the book, help children read the captions at the appropriate time and relate the information to the picture and main text.

Helps students understand text features unique to informational passages.

Develop Fluency

Model reading aloud the first three pages of the book. Emphasize punctuation, phrasing, and pace. Have children chorally repeat. Then have partners reread the book, alternating reading one page at a time.

Content Area Conversation

Talk About Weather Cycles Point out that events in the natural world that seem separate are often connected, or part of a cycle or system. Rainfall, thunder, rainbows, and other parts of a storm are part of a cycle and follow a predictable pattern.

Develop Specialized Vocabulary Ask children to describe in their own words the water cycle. Suggest that they start with a puddle of water and finish with a thunderstorm. Encourage them to use words such as *water vapor, lightning, cloud,* and *spark.* Ask them why they think it is called a water cycle. Ask:

What might happen if rainwater didn't evaporate?

Extending Meaning Through Writing

- Have children write cause-and-effect sentences. They can relate information about thunderstorms, the water cycle, or storm safety. You might provide the following sample to get children started: *Water puddles disappear because the hot air turns the water into water vapor. The water vapor is a gas that rises into the air.* **(Expository)**

- Have children create a thunderstorm safety poster. They should list the safety tips they learned from the book and other tips they may know. **(Persuasive)**

Other Books

Down Comes the Rain by Franklyn N. Branley

I Can Read About Thunder and Lightning by Paddy Cutts

Extends meaning through writing and expanded reading lists.

SCHOLASTIC

USING THE TEACHING CARDS:
NONFICTION FOCUS

The author, genre, level, and word count (for Levels A–K) are provided.

All texts have features that make it easier for the reader to make meaning. Those features are highlighted to assist you as you guide students through the book.

A summary is included to familiarize yourself with the book or give you a brief reminder of its content.

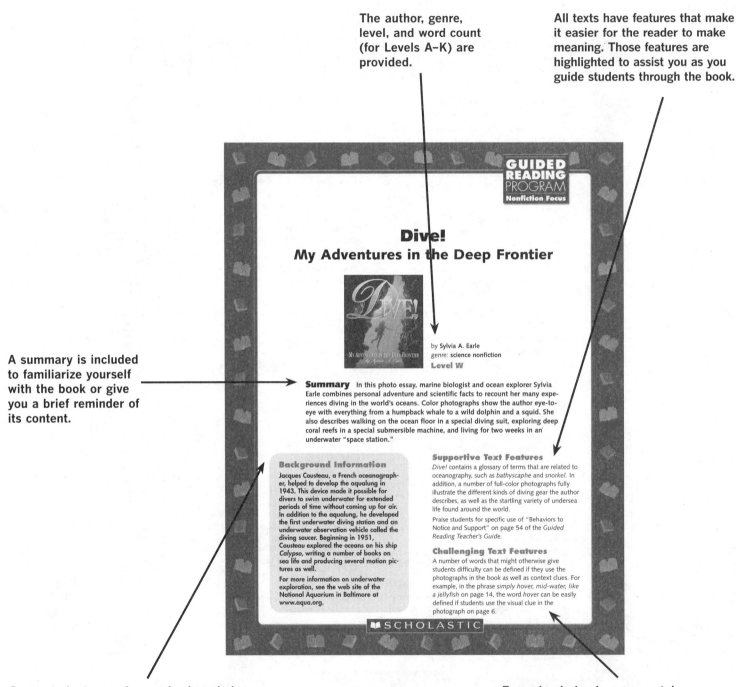

GUIDED READING PROGRAM
Nonfiction Focus

Dive!
My Adventures in the Deep Frontier

by Sylvia A. Earle
genre: **science nonfiction**
Level W

Summary In this photo essay, marine biologist and ocean explorer Sylvia Earle combines personal adventure and scientific facts to recount her many experiences diving in the world's oceans. Color photographs show the author eye-to-eye with everything from a humpback whale to a wild dolphin and a squid. She also describes walking on the ocean floor in a special diving suit, exploring deep coral reefs in a special submersible machine, and living for two weeks in an underwater "space station."

Background Information
Jacques Cousteau, a French oceanographer, helped to develop the aqualung in 1943. This device made it possible for divers to swim underwater for extended periods of time without coming up for air. In addition to the aqualung, he developed the first underwater diving station and an underwater observation vehicle called the diving saucer. Beginning in 1951, Cousteau explored the oceans on his ship *Calypso*, writing a number of books on sea life and producing several motion pictures as well.

For more information on underwater exploration, see the web site of the National Aquarium in Baltimore at www.aqua.org.

Supportive Text Features
Dive! contains a glossary of terms that are related to oceanography, such as *bathyscaphe* and *snorkel*. In addition, a number of full-color photographs fully illustrate the different kinds of diving gear the author describes, as well as the startling variety of undersea life found around the world.

Praise students for specific use of "Behaviors to Notice and Support" on page 54 of the *Guided Reading Teacher's Guide.*

Challenging Text Features
A number of words that might otherwise give students difficulty can be defined if they use the photographs in the book as well as context clues. For example, in the phrase *simply hover, mid-water, like a jellyfish* on page 14, the word *hover* can be easily defined if students use the visual clue in the photograph on page 6.

■ SCHOLASTIC

Some students may have prior knowledge gaps that will impede comprehension. The background information is included to be shared with students prior to reading. Use the information to determine students' level of background knowledge. Clarify or add to existing knowledge. In addition, a web site is provided for further research and resources.

Even simple books may contain text features that may hinder a student's comprehension. These are noted so that you can be on the "lookout" for them as students read, and assist students in dealing with challenging features.

Lessons for one to two comprehension strategies are provided. In each lesson, the skill is defined and sample questions are included for you to teach the skill and assess students' mastery.

Much can be done to build students' listening and speaking vocabularies. This section engages students in conversations about the book to check their comprehension, use newly-learned words, and extend understanding.

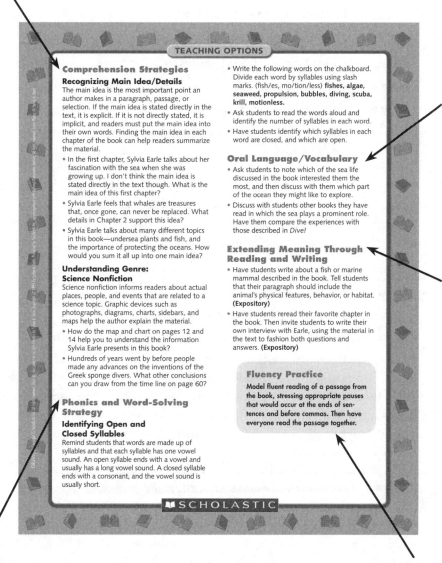

TEACHING OPTIONS

Comprehension Strategies

Recognizing Main Idea/Details
The main idea is the most important point an author makes in a paragraph, passage, or selection. If the main idea is stated directly in the text, it is explicit. If it is not directly stated, it is implicit, and readers must put the main idea into their own words. Finding the main idea in each chapter of the book can help readers summarize the material.

• In the first chapter, Sylvia Earle talks about her fascination with the sea when she was growing up. I don't think the main idea is stated directly in the text though. What is the main idea of this first chapter?

• Sylvia Earle feels that whales are treasures that, once gone, can never be replaced. What details in Chapter 2 support this idea?

• Sylvia Earle talks about many different topics in this book—undersea plants and fish, and the importance of protecting the oceans. How would you sum it all up into one main idea?

**Understanding Genre:
Science Nonfiction**
Science nonfiction informs readers about actual places, people, and events that are related to a science topic. Graphic devices such as photographs, diagrams, charts, sidebars, and maps help the author explain the material.

• How do the map and chart on pages 12 and 14 help you to understand the information Sylvia Earle presents in this book?

• Hundreds of years went by before people made any advances on the inventions of the Greek sponge divers. What other conclusions can you draw from the time line on page 60?

Phonics and Word-Solving Strategy

**Identifying Open and
Closed Syllables**
Remind students that words are made up of syllables and that each syllable has one vowel sound. An open syllable ends with a vowel and usually has a long vowel sound. A closed syllable ends with a consonant, and the vowel sound is usually short.

• Write the following words on the chalkboard. Divide each word by syllables using slash marks. (fish/es, mo/tion/less) **fishes, algae, seaweed, propulsion, bubbles, diving, scuba, krill, motionless.**

• Ask students to read the words aloud and identify the number of syllables in each word.

• Have students identify which syllables in each word are closed, and which are open.

Oral Language/Vocabulary

• Ask students to note which of the sea life discussed in the book interested them the most, and then discuss with them which part of the ocean they might like to explore.

• Discuss with students other books they have read in which the sea plays a prominent role. Have them compare the experiences with those described in *Dive!*

Extending Meaning Through Reading and Writing

• Have students write about a fish or marine mammal described in the book. Tell students that their paragraph should include the animal's physical features, behavior, or habitat. **(Expository)**

• Have students reread their favorite chapter in the book. Then invite students to write their own interview with Earle, using the material in the text to fashion both questions and answers. **(Expository)**

Fluency Practice
Model fluent reading of a passage from the book, stressing appropriate pauses that would occur at the ends of sentences and before commas. Then have everyone read the passage together.

■SCHOLASTIC

Reading and writing are reciprocal processes. Writing prompts for narrative, expository, descriptive, and persuasive writing are provided. Some help to further assess comprehension of text. Others offer writing process prompts for fuller, richer writing experiences.

Lessons for one to two phonics and word-solving strategies are also provided. These lessons will help students decode unfamiliar words and use their knowledge of common spelling patterns as they read.

This section offers fluency-building activities. Students need opportunities to read and reread books to develop their automaticity with word recognition. In addition, they need opportunities to hear fluent reading models and discuss the importance of fluency, and guided practice sessions to develop fluency.

ASSESSMENT
OBSERVATION

Overview

We define assessment as the collection of information about a student's learning, and evaluation as the judgment about the student's strengths and specific needs based on this information. Assessment should be continuous—based on observation and informal measures of reading performance. Evaluation should provide a guide for teaching decisions that will help the student's learning.

To assess and evaluate a student's literacy development, information needs to be collected to demonstrate the following:

- **how a student uses and responds to oral language in various settings.**
- **what a student knows about reading and writing.**
- **how a student uses reading and writing in various settings.**
- **how a student values reading and writing.**

The Guided Reading Program is structured to give information on different kinds of literacy skills for students with varied learning needs. The program supports literacy development in reading, writing, listening, and speaking. These literacy activities provide a wealth of assessment information.

Purposes of Assessment

As a student progresses from a beginning reader and writer to a fluent reader and writer, assessment may have several purposes:

- **to establish what a student initially knows about literacy.**
- **to identify a student's instructional reading level.**
- **to monitor a student's pattern of strengths.**
- **to establish a student's facility with informational text.**

Assessment needs to take place at the beginning of the school year to know what foundational skills students have and to identify potential skill needs. All school-age students know something about oral and written language and are ready to learn more. Some may have knowledge about environmental print but little experience with books or with writing. Others may be confident with books and with some writing.

Observation

One of the best ways to assess an individual student's learning is through observation. For a well-rounded view of the student, try to observe him or her throughout the day in a variety of settings, such as during small-group and whole-class instruction, during independent reading time, or in the classroom library. What exactly can you observe?

Some suggestions include:

- oral language ability
- attitudes
- choices during "free time"
- specific behaviors related to print
- interests
- book-handling behaviors
- peer relationships

Ask yourself questions such as the following when observing a student's behaviors related to print:

- When the student reads or works with print, does he or she approach the task confidently?
- Does the student have a strategy for attempting unfamiliar words in reading and writing?
- Does the student read and write for different purposes?
- Can the student retell what he or she reads in a logical order?
- Does the student select reading materials suited to his or her personal interests?
- Does the student select reading materials suited to his or her level of reading development?

Answers to these kinds of questions will help you make instructional decisions and set goals for an individual student, and will help the student progress in learning.

Make your observations systematic rather than random. Decide whom to focus on. Select one student or several at a time to closely watch. Keep a record for each student, noting what you see by recording it on self-adhesive stickies or peel-off labels that can be attached to the student's personal folder. Alternatively, keep a class list for easy referral.

When behaviors are observed, a check (✓) may be used. You may also wish to make a slash (/) the first time the behavior is observed and convert the slash to an X when you feel the behavior is performed with frequency. Indicating dates is helpful.

Decide when to observe. Observe during a time students are normally using books, when they first come into the room in the morning, or during a time they are involved in various learning centers. You may need to initiate the experience with students who do not independently go to books. Collect pertinent data, including written work samples and recordings of oral reading, and keep anecdotal records. Speak with parents for additional input.

ASSESSMENT
RUNNING RECORDS

An effective reader uses the visual information, based on knowledge of language and the content, to predict what comes next in the text, to check this prediction by taking in new visual information or by thinking about whether the prediction makes sense, and to confirm or reject this prediction in the light of this new information. If the prediction is rejected, the reader self-corrects.

When a student reads aloud, you can record what is read and look more closely at what the student is thinking and doing. Oral reading miscues reveal a student's reading strategies. Any miscues can be analyzed to make teaching decisions about the suitability of the level of the guided reading books being read and about the type of help a student may need. One way of doing this is to take a running record of oral reading.

Using a Running Record
Follow this assessment procedure to periodically monitor reading strategies.

First Step	Select something that is known to the student for him or her to read orally. (If it is too familiar, the reading may not reveal much information about the child's thinking.) This may be: • **a guided reading book;** • **a poem;** • **a dictated piece of the student's writing;** • **some of the student's published personal writing.**
Second Step	Ask the student to read the selected piece aloud. Record the student's reading in one of these ways: • **Record the correct reading and miscues on a blank piece of paper as the student reads, keeping the same linear arrangement of the text.** OR • **Make a copy of the text and mark the miscues on it as the student reads.**
Third Step	Tabulate the miscues. Use symbols to indicate what the student is doing. Some usual conventions follow.

Accurate reading	✓✓✓	(checks follow test pattern)
Substitution	wet (*child*)	
	Went (*text*)	
Attempt	w-we-wet	
	went	
Self-correction	wet	
	Went SC	
Omission	-	(or circle word)
	went	
Insertion	is	(or use carat)
	went	
Teacher told	-	(or underline word)
	Went T	
Repetition (of word or sentence)	R2 (numeral indicated number of repeats)	(or wavy underlines)

Evaluation: Analysis of the Running Record

Miscues in oral reading performance help you to identify the strategies a student uses. Ask yourself why the student makes each error. To determine what cues the student depends on, consider the following:

- Does the student use visual cues from letters and words, such as *they* for *them*?

- Does the student use context clues to construct meaning? Inaccurate reading that makes sense indicates the student is probably using prior knowledge or familiar oral language.

- Does the student use knowledge of the grammatical structure of language? Again, the student's own oral language may influence a response.

Make your best guess as to what cues the student uses, recording by the miscues *v* for visual cues, *m* for meaning, and *s* for structure. One or more types of cues might be used for any miscue. By analyzing each miscue in this way you can get an indication of the strategies the student is using, as well as those not being used or those being overused. Also notice instances of self-correction. Self-correction is an important skill in good reading.

Finally, make any notes on the running record about behaviors during the session. All of this information will assist you in assessing the student.

Running Records as a Regular Monitoring Tool

For each student who is able to read some type of continuous text, it is useful to take a running record about every six weeks. Repeat more often for students for whom you have concerns. For fluent readers it would only be necessary at the beginning, middle, and end of the school year.

Establish a system. For example, you might choose one student per school day, keeping the dated record and analysis in each student's portfolio to monitor the progress during the year. Select a time when you can hear the student read without interruptions, such as when other students are engaged in individual quiet reading.

Sample Running Record

Name: _____ Date: _____

Title: _____

PAGE	TEXT INFORMATION USED	RUNNING RECORD	
4	The animals had a picnic	✓ ✓ have ✓ ✓	v, m
	To celebrate the fair.	✓ ✓ ✓ ✓	
	They all brought something tasty	✓ ✓ bought ✓ t/testy/SC	v, m, s
	For everyone to share.	✓ ✓ ✓ ✓	
7	The lambs brought yams.	✓ ✓ bought ✓	v, m, s
	The bees brought peas.	✓ ✓ bought ✓	v, m, s
	The poodles brought noodles	✓ ✓ bought ✓	v, m, s
	All sprinkled with cheese.	✓ sprin/sprinkle/SC ✓	
8	The cheetahs brought pitas.	✓ ✓ bought pasta/T	v, m, s
	The mice brought rice.	✓ ✓ bought ✓	v, m, s
	The moose brought juice	✓ ✓ bought ✓	v, m, s
	And a bucket of ice.	✓ ✓ ✓ ✓	
11	The pigs brought figs.	✓ ✓ bought ✓	v, m, s
	The bears brought pears.	✓ ✓ bought ✓	v, m, s
	The apes brought grapes	✓ ✓ bought ✓	v, m, s
	And some picnic chairs.	✓ ✓ ✓ ✓	
12	The raccoons brought spoons.	✓ ✓ ✓ ✓	
	The moles brought bowls.	✓ ✓ ✓ ✓	
	The storks brought forks	✓ ✓ ✓ fo/fork/SC	
	And some cinnamon rolls.	✓ ✓ c/cam/camon/T	v
15	The snakes brought cakes	✓ snake bought ✓	v, m, s
	And I brought the tea.	✓ ✓ ✓ ✓ ✓	
	It was a wild picnic –	✓ ✓ ✓ ✓ ✓	
	Just the animals and me!	✓ ✓ ✓ ✓ ✓	

v=visual, m=meaning, s=structure

Calculations

Note: In the example the student repeatedly misread the word *brought* as *bought*. There are two approaches to counting this error: as one error that is repeated or as multiple errors (which the student failed to self-correct).

- **Calculation of Accuracy Rate**

  If *bought* is counted as only one error, accuracy rate is calculated as follows:

  $$102-(5/102 \times 100)=95\%$$

  If *bought* is counted as an error each time it is misread, the accuracy rate is calculated as follows:

  $$102-(15/102 \times 100)=85\%$$

  The calculation of the accuracy rate is expressed by the following generic formula:

  $$T-(E/T \times 100)=AR$$

- **Calculation of Self-Correction Rate**

  If *bought* is counted as only one error, self-correction rate is $(5+3)/3=2.6$

  If *bought* is counted as an error each time it is misread, self-correction rate is $(15+3)/3=6$

  The calculation of the self-correction rate can be expressed by the following formula:

  $$(E+SC)/SC=SCR$$

T=total number of words	E=number of errors
AR=accuracy rate	SC=number of self-corrections
SCR=self-correction rate	

Teacher's Notes

Adib told the story (pointing to picture) and answered questions. Adib is using all strategies when reading and seems to have cross-checked one cue against another to self-correct. I could draw his attention to the difference between brought *and* bought. *This book is at a suitable level of difficulty for instruction.*

Note that space has also been provided for you to ask your own comprehension questions and record children's responses.

Evaluation of Suitability of Books

If a student is reading at an appropriate instructional level, approximately 94% of the text should be read accurately. An attempt at a word that is eventually correct is not an error; record this as a self-correction and tally it as accurately read. By calculating the percentage of accurately read words and analyzing the types of errors, you'll be able to determine whether the student is reading books at the appropriate instructional level, and you'll be able to choose the right guided reading books for individuals and groups.

Students may select a guided reading book to have it read to them or to read with a partner. In these instances the book may be easier or harder than the instructional level.

RUNNING RECORD
BENCHMARK BOOK LEVEL A

Running Record Sheet
Helping

Name _____   Date _____

24 Words   Level A   Accuracy Rate _____

PAGE	TEXT	RUNNING RECORD ANALYSIS
Page 3	I help my mom.	
Page 5	I help my dad.	
Page 7	I help my sister.	
Page 9	I help my cat.	
Page 11	I help my dog.	
Page 12	I like to help.	

Comprehension:

1) _____

_____

_____

_____

2) _____

_____

_____

_____

RUNNING RECORD
BENCHMARK BOOK LEVEL B

Running Record Sheet
Off to the City

Name _____   Date _____

43 Words   Level B   Accuracy Rate _____

PAGE	TEXT	RUNNING RECORD ANALYSIS
Page 2	Dad and Kim went off to the city.	
Page 3	They went past the pond.	
Page 4	They went past the red barn.	
Page 5	They went past the train station.	
Page 6	They went past the school.	
Page 7	Dad and Kim went to see Grandma.	
Page 8	Dad and Kim went back home.	

Comprehension:

1) _____

_____

_____

_____

2) _____

_____

_____

_____

RUNNING RECORD
BENCHMARK BOOK LEVEL C

Running Record Sheet
The Big Blue Sea

Name _____   Date _____
68 Words   Level C   Accuracy Rate _____

PAGE	TEXT	RUNNING RECORD ANALYSIS
Page 2	A little fish lives in the big blue sea.	
Page 4	A big turtle lives in the big blue sea.	
Page 6	A little sea star lives in the big blue sea.	
Page 8	A big jellyfish lives in the big blue sea.	
Page 10	A little sea horse lives in the big blue sea.	
Page 12	A big, big octopus lives in the big blue sea.	
Page 14	Big animals and little animals live in the big blue sea.	

Comprehension:

1) _____

_____

_____

_____

2) _____

_____

_____

_____

RUNNING RECORD
BENCHMARK BOOK LEVEL D

Running Record Sheet
The Little Red Hen

Name _____   Date _____

50 Words   Level D   Accuracy Rate _____

PAGE	TEXT	RUNNING RECORD ANALYSIS
Page 2	There was a little red hen. She found a grain of wheat. The little red hen said, "Who will plant this grain of wheat?"	
Page 3	"Not I," said the duck. "Not I," said the dog. "Not I," said the cat. "Then I will plant the wheat," said the little red hen.	

Comprehension:

1) _____

_____

_____

_____

2) _____

_____

_____

_____

RUNNING RECORD
BENCHMARK BOOK LEVEL E

Running Record Sheet
Fred's Wish for Fish

Name _____   Date _____

128 Words   Level E   Accuracy Rate _____

PAGE	TEXT	RUNNING RECORD ANALYSIS
Page 2	Fred and Dad went to the pet store. Dad said, "Look at the fish, Fred!" Fred said, "I wish I had some fish." Fred did not have any fish. Fred said, "Can we get some fish, please?" Dad said, "Okay!"	
Page 4	Kate from the pet store came to help. Fred said, "I want orange fish. I want black and white fish. I want fish with lots of colors!" Kate put the fish in a bag with water. Fred and Dad went home.	
Page 6	Fred looked at his fish. He had orange fish. He had black and white fish. He had fish with lots of colors. Fred was happy!	
Page 8	Dad said, "Now you have a lot of fish." Fred said, "Thank you, Dad! I love my fish! And I love **you**!"	

Comprehension:

1) _____

_____

_____

_____

2) _____

_____

_____

_____

RUNNING RECORD
BENCHMARK BOOK LEVEL F

Running Record Sheet
The Country Mouse and the Town Mouse

Name _____   Date _____

126 Words   Level F   Accuracy Rate _____

PAGE	TEXT	RUNNING RECORD ANALYSIS
Page 2	What did Country Mouse do? She called Town Mouse. She asked Town Mouse to dinner.	
Page 4	What did Country Mouse do? She put nuts and berries in a basket.	
Page 6	What did Country Mouse do? She met Town Mouse at the door.	
Page 8	What did Country Mouse do? She gave Town Mouse berries and nuts. "Do you like the dinner?" asked Country Mouse. "I do, but I have more to eat in town. Come for dinner! You will see," said Town Mouse.	
Page 10	What did Country Mouse do? She left her country home.	
Page 11	What did Country Mouse do? She went to town. She went to Town Mouse's home.	
Page 12	What did Country Mouse do? She saw a lot of food. "This is how a mouse eats in town!" said Town Mouse.	

Comprehension:

1) _____

_____

2) _____

_____

RUNNING RECORD
BENCHMARK BOOK LEVEL G

Running Record Sheet
Justin's New Bike

Name _____   Date _____

122 Words   Level G   Accuracy Rate _____

PAGE	TEXT	RUNNING RECORD ANALYSIS
Page 3	Danny and Justin went to the bike track. Justin had a new bike. Danny's bike was old.	
Page 4	They looked at the other kids riding up and down the hills on the track.	
Page 6	Justin looked at Danny going around the track.	
Page 7	"I can do that," said Danny. "Look at me!" he shouted.	
Page 8	Danny was going very fast! He made lots of dust.	
Page 9	Justin looked down at his new bike. He looked at Danny speeding around the bike track.	
Page 10	"I can go faster than you," shouted Justin.	
Page 11	Justin took off down the first hill. "Look out, Danny," shouted Justin. "Here I come!"	
Page 12	Justin went speeding around the track after Danny. Dust flew up from the track. The boys went flying over the little hills ...	

Comprehension:

1) _____

_____

_____

2) _____

_____

_____

RUNNING RECORD
BENCHMARK BOOK LEVEL H

Running Record Sheet
Sammy the Seal

Name _____   Date _____

113 Words   Level H   Accuracy Rate _____

PAGE	TEXT	RUNNING RECORD ANALYSIS
Page 7	It was feeding time at the zoo. All the animals were getting their food.	
Page 8	The lions ate their meat.	
Page 9	The elephants ate their hay.	
Page 10	The monkeys ate their bananas.	
Page 11	The bears ate their honey.	
Page 12	Then it was time for the seals to be fed. Mr. Johnson took them fish.	
Page 13	"Hooray for fish!" said the seals. They jumped in the water.	
Page 14	Soon the basket was empty. "That is all there is," said Mr. Johnson. "There is no more."	
Page 15	"Thank you for the fish," said the seals. "They were good." The seals were happy.	
Page 16	But one little seal was not happy. He sat by himself. He looked sad. "What is wrong, Sammy?" said Mr. Johnson.	

Comprehension:

1) _____

_____

_____

2) _____

_____

_____

RUNNING RECORD
BENCHMARK BOOK LEVEL I

Running Record Sheet
Mama Zooms

Name _____   Date _____

144 Words   Level I   Accuracy Rate _____

PAGE	TEXT	RUNNING RECORD ANALYSIS
Page 4	Mama's got a zooming machine and she zooms me everywhere.	
Page 6	Every morning Daddy puts me in Mama's lap and we're off!	
Page 8	Mama zooms me across the lawn and she's my racehorse.	
Page 10	Mama zooms me through a puddle and she's my ship at sea.	
Page 12	Mama zooms me down a smooth sidewalk and she's my race car.	
Page 14	Mama zooms me fast down ramps. We love ramps!	
Page 16	Mama zooms me across a bridge and she's my airplane.	
Page 18	Mama zooms me through a dark hall and she's my train in a tunnel.	
Page 20	Mama zooms me over a bumpy road and she's my buckboard wagon.	
Page 22	Mama zooms me along the ocean boardwalk and she's my wave.	
Page 24	Mama has very strong arms from all our zooming.	
Page 26	Daddy and I push her up only the very steepest hills. When we get to the top, Daddy says, "See you back on earth!"…	

Comprehension:

1) _____

_____

2) _____

_____

RUNNING RECORD
BENCHMARK BOOK LEVEL J

Running Record Sheet
Poppleton Has Fun

Name _____   Date _____

129 Words   Level J   Accuracy Rate _____

PAGE	TEXT	RUNNING RECORD ANALYSIS
Page 24	Poppleton and his neighbor Cherry Sue went to a fair. There they saw quilts.	
Page 26	The quilts had pictures on them and names and buttons from people's clothes.	
Page 27	"We should make our own quilt," Poppleton said to Cherry Sue. "What fun!" said Cherry Sue. "We will ask Hudson and Fillmore to help," said Poppleton. "Perfect!" said Cherry Sue.	
Page 28	Poppleton called his friends. "We are making a quilt on Saturday," Poppleton told Hudson. "Can you come?" "Sure!" said Hudson.	
Page 30	Poppleton called Fillmore. "We are making a quilt on Saturday," said Poppleton. "Can you come?" "Certainly!" said Fillmore.	
Page 31	On Saturday everyone met at Poppleton's house. Fillmore had some old shirts. Hudson had some old trousers.	
Page 32	Poppleton had some old curtains. And Cherry Sue had a bucket of buttons. "Let's sew!" said Poppleton.	

Comprehension:

1) _____

_____

_____

2) _____

_____

_____

RUNNING RECORD
BENCHMARK BOOK LEVEL K

Running Record Sheet
The Frog Prince

Name _____   Date _____

139 Words   Level K   Accuracy Rate _____

PAGE	TEXT	RUNNING RECORD ANALYSIS
Page 5	Once upon a time there was a beautiful princess. She had a golden ball, and it was her favorite plaything. She took it wherever she went.	
Page 6	One day the princess was playing in the woods, near a well. She threw her ball high into the air. It fell—**splash!**—into the well.	
Page 7	The princess watched her golden ball sink deep into the water of the well, and she began to cry. She cried harder and harder. Suddenly someone said, "What is the matter, princess? Why are you making so much noise?"	
Page 8	The princess looked around. She looked into the well. An ugly little frog was looking up at her. The frog asked again, "What is the matter, princess?" "Oh, it's you, you old water-splasher," the princess said. "My golden ball has fallen into the well. That is why I am crying."	

Comprehension:

1) _____

_____

_____

2) _____

_____

_____

RUNNING RECORD
BENCHMARK BOOK LEVEL L

Running Record Sheet
Miss Nelson Has a Field Day

Name _____   Date _____

153 Words   Level L   Accuracy Rate _____

PAGE	TEXT	RUNNING RECORD ANALYSIS
Page 3	For some weeks now, gloom had blanketed the Horace B. Smedley School. No one laughed or threw spitballs. No one even smiled. Miss Nelson was worried.	
Page 4	Everyone was down in the dumps. Even the cafeteria ladies had lost their sparkle.	
Page 5	Mr. Blandsworth was so depressed he hid under his desk. "It's the worst team in the whole state," he said.	
Page 6	And it was true—the Smedley Tornadoes were just pitiful. They hadn't won a game all year.	
Page 7	They hadn't scored even a single point. And lately they seemed only interested in horsing around and in giving Coach the business. "Why practice?" they said. "We'll only lose anyway."	
Page 8	"We're in for it now," said old Pop Hanson, the janitor. "The big Thanksgiving game is coming up, and the Werewolves from Central are real animals. They'll make mincemeat out of our team." "What's to be done?" said Miss Nelson. "We need a real expert," said Pop.	

Comprehension:

1) _____

_____

2) _____

_____

RUNNING RECORD
BENCHMARK BOOK LEVEL M

Running Record Sheet
Dancing With the Indians

Name _____   Date _____

118 Words   Level M   Accuracy Rate _____

PAGE	TEXT	RUNNING RECORD ANALYSIS
Page 6	Mama's packed our supper, the sheep are in their pens, it's time to go and visit the Seminole Indians.	
Page 8	Golden threads of sunlight trickle through the trees turning leaves above us into lacy canopies.	
Page 9	We hear about our grandpa, as our wagon creaks along, living with the Indians because slavery was wrong.	
Page 10	He worked on a plantation before he ran away, traveling by night, hiding by day.	
Page 11	Seminoles rescued Grandpa, making him their friend, calling him blood brother, Black and Indian. Each year we go to visit, honoring those he knew, joining in the dancing, watching what they do.	
Page 12	Our wagon nears the camp. Drums pound and move our feet. Soon everyone is swaying to the tom-tom beat.	

Comprehension:

1) _____

_____

2) _____

_____

RUNNING RECORD
BENCHMARK BOOK LEVEL N

Running Record Sheet
Suitcase

Name _____   Date _____

119 Words   Level N   Accuracy Rate _____

PAGE	TEXT	RUNNING RECORD ANALYSIS
Page 34	Xander walked from school through the park. He passed the flying rings, the hand-over-hand ladder, and the trapeze. None of these interested him. He made his way to a wire stretched close to the ground. This wire was used to increase balance skills. Xander called it "the steady tester." As he came closer to the wire he was surprised to see Jeff there with a group of men.	
Page 35	Xander moved to watch as, one at a time, the men tried to walk across the wire. He stood in awe, even though their arms flailed and they fell off almost immediately. As many times as he had tried, he had never even been able to get on the wire.	

Comprehension:

1)_____

_____

_____

_____

2)_____

_____

_____

_____

RUNNING RECORD
BENCHMARK BOOK LEVEL O

Running Record Sheet
Chocolate Fever

Name _____   Date _____

115 Words   Level O   Accuracy Rate _____

PAGE	TEXT	RUNNING RECORD ANALYSIS
Page 34	In later years, Henry couldn't remember who screamed first. All he could recall was that both he and Mrs. Kimmelfarber were yelling their heads off. And that Nurse Molly Farthing was as cool as a cantaloupe. "Calm down now, both of you," she said. "Mrs. Kimmelfarber, you go and call Mrs. Green on the telephone. Tell her we're taking Henry to the City Hospital." Mrs. Kimmelfarber didn't move. She just stood there with her mouth open, staring at Henry.	
Page 35	"You scoot now," insisted Nurse Farthing in a stern tone. "Shoosh... off with you!" "And you, Henry Green," she said as Mrs. Kimmelfarber left the room, "are coming with me. Let us go. Quietly. Calmly."	

Comprehension:

1) _____

_____

_____

_____

2) _____

_____

_____

_____

RUNNING RECORD
BENCHMARK BOOK LEVEL P

Running Record Sheet
Who Stole The Wizard of Oz?

Name _____   Date _____

130 Words   Level P   Accuracy Rate _____

PAGE	TEXT	RUNNING RECORD ANALYSIS
Page 3	My sister Becky and I were stretched out on the front porch one morning thinking out loud about how we should spend our summer vacation. It was too hot to do much more. At about nine-thirty, a police car turned down our street, then stopped in front of the Checkertown Library. Checkertown, Ohio—that's our town. Anyway, we watched the policeman go into the library, then we went back to making plans. But half an hour later, the phone rang. Becky jumped up, ran inside, and grabbed it. "Hello?" "Is this Becky?" "Yes." "This is Mrs. Brattle. The Checkertown librarian."	
Page 4	"Oh, hi." "Becky, there's a policeman here who wants to talk to you. Can you come over now?" "What for?" "There's been a robbery at the library, Becky," said Mrs. Brattle.	

Comprehension:

1) _____

_____

2) _____

_____

RUNNING RECORD
BENCHMARK BOOK LEVEL Q

Running Record Sheet
Just Juice

Name _____ Date _____

161 Words   Level Q   Accuracy Rate _____

PAGE	TEXT	RUNNING RECORD ANALYSIS
Page 32	Someone is knocking on the front door, but we ignore it. No one but salesmen ever come calling round front. And besides, we are in the back, dancing to Pa's fiddle. Pa fiddles whenever Ma asks. Ma says it soothes her nerves and makes that teensy baby inside her settle right on down. Wait till that baby comes out and finds Pa's fiddle isn't supposed to settle anything down. Pa's fiddle swings us. It sends us sashaying across the kitchen floor. But it does not settle us down.	
Page 33	I don't know how long the person knocks around front. Finally a face appears at the back door. "Mrs. Faulstich?" Ma makes her way across the kitchen. "Mrs. Faulstich, my name is Geneva Long. Is this a good time for a visit?" Geneva Long is a big woman. Nearly as big as Ma. Ma says, "Come on, come right on in, Geneva." For a stranger, Geneva sure looks at home in our kitchen.	

Comprehension:

1)_____

_____

_____

2)_____

_____

_____

RUNNING RECORD
BENCHMARK BOOK LEVEL R

Running Record Sheet
The Trumpet of the Swan

Name _____   Date _____

167 Words   Level R   Accuracy Rate _____

PAGE	TEXT	RUNNING RECORD ANALYSIS
Page 15	One day, almost a week later, the swan slipped quietly into her nest and laid an egg. Each day she tried to deposit one egg in the nest. Sometimes she succeeded, sometimes she didn't. There were now three eggs, and she was ready to lay a fourth. As she sat there, with her husband, the cob, floating gracefully nearby, she had a strange feeling that she was being watched. It made her uneasy. Birds don't like to be stared at. They particularly dislike being stared at when they are on a nest. So the swan twisted and turned and peered everywhere. She gazed intently at the point of land that jutted out into the pond near the nest. With her sharp eyes, she searched the nearby shore for signs of an intruder. What she finally saw gave her the surprise of her life. There, seated on a log on the point of land, was a small boy. He was being very quiet, and he had no gun.	

Comprehension:

1) _____

_____

_____

2) _____

_____

_____

RUNNING RECORD
BENCHMARK BOOK LEVEL S

Running Record Sheet
Granny Torrelli Makes Soup

Name _____

Date _____

154 Words   Level S

Accuracy Rate _____

PAGE	TEXT	RUNNING RECORD ANALYSIS
Page 7	Why I liked Bailey in the first place: Bailey was always there, born next door to me, one week after me, the two of us just two babies growing up side by side, our mothers together, and me and Bailey together, on the lawn, on the porch, on the floor, playing with pots and pans and mud and worms and snow and rain and puddles. *Help Bailey* was what our mothers said to me. *Help him, will you, Rosie?* And I did. I always helped Bailey. He was my buddy, my pal, my friend. Went to the zoo, went to the park, had birthdays together.	
Page 8	What a smile that Bailey had! He was smiling mostly all the time, his hands waving out in front of him, sweeping the air. Freckles on his face, sticking-up hair very soft, very quiet Bailey boy, but not too quiet, and not pushy, not selfish, not mean, not usually.	

Comprehension:

1) _____

_____

_____

_____

2) _____

_____

_____

_____

RUNNING RECORD
BENCHMARK BOOK LEVEL T

Running Record Sheet
The Power of Un

Name _____   Date _____

147 Words   Level T   Accuracy Rate _____

PAGE	TEXT	RUNNING RECORD ANALYSIS
Page 35	I grabbed Roxy and covered her mouth as the nearby woods came alive with the scuttlings and flutterings of unseen creatures. My own heart banged against my ribs. There's nothing like the sound of pure terror to get your blood fizzing with adrenaline. "Who's there?" I said, trying hard to keep my voice steady. "Gib? It's just me, Ash!" I let the breath out of my lungs in a long, deep rush. It wasn't all relief. Some of it was embarrassment. My flashlight beam came to rest on Ash's familiar freckled face and well-worn Giants baseball cap. He was laughing. "Hey, it's not funny, all right?" I said. "You shouldn't sneak up on people in the dark." Then, realizing how	
Page 36	wimpy that sounded, I went on in a hurry. "I mean, not me. Little kids like Roxy. You could give her nightmares doing that kind of stuff."	

Comprehension:

1) _____

_____

_____

2) _____

_____

_____

RUNNING RECORD
BENCHMARK BOOK LEVEL U

Running Record Sheet
Tangerine

Name _____   Date _____

156 Words   Level U   Accuracy Rate _____

PAGE	TEXT	RUNNING RECORD ANALYSIS
Page 84	The *Tangerine Times* printed a special pullout section on the Lake Windsor Middle School sinkhole. The photos were spectacular. They had one huge shot of the splintered walkways sticking up in all directions, like Godzilla had just trampled through there. The newspaper ran a letter from Mrs. Gates to the parents of all seventh and eighth graders. We're all supposed to attend a special disaster meeting on Friday night at seven-thirty in the high school gymnasium. The letter said that "state and county officials are planning to attend," and that "they are currently working out an emergency relocation plan that will be presented at this meeting." I'll bet they are. Think about it: There are 25 portables that are completely trashed, completely out of commission. Let's say there are 25 kids assigned to each of those portables. And each kid has 7 class periods a day. That's 625 kids and 175 class periods to relocate. Awesome.	

Comprehension:

1) _____

_____

_____

2) _____

_____

_____

RUNNING RECORD
BENCHMARK BOOK LEVEL V

Running Record Sheet
The Firework-Maker's Daughter

Name _____   Date _____

156 Words   Level V   Accuracy Rate _____

PAGE	TEXT	RUNNING RECORD ANALYSIS
Page 55	She pulled herself up with shaking arms, and stepped inside. The floor was baking hot and the air was hardly breathable. She walked on, deeper into the earth, deeper than the moonlight went, and heard nothing but silence, and saw nothing but dark rock. Harsh, barren walls rose to left and right; she felt them with her bleeding hands. Then the tunnel opened out into a great cavern. She had never seen anything so gloomy and empty of life, and her heart sank, because she had come all this way and there was nothing here. She sank to the floor. And, as if that were a signal, a little flame licked out of the rocky wall for an instant, and went out. Then another, in a different place. Then another. Then the earth shook and groaned, and with a harsh	
Page 56	grating sound, the rocky wall tore itself open, and suddenly the cavern was full of light.	

Comprehension:

1) _____

_____

_____

2) _____

_____

_____

RUNNING RECORD
BENCHMARK BOOK LEVEL W

Running Record Sheet
Tunnels

Name _____   Date _____

152 Words   Level W   Accuracy Rate _____

PAGE	TEXT	RUNNING RECORD ANALYSIS
Page 44	The next day after school, Will and Chester resumed their work at the excavation. Will was returning from dumping the spoils, his wheelbarrow stacked high with empty buckets as he trundled to the end of the tunnel where Chester was hacking away at the stone layer. "How's it going?" Will asked him. "It's not getting any easier, that's for sure," Chester replied, wiping the sweat from his forehead with a dirty sleeve and smearing dirt across his face in the process. "Hang on, let me have a look. You take a break." "OK." Will shone his helmet lamp over the rock surface, the subtle browns and yellows of the strata gouged randomly by the tip of the pickax, and sighed loudly. "I think we'd better stop and think about this for a minute. No point banging our heads on a sandstone wall! Let's have a drink." "Yeah, good idea," Chester said gratefully.	

Comprehension:

1) _____

_____

_____

2) _____

_____

_____

RUNNING RECORD
BENCHMARK BOOK LEVEL X

Running Record Sheet
A Break With Charity

Name _____   Date _____

152 Words   Level X   Accuracy Rate _____

PAGE	TEXT	RUNNING RECORD ANALYSIS
Page 32	The hour was late by the time I got to Salem Town, where candlelight from all the house windows threw a soft glow out on darkened streets. I knew I was in trouble, for in the cart I still had many of the items I was supposed to have distributed to the poor of Salem Village: precious packets of needles and skeins of wool, an iron cook pot or two, bolts of warm flannel, some molasses, flour, and salted codfish. Mama would want to know why I had returned with my cargo. And so it was that I determined to lie. I was not practiced in the art of dissembling, the word given to such a sin. There had been no need in	
Page 33	my life, up until now, to keep any of my doings from my parents. But in the next few months I was to learn the art of dissembling well.	

Comprehension:

1) _____

_____

_____

_____

2) _____

_____

_____

_____

RUNNING RECORD
BENCHMARK BOOK LEVEL Y

Running Record Sheet
Larklight

Name _____   Date _____

143 Words   Level Y   Accuracy Rate _____

PAGE	TEXT	RUNNING RECORD ANALYSIS
Page 35	We saw no more of the spiders as we flew down the stairs to the lifeboat house. We knew the lifeboats well, for Father had made us practise in them lest there should ever be a fire at Larklight. They were barrel-shaped objects, squatting on	
Page 36	spring-loaded projector plates in the middle of the shadowy boathouse. We checked about nervously for spiders before we heaved open the hatch of the nearer one and pulled ourselves inside. 'Are we to wait for Father?' wondered Myrtle, but she was looking very solemnly at me, as though she already knew the answer. I shook my head. 'Were there a very great number of those awful creatures?' she asked. I nodded. 'And did they devour him?' Myrtle whispered. I shrugged, and shook her away when she said, 'Poor Art! Then we are orphans!' and tried to hug me.	

Comprehension:

1) _____

_____

_____

2) _____

_____

_____

RUNNING RECORD
BENCHMARK BOOK LEVEL Z

Running Record Sheet
Harry Potter and the Deathly Hallows

Name _____   Date _____

170 Words   Level Z   Accuracy Rate _____

PAGE	TEXT	RUNNING RECORD ANALYSIS
Page 350	Without realizing it, he was digging his fingers into his arms as if he were trying to resist physical pain. He had spilled his own blood more times than he could count; he had lost all the bones in his right arm once; this journey had already given him scars to his chest and forearm to join those on his hand and forehead, but never, until this moment, had he felt himself to be fatally weakened, vulnerable, and naked, as though the best part of his magical power had been torn from him. He knew exactly what Hermione would say if he	
Page 351	expressed any of this: The wand is only as good as the wizard. But she was wrong; his case was different. She had not felt the wand spin like the needle of a compass and shoot golden flames at his enemy. He had lost the protection of the twin cores, and only now that it was gone did he realize how much he had been counting upon it.	

Comprehension:

1) _____

_____

_____

2) _____

_____

_____

GUIDELINES FOR **ASSESSING** READING COMPREHENSION THROUGH **RETELLING**

Select similar texts.	When comparing a student's retelling over time, use the same type of text each time. Compare narratives with other narratives and nonfiction texts with other nonfiction texts. Also select similar levels unless you are purposely moving a struggling reader down a level to discover an independent reading level or moving a reader up to a more challenging level.
Prepare a guide sheet.	In preparation for retelling, preview a text to determine what kinds of ideas and information you will be listening for in the student retelling. You may want to create a guide sheet or checklist that you can refer to and use for taking notes.

For fiction texts, include on your checklist:

- **title and author name**
- **genre**
- **character names and a note whether they are major or minor characters**
- **note about the setting, including any changes in setting**
- **brief description of the problem, conflict, or goal in the story**
- **list of important events in sequential order in the beginning, middle, and end**
- **brief description of how the problem or conflict is solved, or the goal reached**

For nonfiction texts, include on your checklist:

- **title and author name**
- **genre**
- **book topic**
- **main idea of the book and of any sections or chapters**
- **important details that support main ideas**
- **important people included if the book is a narrative**
- **important events listed in sequential order**
- **text features such as photographs or illustrations, diagrams, charts, and maps**

Ask the student to retell the text.	Make sure the student has recently read the text selected for the retelling. Then ask the student to retell the story or information, starting at the beginning and telling what happened or what the author said about the topic. As the student retells, make checks or notes on your guide sheet that will help you recall what the student included and the sequence of information. If you find it difficult to make checks or notes, it may be because the student is retelling information out of sequential order, has omitted important ideas, is focusing on unimportant information, or has not comprehended the main idea or the plot. For events or information told out of sequence, you may want to number the order of ideas students express instead of just checking them off.

Listen for what the student says and does not say.

When you listen to a retelling, listen for what the student says and how the student retells a fiction or nonfiction text. What the student leaves out is as important as what he or she says as an indicator of comprehension and understanding.

In a fiction retelling, listen for:

- **characters' names**
- **important events in sequence**
- **important details**
- **use of language and vocabulary from the story**
- **understanding of how the story is organized**
- **understanding of the genre, such as whether a student knows a story is realistic, a fantasy, or a special type of literature such as a folktale, fable, or mystery, as evidenced by mention of setting, understanding that characters are imaginary, connection with realistic situations and people, or a description of clues that lead to solving a mystery**

In a nonfiction retelling, listen for:

- **statement of what the text is about**
- **statements of main ideas**
- **key ideas and facts**
- **mention of text features from which the student derived information, such as a photograph or illustration, chart, diagram, or map**
- **use of language and vocabulary from the text**
- **understanding of the genre, such as whether the student points out that the text describes or explains a topic, tells about the life of a person or is told by that person, or narrates an important time or event in history**
- **understanding of how the text is organized by mention of details that support main ideas, or how the author explained or described a topic, presented a problem and solution, showed causes and effects, or compared and contrasted people, things, or ideas**

Provide prompts if needed.

When a student is retelling, let him finish without prompting for information. If the retelling is incomplete, out of order, or leaves out important information, you may want to prompt with more specific questions about parts of the text the student misunderstood or did not include. Note how many prompts are needed to complete the retelling.

Summarize and evaluate the retelling.

Using your guide sheet, discuss and review the retelling with the student to help her understand what can be improved and how. This process also helps you develop instructional goals for future sessions.

You can also use your guide sheet to help you evaluate the retelling at a later time and determine what level the student is on and what instruction she needs. Keep your guide sheets for each student retelling to give you information for determining student progress and points for intervention.

Evaluating Students' Retellings

Students' retellings of fiction and nonfiction will give you a snapshot of where students fall in their ability to process and comprehend text. The following criteria for establishing levels can aid you in placing a student at a particular level and help you plan for instruction.

FICTION

Level	Criteria for Establishing Level
3	Most-complete retellings: • Indicate an understanding of the genre through description of and connections made to setting, characters, and plot • Present a sequence of actions and events • Provide explanations for the motivations behind characters' actions • Include character names • Elaborate using important details from the story • Comment on or evaluate the story • Do not require prompts during retelling
2	Less complex retellings: • Indicate a basic understanding of genre in brief comments of characters, setting, and plot • Present concrete events in sequence • Supply missing information through appropriate inferences • Include some explanation of the causes of events or characters' motivations • Include some important details • Require one or two prompts during retelling
1	Simple descriptive retellings: • Are partial or limited • Indicate a lack of awareness of genre through no mention of a genre's features • Have simple beginning, middle, and end • May include events out of sequence • May describe a setting • Present an initiating event and the outcome of a problem • Include misinterpretations • Refer to characters as "he" or "she" rather than by name • Require three or more prompts during retelling

NONFICTION

Level	Criteria for Establishing Level
3	Most-complete retellings: • **Show a comprehension of the topic** • **Indicate an understanding of the genre in a description of the text, its purpose, and how it is organized** • **Present main ideas of whole text and parts of text** • **Provide important details that support main ideas** • **Include key ideas and facts** • **Elaborate using details enhanced by prior knowledge** • **Comment on or evaluate the text** • **Do not require prompts during retelling**
2	Less complex retellings: • **Show a basic comprehension of the topic** • **Indicate a basic understanding of the genre and text organization in a description of the book** • **Present concrete related facts or events in sequence** • **Supply missing information through appropriate inferences** • **Include some main ideas** • **Provide some important details that support main ideas** • **Mention some key ideas and facts, but omit others** • **Require one or two prompts during retelling**
1	Simple descriptive retellings: • **Are partial or limited** • **Provide the topic of the text** • **Include misinterpretations** • **Include general ideas without focusing on specific main ideas** • **Omit important details to support main ideas** • **Do not include comments on text structure** • **Require three or more prompts during retelling**

BENCHMARK BOOKS

Level	Benchmark Book
Level A	Helping
Level B	Off to the City
Level C	The Big Blue Sea
Level D	The Little Red Hen
Level E	Fred's Wish for Fish
Level F	The Country Mouse and the Town Mouse
Level G	Justin's New Bike
Level H	Sammy the Seal
Level I	Mama Zooms
Level J	Poppleton Has Fun
Level K	The Frog Prince
Level L	Miss Nelson Has a Field Day
Level M	Dancing With the Indians
Level N	Suitcase
Level O	Chocolate Fever
Level P	Who Stole *The Wizard of Oz*?
Level Q	Just Juice
Level R	The Trumpet of the Swan
Level S	Granny Torrelli Makes Soup
Level T	The Power of Un
Level U	Tangerine
Level V	The Firework-Maker's Daughter
Level W	Tunnels
Level X	A Break With Charity
Level Y	Larklight
Level Z	Harry Potter and the Deathly Hallows

READING LEVEL CORRELATIONS*

Grade Level (Basal)	Guided Reading Levels	DRA Levels	Success For All Levels	Reading Recovery Levels	Stages of Reading	Lexiles	DRP Text
Kindergarten	A B	A 2	1–3	A–B, 2	Emergent		
Pre-Primer	C D E	3–4 6 8	4–25 25	3–4 5–6 7–8	Emergent/ Early	BR–200	
Primer	F G	10 12	26–27	9–10 12	Early/ Transitional	200–300	
1st Grade	H I	14 16	38–48	14 16	Early/ Transitional	300–400	25–30
2nd Grade	J–K L–M	16–18 20–24	2.0	18 20	Transitional Fluency/ Extending	400–550	30–44
3rd Grade	N O–P	28–30 34–38	3.0	22 24	Fluency/ Extending	600–700	44–54
4th Grade	Q–R	40	4.0	26	Fluency/ Extending Advanced	750–900	46–55
5th Grade	S–V	50	—	26–28	Fluency/ Extending Advanced	850–950	49–57
6th Grade	W–Y Z	60 70–80	—	30 32–34	Advanced	950– 1050	51–60

*See **Text Gradient Chart** on the back of your materials folder. This chart identifies the overlapping level ranges for each grade in the *Scholastic Guided Reading Program*.

USING THE
GUIDED READING PROGRAM

Characteristics of Text

The easiest books are included in Levels A and B. We suggest that children begin using Level A books for guided reading after they have listened to many stories and participated in shared reading. They should have some familiarity with print and understand that you read print and move from left to right in doing so. Children need not know all the letters of the alphabet and their sounds before reading Level A books.

Level A includes picture books without words, some with simple labels or captions, and some with as many as five or six words, often on one line.

In general, these books have clear, easy-to-read print with generous space between words. These simple formats enable young children to focus on print and reading from left to right, while gradually increasing their control over more words. Many of the books have high-frequency words and repeating language patterns. Print is presented in a variety of ways, which helps children become flexible readers from the start. In general, the books focus on topics that are familiar to most children. Books with more complex topics usually have fewer words and will require more of an introduction and teacher-child interaction to support understanding.

Behaviors to Notice and Support

	Child's Name							
Understands familiar concepts in stories and illustrations								
Differentiates print from pictures								
Holds the book and turns pages from right to left								
Reads words from left to right								
Begins to match word by word, pointing with one finger under words								
Locates both known and new words								
Remembers and uses language patterns								
Relates the book to his/her experience								

USING THE
GUIDED READING PROGRAM

Characteristics of Text

Level B books generally have simple story lines or a single idea. The print is easy to read, with adequate space between words so that children can point to words as they read. Books at this level generally have one or two lines of print on a page, somewhat longer sentences, and a variety of punctuation.

There is direct correspondence between the text and pictures, and repeating patterns support the reader. Topics are generally familiar to most children. If more complex concepts are involved, the reading of the book will require teacher-child interaction to support understanding.

Behaviors to Notice and Support

	Child's Name							
Demonstrates control of left-to-right movement and return sweep								
Begins to control word-by-word matching across two lines of text, pointing with one finger								
Notices and interprets detail in pictures								
Talks about ideas in the text								
Remembers and uses language patterns in text								
Uses knowledge of high-frequency words to check on reading								
Uses word-by-word matching to check on reading								
Notices mismatches in meaning or language								
Uses visual information, such as the first letter of the word, to read known and new words								
Pays close attention to print								
Notices features of letters and words								
Begins to self-monitor, noticing mismatches in meaning or language								
Rereads to confirm or figure out new words								

USING THE GUIDED READING PROGRAM

Characteristics of Text

Level C books have simple story lines and topics that are familiar to most children. Some may offer a new viewpoint on a familiar topic. Level C books generally have more words and lines of print than books at earlier levels. Print is clear and readable, with adequate space between words. Most sentences are simple, but some have more complex structure, offering readers a challenge. While Level C books include some repeating language patterns, these are more complex and there is a shift to more varied patterns. Language patterns are more likely to change from page to page, so children cannot rely on them to make predictions and must pay closer attention to print. Level C books include many high-frequency words, as well as easily decodable words.

Behaviors to Notice and Support

	Child's Name						
Demonstrates control of left-to-right directionality and word-by-word matching across several lines of print							
Begins to track print with eyes							
Rereads to solve problems, such as figuring out new words							
Demonstrates awareness of punctuation by pausing and using some phrasing							
Uses picture details to help figure out words							
Remembers and uses language patterns in text							
Rereads to confirm or figure out new words							
Solves some new words independently							
Controls directionality and word-by-word matching with eyes, using finger at points of difficulty							
Uses visual information to predict, check, and confirm reading							
Recognizes known words quickly and uses them to figure out the meaning of new words							
Searches for understanding while reading							

USING THE
GUIDED READING PROGRAM

Characteristics of Text

Stories at Level D are slightly more complex than at previous levels. Generally, Level D books have topics that are familiar to most children, but also include some abstract or unfamiliar ideas. Text layout is still easy to follow, with both large and small print. Sentences are a little longer than at Level C. Some are carried over to the next page or several pages and use a full range of punctuation. There are more compound words, multisyllabic words, and words with a variety of inflectional endings. Illustrations are still supportive, but less so than at the previous level, requiring the reader to pay more attention to print.

Behaviors to Notice and Support

	Child's Name						
Remembers language patterns and repeating events over longer stretches of text							
Self-corrects, using visual information							
Controls directionality and word-by-word matching with eyes, using finger only at points of difficulty							
Searches for understanding while reading							
Remembers details from the text and pictures							
Pays close attention to words and their structural features (for example, endings)							
Reads fluently, with phrasing							
Rereads to confirm or figure out new words							
Solves new words using knowledge of sound/letter relationships and word parts							

USING THE
GUIDED READING PROGRAM

Characteristics of Text

Level E books are generally longer than books at previous levels, with either more pages or more lines of text on a page. Some have sentences that carry over several pages and have a full range of punctuation. The text structure is generally more complex: stories have more or longer episodes, and informational books have more difficult ideas and concepts. However, in texts with more difficult concepts, there are usually repeating language patterns that offer some support. There are more multisyllabic and compound words at this level.

Behaviors to Notice and Support

	Child's Name							
Tracks print with eyes except at points of difficulty								
Uses language syntax and meaning to read fluently, with phrasing								
Demonstrates awareness of punctuation by pausing, phrasing, and reading with inflection								
Rereads to self-monitor or self-correct phrasing and expression								
Recognizes many words quickly and automatically								
Figures out some longer words by taking them apart								
Relates texts to others previously read								
Reads for meaning but checks with the visual aspects of print (letters, sounds, words)								
Rereads to search for meaning and accuracy								
Remembers details and uses them to clarify meaning								
Demonstrates understanding by talking about text after reading								

USING THE
GUIDED READING PROGRAM

Characteristics of Text

In general, texts at Level F are longer and have more story episodes than at previous levels. There are also shorter texts with some unusual language patterns. Books have some concepts unfamiliar to children and some are even abstract, requiring reflection. Pictures continue to support reading, but closer attention to print is required. Language patterns are more characteristic of written language than of spoken language. Some Level F books have smaller print and more words and lines of text. There are many more new words and a greater variety of high-frequency words. A full range of punctuation is used to enhance meaning.

Behaviors to Notice and Support

	Child's Name							
Tracks print with eyes, using the finger only at points of difficulty								
Demonstrates awareness of punctuation by pausing, phrasing, and reading with inflection								
Uses syntax of written language to figure out new words and their meaning								
Uses sound/letter relationships, word parts, and other visual information to figure out new words								
Uses known words to figure out new words								
Uses multiple sources of information to search and self-correct								
Figures out longer words while reading for meaning								
Rereads to figure out words, self-correct, or improve phrasing and expression								
Rereads to search for meaning								
Recognizes most words quickly and automatically								
Moves quickly through the text								
Reads fluently, with phrasing								
Talks about ideas in the text and relates them to his/her experiences and to other texts								

USING THE
GUIDED READING PROGRAM

Characteristics of Text

Most books at Level G are not repetitive. These books include a variety of patterns. Knowledge of punctuation is important in understanding what the sentence means and how it should be spoken. Vocabulary is more challenging, with a greater range of words and more difficult words, including some that are technical and require content knowledge. Concepts and ideas may be less familiar than at previous levels. Level G books have a greater variety of styles of print and text layout, requiring close attention to print and flexibility on the part of the reader.

Behaviors to Notice and Support

	Child's Name							
Reads fluently and rapidly, with appropriate phrasing								
Follows print with eyes, occasionally using finger at points of difficulty								
Notices and uses punctuation to assist smooth reading								
Recognizes most words quickly and automatically								
Uses sound/letter relationships, known words, and word parts to figure out new words								
Uses meaning, visual information, and language syntax to figure out words								
Rereads to figure out words, self-correct, or improve phrasing and expression								
Rereads to search for meaning								
Remembers details to support the accumulation of meaning throughout the text								
Uses pictures for information but does not rely on them to make predictions								

USING THE
GUIDED READING PROGRAM

Characteristics of Text

Level H books are similar in difficulty to Level G, but Level H has a wider variety, including books with poetic or literary language. Sentences vary in length and difficulty, and some complex sentences carry over several pages. Children will need to be familiar with the syntactic patterns that occur.

Books have fewer repeating events and language patterns, requiring more control of aspects of print. The vocabulary is expanded and includes words that are less frequently used in oral language. The size of print varies widely.

Behaviors to Notice and Support

	Child's Name							
Reads fluently and rapidly, with appropriate phrasing								
Follows the text with eyes, using finger only at points of particular difficulty								
Notices and uses punctuation to assist smooth reading								
Recognizes most words rapidly								
Uses sound/letter relationships, known words, and word parts to figure out new words								
Uses meaning, visual information, and language syntax to solve problems								
Rereads phrases to figure out words, self-correct, or improve phrasing and expression								
Rereads to search for meaning								
Remembers details to support meaning accumulated through the text								
Uses pictures for information but does not rely on them to make predictions								
Searches for meaning while reading, stopping to think or talk about ideas								

USING THE
GUIDED READING PROGRAM

Characteristics of Text

In general, the books at Level I are longer and more complex than at Levels G and H. The size of print is smaller and there are many more lines of print on the page. Books have longer sentences and paragraphs. There are more multisyllabic words, requiring complex word-solving skills. This level offers a greater variety of texts, including some that are informational, with technical language. Events in the text are more highly elaborated. Illustrations enhance the story, but provide low support for understanding meaning.

Behaviors to Notice and Support

	Child's Name							
Actively figures out new words, using a range of strategies								
Follows the print with eyes								
Reads fluently, slowing down to figure out new words and then resuming speed								
Begins to silently read some of the text								
In oral reading, rereads some words or phrases to self-correct or improve expression								
Rereads to search for meaning								
Flexibly uses meaning, language syntax, and visual information to figure out new words and to monitor reading								
Self-corrects errors that cause loss of meaning								
Rereads when necessary to self-correct, but not as a habit								
Demonstrates understanding of the story and characters								
Goes beyond the text in discussions and interpretations								
Sustains problem solving and development of meaning through a longer text and over a two- or three-day period								

USING THE
GUIDED READING PROGRAM

Characteristics of Text

Although it supports essentially the same reading behaviors, Level J offers books that are more difficult and varied than those at Level I. It includes informational books with new concepts and beginning chapter books with complex narratives and memorable characters. The amount of print varies; some Level J books have full pages of text with few illustrations. Generally, illustrations enhance the text but offer little support for understanding text meaning or figuring out new words. The difficulty of the language also varies. There are books with easy and familiar language and others with literary language or other challenges. Texts have many high-frequency words but may also have unfamiliar and/or technical words.

Behaviors to Notice and Support

	Child's Name						
Uses multiple sources of information to process text smoothly							
Uses multiple strategies to figure out new words while focusing on meaning							
Analyzes words from left to right, using knowledge of sound/letter relationships							
Uses known words and word parts to figure out new words							
Reads fluently, slowing down to figure out new words and then resuming speed							
Flexibly uses meaning, language syntax, and visual information to monitor reading							
Self-corrects errors that cause loss of meaning							
Rereads when necessary to self-correct, but not as a habit							
Rereads to search for meaning							
Demonstrates understanding of the story and characters							
Goes beyond the text in discussions and interpretations							
Sustains problem-solving and development of meaning through a longer text read over several days							
Silently reads sections of text							
Makes inferences, predicts, and analyzes character and plot							

USING THE
GUIDED READING PROGRAM

Characteristics of Text

The Level K collection includes longer chapter books with memorable characters, shorter informational books with technical language and new concepts, and literary texts with illustrations that enhance meaning. Stories have multiple episodes related to a single plot. Some stories have to do with times, places, and characters outside children's experience.

Readers will need to use a variety of strategies to figure out new writing styles. At this level, most reading will be silent, although teachers will always sample oral reading or invite children to read aloud for emphasis or enjoyment in group sessions. It will take more than one sitting for children to read some of the longer chapter books.

Behaviors to Notice and Support

	Child's Name							
Integrates multiple sources of information while reading with fluency								
When reading orally, reads rapidly, with phrasing, slowing down to problem solve and then resuming speed								
Reads silently much of the time								
Demonstrates understanding of the text after silent reading								
Makes inferences, predicts, and analyzes character and plot								
Flexibly uses multiple word-solving strategies while focusing on meaning								
Goes beyond the text in understanding of problems and characters								
Demonstrates facility in interpreting the text								
Sustains attention to meaning and interpretation of a longer text read over several days								

USING THE
GUIDED READING PROGRAM

Characteristics of Text

In general, reading behaviors for Level L are the same as for Level K except they are applied to longer and/or more complex books. At Level L there is greater variety of texts, including informational books, biographies, chapter books, and some longer, highly literary, or informational picture books.

Chapter books have more sophisticated plots and characters that are developed throughout the text. Some books have abstract or symbolic themes that require higher-level conceptual understandings. Texts contain an expanded vocabulary with many multisyllabic words.

Behaviors to Notice and Support

Child's Name								
Integrates multiple sources of information while reading with fluency								
When reading orally, reads rapidly, with phrasing								
Reads orally, with accuracy, not stopping to self-correct in the interest of fluency and phrasing								
In oral reading, uses multiple word-solving strategies with longer words								
Reads silently most of the time								
Demonstrates understanding and facility in interpreting the text after silent reading								
After reading longer sections of a text, predicts events, outcomes, problem resolutions, and character changes								
Makes connections between the text read and other books								
Sustains attention to meaning and interpretation of a longer text read over several days								

USING THE
GUIDED READING PROGRAM

Characteristics of Text

Level M books have a variety of formats. Topics vary widely, and include subjects that will be familiar to students as well as those that are new. Literary selections have complex language and subtle meanings that require interpretation and background knowledge.

Chapter books are longer with few pictures. This requires readers to have mastery of the text. Many books have small print and little space between words. Vocabulary is expanded, and many words require background knowledge for comprehension.

Behaviors to Notice and Support

	Student's Name							
Uses multiple sources of information to figure out words rapidly while focusing on meaning								
Flexibly applies word-solving strategies to more-complex, multisyllabic words								
Demonstrates facility in interpreting text while reading orally, with fluency and phrasing								
Reads orally with high accuracy in most instances, not stopping to self-correct errors in the interest of fluency and phrasing								
Reads silently, except during assessment or to demonstrate text interpretation								
After reading longer sections of text, predicts outcomes, problem resolutions, and character changes								
Remembers details and sustains attention to meaning through a longer text								
Demonstrates understanding and facility at interpretation after silent reading								
Makes connections between the text read and other books								
Goes beyond the text to make more sophisticated interpretations								

USING THE
GUIDED READING PROGRAM

Characteristics of Text

The Level N collection includes longer texts in a variety of genres. There are chapter books that present memorable characters developed through literary devices such as humor, irony, and whimsy. There are informational books and books that offer mystery and suspense. Level N also has shorter selections that provide opportunity to interpret texts and go beyond them. Vocabulary continues to expand, and topics go well beyond students' own experience.

Behaviors to Notice and Support

Student's Name							
Uses multiple strategies to figure out new words quickly							
Demonstrates facility in text interpretation while reading orally, with fluency and phrasing							
Reads silently, except during assessment or when demonstrating text interpretation							
Remembers details from one section of text to the next							
Sustains attention to a longer text, remembering details and revising interpretations							
Notices how illustrations convey the author's meaning							
Demonstrates sophisticated interpretation of characters and plot							
Makes connections among a wide variety of texts							
Goes beyond the text to speculate on alternative meanings							

USING THE
GUIDED READING PROGRAM

Characteristics of Text

Books at Level O include selections from children's literature and chapter books. Books at this level explore more mature themes and topics that go beyond students' experience and expand it. Students can empathize with characters and learn about the lives of others. The vocabulary is sophisticated and varied. Most words will be known or within students' control; however, many will require interpretation of meaning. Many new multisyllabic words are included. Sentences are more complex and use a full range of punctuation.

Behaviors to Notice and Support

	Student's Name							
Solves words quickly and automatically while focusing on meaning								
Searches to understand the subtle shades of meaning that words can convey								
Demonstrates facility in text interpretation while reading orally, with fluency and phrasing								
In oral reading, figures out new words rapidly while reading smoothly and expressively								
Sustains attention to a text read over several days, remembering details and revising interpretations as new events are encountered								
After reading silently, demonstrates understanding and sophistication in text interpretation								
Makes connections among texts to enhance interpretation								
Goes beyond the text to speculate on alternative meanings								
Shows the ability to summarize the text in writing								

USING THE
GUIDED READING PROGRAM

LEVEL P

Characteristics of Text

In general, books at this level are longer and ideas and language are more complex than at previous levels. Level P has a variety of informational texts, including history and biography. Through this variety, students become familiar with texts that are organized differently and learn how to gain information from them. Other genres include chapter books that explore the problems of early adolescence.

Behaviors to Notice and Support

	Student's Name							
When reading silently, reads rapidly and with attention to meaning								
Actively acquires new vocabulary through reading								
Demonstrates facility in text interpretation while reading orally, with fluency and phrasing								
In oral reading, figures out new words rapidly while reading smoothly and expressively								
Sustains attention to a text read over many days, remembering details and revising interpretations as new events are encountered								
Demonstrates interest in reading an extended text over a longer time period								
After reading silently, demonstrates understanding and sophistication in interpreting meaning								
Compares the text with other books in an analytic way								
Goes beyond the text to speculate on alternative meanings								
Shows the ability to summarize and extend the text in writing								

USING THE
GUIDED READING PROGRAM

Characteristics of Text

Level Q includes literature selections with sophisticated humor, complex plots, and memorable characters. Themes at this level are sophisticated and require interpretation. They serve as a good foundation for group discussion. Illustrations and their relationship to the text can be examined as well. Books have complex structure and difficult words that offer challenges. There are some words from languages other than English. Longer texts require an extended time period to read.

Behaviors to Notice and Support

	Student's Name							
Reads rapidly, with attention to meaning, when reading silently								
Actively acquires new vocabulary through reading								
Demonstrates facility in text interpretation while reading orally, with fluency and phrasing								
In oral reading, figures out new words rapidly while reading smoothly and expressively								
Sustains attention to a text read over many days, remembering details and revising interpretations as new events are encountered								
Demonstrates interest in reading an extended text over a longer time period								
Uses illustrations to help analyze text meaning								
After reading silently, demonstrates understanding and sophistication in interpreting meaning								
Compares the text to other books in an analytic way								
Goes beyond the text to speculate on alternative meanings								
Goes beyond the text to interpret characters' thoughts and feelings								
Shows the ability to analyze and extend the text in writing								

USING THE
GUIDED READING PROGRAM

Characteristics of Text

At Level R, both fiction and nonfiction have a range of historical place and time settings, giving students an opportunity to empathize with characters and learn about their lives and the times and places in which they lived. In general, skills are the same as at Level Q, but are extended over a wider variety of texts. Some books require sustained reading over a longer time period. Vocabulary and language are sophisticated and offer challenges to the reader.

Behaviors to Notice and Support

Student's Name								
Reads rapidly, both orally and silently, while focusing on meaning								
Actively acquires new vocabulary through reading								
Sustains attention to a text read over many days, remembering details and revising interpretations as new events are encountered								
Demonstrates interest in reading an extended text over a longer time period								
Extends the text in various ways, including through research								
Demonstrates interest and ability in interpreting shorter selections								
Uses illustrations to help analyze text meaning								
After reading silently, demonstrates understanding and sophistication in interpreting meaning								
Uses comparison with other texts to assist interpretation								
Goes beyond the text to interpret characters' thoughts and feelings and to speculate on alternative meanings								
Demonstrates all interpretive and analytic skills in writing								

USING THE
GUIDED READING PROGRAM

Characteristics of Text

Level S includes literary selections, highly literary or informational picture books, and chapter books in a variety of genres. The collection reflects a wide variety of topics, cultures, and historical settings. Sentences and paragraphs at this level are complex.

Words present many shades of meaning which readers must interpret from the text and their own background knowledge. Selections offer opportunities for readers to make connections with other books they have read at earlier levels.

Behaviors to Notice and Support

	Student's Name						
Reads rapidly, both orally and silently, with attention to meaning							
Rapidly acquires new vocabulary through reading							
Sustains attention to a text read over many days, remembering details and revising interpretations as new events are encountered							
Demonstrates interest and ability in interpreting shorter selections							
Demonstrates flexibility in reading many different kinds of texts							
After reading silently, demonstrates understanding and sophistication in interpreting meaning							
Goes beyond the text to interpret characters' thoughts and feelings and to speculate on alternative meanings							
Demonstrates all analytic and interpretive skills in writing							
Extends text meaning through research, writing, or the arts							

USING THE
GUIDED READING PROGRAM

Characteristics of Text

The Level T collection has a great variety of genres. Short selections include informational books, legends, historical fiction, and folktales. Chapter books include autobiographies, historical narratives, realistic fiction, science fiction, and other fantasy stories. Some chapter books are quite long and require reading over an extended time. Judgment is needed as to whether students can sustain interest for these longer selections. Selections contain many sophisticated, multisyllabic words, and readers will need to consider both their literal and connotative meanings.

Behaviors to Notice and Support

	Student's Name							
Reads rapidly, both orally and silently, with attention to meaning								
In oral and silent reading, figures out new words automatically and easily interprets word meaning								
Sustains attention to a text read over many days, remembering details and revising interpretations as new events are encountered								
Demonstrates interest and ability in interpreting shorter selections								
Demonstrates flexibility in reading texts of different styles and genres								
After reading silently, demonstrates understanding and ability to analyze characters and plot								
Reflects knowledge of literary genre in conversation and writing								
Extends and demonstrates understanding of the text through writing in a variety of genres								
Extends and demonstrates understanding of the text through public speaking, research, or the arts								

USING THE
GUIDED READING PROGRAM

Characteristics of Text

Text at Level U requires readers to employ a wide range of sophisticated reading strategies that approach adult levels. The difference, of course, is that elementary and middle school students are still gaining the world experience and content knowledge, or the accumulation of text experience, needed to deeply understand the more complex texts they will be reading at Levels U through Z. By this time, students have built an integrated processing system, but they need to apply their strategies to increasingly difficult levels of text. As they do so, reading with fluency and understanding, they will expand and build their reading strategies.

Fiction texts at Level U may have several different themes and multiple story lines. Texts are increasingly literary, with writers expressing layers of meaning through symbolism. Themes are more abstract; creative formats may be used, such as collections of short stories that build meaning over different texts, or novels that incorporate diaries, poetry, or stories within stories. Generally, there are more characters to follow and their development is more complex; there are plots and subplots. Informational texts at Level U cover a wide range of topics and present specific, technical information. As with earlier levels, illustrations require interpretation and connection to text.

Behaviors to Notice and Support

Student's Name							
Notices graphic illustrations and gets information from them							
Synthesizes information from graphic information with the body of the text							
Uses the table of contents to help in understanding the organization of the text							
Grasps "layers" of meaning in a story; for example, specific understandings plus the "bigger picture"							
Reads, understands, and appreciates literary language							
Interprets illustrations and their connections to the text							
Keeps up with several different themes and many characters							
Interprets characters' motives and the influences on their development							
Recognizes and appreciates a wide range of genres, both fiction and nonfiction							
Notices and uses a full range of punctuation, including more rarely used forms such as dashes							
Learns technical words from reading							
Uses reading to learn about self and others							

USING THE
GUIDED READING PROGRAM

Characteristics of Text

At Level V, readers employ essentially the same range of strategies as at the previous level, but more background knowledge will be required for true understanding. Also, students will be rapidly adding to their reading vocabularies. Fiction includes science fiction that presents sophisticated ideas and concepts. In many works of realistic or historical fiction, the writer is conveying a significant message beyond the story. Readers must think critically and sustain attention, memory, and understanding of theme over much longer texts. Full appreciation of

texts requires noticing aspects of the writer's craft, including metaphor, simile, and symbolism. Many long texts have print in a much smaller font. Informational texts present complex ideas and may use language that is more technical. Topics are more often distant from students' experience in time and place. Biographies provide a significant amount of historical information. Many focus on harsh themes. Other, longer biographies are told in narrative style but present complex themes.

Behaviors to Notice and Support

	Student's Name						
Understands and talks about complex themes, analyzing them and applying them to current life situations							
Understands many different perspectives that are encountered in fiction and nonfiction texts							
Evaluates both fiction and nonfiction texts for their authenticity and accuracy							
Deals with mature topics such as death, war, prejudice, and courage							
Thinks critically about and discusses the content of a literary work or the quality of writing							
Notices aspects of the writer's craft and looks at the text from a writer's point of view							
Sustains attention and thinking over the reading of texts that are long and have smaller fonts							
Tries new genres, topics, and authors, and is able to compare them with known genres, topics, and authors							
Makes connections across texts to notice an author's style or technique							
Understands symbolism in both realistic fiction and fantasy; discusses what symbols mean in terms of today's society							
Brings prior knowledge to bear in understanding literary references							
Learns technical language and concepts through reading							
Learns about self and others through reading, especially about societies that are different from one's own							

USING THE
GUIDED READING PROGRAM

Characteristics of Text

Texts at Level W have themes that explore the human condition, with the same kinds of social problems mentioned at earlier levels. Fiction and nonfiction texts present characters who suffer hardship and learn from it. The writing is sophisticated, with complex sentences, literary language, and symbolism. Texts vary in length; print is generally in a small font. Comprehending texts at this level will require awareness of social and political issues; through them, readers can learn to understand current social problems at deeper levels.

Fantasy includes science fiction as well as "high" fantasy that introduces heroic characters, questions, and contests between good and evil. Informational texts may present complex graphic information and require readers to possess a wide range of content knowledge and to understand all of the basic organizational structures for nonfiction. Narrative-style biographies include many details of their subjects' lives and prompt readers to make inferences about what motivated their achievements.

Behaviors to Notice and Support

	Student's Name							
Sustains reading over longer and more complex texts; is not intimidated by varying layouts and styles of print								
Builds understanding of a wide variety of human problems								
Uses reading to expand awareness of people who are different from oneself								
Understands and learns from characters' experiences								
Learns about self and others through reading; actively seeks understanding of people different from oneself by culture, period of history, or other variation								
Deals with mature themes such as prejudice, war, death, survival, and poverty, and is able to discuss them in relation to one's own experiences								
Understands the complexities of human characters as they develop and change; discusses one's own point of view and relationship to characters								
Integrates understandings derived from graphic illustrations and the text								
Expands world knowledge through reading								
Flexibly and automatically uses tools such as glossary, references, index, credentials for authors, legends, charts, and diagrams								

USING THE GUIDED READING PROGRAM

LEVEL X

Characteristics of Text

Texts at Level X include the same wide range of genres shown at previous levels, but the themes explored are increasingly mature. Fantasy depicts quests and the struggle between good and evil. High fantasy includes complex, extended symbolic narratives that require knowledge of previously read texts for full understanding. Readers are required to go substantially beyond the literal meaning of the text to construct a writer's implied meaning. In addition, texts require interpretation of theme and plot. In fiction texts, there may be many characters to follow and understand. There is a continuing increase in the sophistication of vocabulary, language, and topics. Nonfiction texts require extensive prior knowledge for full understanding. In addition, texts are designed to present a great deal of new knowledge, sometimes in a dense way. Graphic illustrations are helpful to readers but also require interpretation.

Behaviors to Notice and Support

	Student's Name						
Sustains attention over longer texts with more abstract, mature, and complex themes							
Notices, understands, and discusses a wide range of literary devices, such as flashbacks and stories within stories							
Deals with mature themes, such as family relationships, death, social injustice, and the supernatural							
Appreciates, understands, and discusses irony and satire							
Uses descriptive text as a way to understand settings and their importance to the plot or character development							
Discusses the setting as an element of the text, deciding whether it is important or unimportant							
Flexibly and automatically uses tools such as glossary, references, index, credentials for authors, legends, charts, and diagrams							
Notices aspects of the author's craft, including the way characters are described and presented as "real"							
Talks about the text in an analytic way, including finding specific evidence of the author's style							
Understands and is able to use the sophisticated, scholarly, and technical language that is found in informational texts							

USING THE
GUIDED READING PROGRAM

Characteristics of Text

Books categorized as Level Y present subtle themes and complex plots. As with earlier levels, they include a whole range of social problems as themes, but more explicit details (for example, about death or prejudice) may be provided. Readers will need to bring considerable world experience and reading experience to their understanding of these more mature texts. Writers use symbolism, irony, satire, and other literary devices that require readers to think beyond the literal meaning of the text.

Books at Level Y include many more complex works of fantasy that depict hero figures and heroic journeys. Readers are required to discern underlying lessons and also to analyze texts for traditional elements. Informational texts explore an ever-widening world of history and science; topics require extensive prior knowledge of complex concepts, as well as vocabulary. Readers are required to gather new information from reading and synthesize it with their current knowledge. A wide range of critical reading skills are also required, so that students continuously evaluate the quality and objectivity of the texts they read.

Behaviors to Notice and Support

	Student's Name						
Understands and discusses subtle and complex plots and themes							
Understands, discusses, and deals in a mature way with a wide range of social problems, including social injustice and tragedy							
Understands and discusses in a mature way texts that present explicit details of social problems							
Understands literary irony and satire as they are used to communicate big ideas							
Understands complex fantasy, entering into whole new worlds, and understands concepts in relation to the imagined setting							
Understands and discusses the fact that words can have multiple meanings in relation to the context in which they are used							
Flexibly and automatically uses tools such as glossary, references, index, credentials for authors, legends, charts, and diagrams							
Interprets events in light of the setting—time, place, and culture							
Engages in critical thinking about fiction and nonfiction texts							
Critically evaluates nonfiction texts for accuracy and presentation of information							

USING THE
GUIDED READING PROGRAM

Characteristics of Text

Level Z captures books that require reading strategies similar to those needed at lower levels, but which present such mature themes that readers simply need more experience to deal with them. Some students who are widely read may need this challenge. Some informational books present complex and technical information, sometimes within a denser text. Others deal with controversial social concepts and political issues that require readers to evaluate several points of view. Critical reading is essential, and readers often have to reevaluate and revise their own previously held beliefs. Historical texts have detailed accounts of periods of history that are less well known. Readers learn new ways of finding technical information, and encounter complex examples of the basic organizational structures for informational texts. Fiction texts explore a wide range of human themes, often with graphic details of hardship, violence, or tragedy. High fantasy presents heroic quests, symbolism, and complex characters, and involves the reader in considering the meaning of life.

Behaviors to Notice and Support

Student's Name							
Sustains reading and understanding over much longer texts							
Deals with a great range of texts—from diaries to narratives to plays							
Switches easily from one genre to another, accessing knowledge of the structure and nature of the text while beginning to read							
Understands and discusses how a text "works" in terms of the writer's organization							
Deals with controversial social and political issues, seeing multiple perspectives							
Uses reading to gain technical knowledge in a wide variety of areas							
Understands the symbolism in heroic quests; applies concepts encountered in fantasy to today's life							
Flexibly and automatically uses tools such as glossary, references, index, credentials for authors, legends, charts, and diagrams							
Deals with and discusses in a mature way graphic details such as accounts of brutality, hardship, or violence							
Notices, understands, appreciates, and discusses literary devices							
Understands and appreciates complex language, archaic language, and cultural motifs							
Learns about epilogues, bibliographies, and forewords							
Builds information across the text, even when very unusual formats are used (for example, brief interviews with many characters)							
Fully understands the subtle differences between fiction and nonfiction							

LEVELED BOOKROOM CHECKOUT SHEET

Date	Teacher Name	Returned

EVALUATION RESPONSE FOR TEXT GRADIENT

adapted from *Guided Reading: Good First Teaching for All Children* (Fountas and Pinnell, 1996)

Directions: Since any gradient is always in the process of construction when it is used with varying groups of students, we expect our list to change every year. We encourage you to try the levels with your students and to provide feedback based on your own experiences. Please suggest changes to existing book levels and suggest new books for the list. Please provide the information requested.

Name: _____ Grade Level You Teach: _____

Telephone: _____ E-mail Address: _____

Address: _____

Book Evaluated

Book Title: _____ Level: _____

Author: _____ Publisher: _____

This book is

_____ A book that I have evaluated by using it with my class.

To what level should it be moved? _____

Why? _____

_____

_____ A book that I am recommending as a benchmark book.

How does it support readers at this level? _____

What challenge does it offer? _____

_____

_____ A new book that I am recommending to the collection.

At what level should it be placed? _____

Why? _____

_____

Copy and mail this form to:
Irene C. Fountas
Lesley University
Suite 2-029
1815 Massachusetts Avenue
Cambridge, MA 02140

LEVELED BOOKROOM AUDIO TITLES

Level	Title
Level I	Leo the Late Bloomer
Level I	Noisy Nora
Level J	Charlie Needs a Cloak
Level K	Corduroy
Level K	Martin's Big Words
Level L	Miss Nelson Is Missing
Level M	George Washington's Mother
Level N	Zen Shorts
Level O	What's the Big Idea Ben Franklin?
Level Q	The True Story of the Three Little Pigs
Level Q	Lon Po Po
Level T	Chasing Vermeer
Level T	Any Small Goodness
Level W	The Invention of Hugo Cabret

TECHNOLOGY

Information on Guided Reading and how to implement it in your classroom is provided at **www.scholastic.com**. In addition, the site contains numerous teacher, student, and parent resources related to books in the Guided Reading Program. Use these resources for independent and group extension activities.

teacher resources

student activities

Scholastic Reading Counts! quizzes are available for all the titles in the Guided Reading Program. These quizzes can be used to monitor student comprehension and make decisions about each student's instructional needs.

Dear Family Member:

Your child is becoming a skilled independent reader! And the guided reading books that your reader will bring home are designed to help in this process.

As part of the *Scholastic Guided Reading Program,* your child will participate in small groups and will receive individualized instruction to develop fluency, oral language, vocabulary, phonics, comprehension, and writing skills. In addition, your child will bring home enjoyable, level-appropriate stories and selections that will help to ensure his or her success as an independent reader.

Here are some suggestions for helping your child before, during, and after reading:

Before

- Look at the book cover with your child. Together, review the illustrations or photographs in the book. Ask your child to predict what the story or selection will be about.

- Discuss what you and your child might already know about the topic of the book you are about to read.

- If your child is a beginning reader, echo-read the story or selection with your child by reading a line first and having your child read it after you. If your child is a more skilled reader, periodically stop and ask questions.

During

- If your child does not recognize a word right away, help him or her to focus on the familiar letters and spelling patterns in the word. Guide your child to think about other words that look like the unfamiliar word.

- Encourage your child to use phonics and decoding skills to sound out any new, unfamiliar words. If necessary, provide the word if your child struggles.

- Encourage your child to read with expression and to enjoy reading!

After

- Encourage your child to reread the story or selection to develop confidence. If the book is long, reread a few favorite sections or chapters. Perhaps your child could read the story or selection to other family members or friends.

- Discuss the story or selection with your child. Ask questions such as: What were your favorite parts? Who were your favorite characters? Why? What interesting fact did you learn?

- Have your child keep a journal of favorite stories and selections and interesting words in those books. Your child might also like to write about the book in this journal.

Have fun with this reading experience and your child will have fun, too!

Sincerely,

Estimado padre o tutor:

Su niño está en el proceso de convertirse en un lector hábil e independiente. Los libros de lectura guiada que su niño llevará a casa han sido concebidos para ayudar en este proceso.

Como parte del Programa de Lectura Guiada de Scholastic, su niño recibirá instrucción en grupos pequeños e individualizada con el objetivo de desarrollar la fluidez, el lenguaje oral, el vocabulario, la fonética, la comprensión y las destrezas de escritura. Además, su niño llevará a casa lecturas amenas y apropiadas a su nivel, que le servirán para garantizar su éxito como lector independiente.

Éstas son algunas sugerencias para ayudar a su niño antes, durante y después de la lectura:

Antes

- Observe con su niño la cubierta del libro. Repasen juntos las ilustraciones o fotografías del libro. Pídale a su niño predecir de qué tratará el cuento o la selección que van a leer.
- Comenten lo que usted y su niño ya sepan sobre el tema del libro que van a leer.
- Si su niño es un lector principiante, lea usted primero una línea y pídale que lea esa misma línea después. Si su niño es un lector más avanzado, haga una pausa de vez en cuando para hacerle preguntas.

Durante

- Si a su niño le resulta difícil reconocer alguna palabra, ayúdelo a fijarse en las letras y patrones ortográficos con los que esté familiarizado. Guíe a su niño en la búsqueda de otras palabras que se parezcan a la palabra desconocida.
- Anime a su niño a usar la fonética y las destrezas de decodificación para leer en voz alta cualquier palabra nueva o desconocida. Si su niño tiene dificultades para hacerlo de manera independiente, lea usted la palabra.
- Anime a su niño a leer de manera expresiva y a disfrutar de la lectura.

Después

- Anime a su niño a volver a leer el cuento o la selección para que gane confianza como lector. Si el libro es demasiado largo, vuelva a leer algunas de las secciones o pasajes favoritos. También puede pedirle que lea el cuento a otros familiares o amigos.
- Comente con su niño el cuento o la selección. Hágale preguntas como las siguientes: ¿Qué partes te gustaron más? ¿Qué personajes son tus favoritos? ¿Por qué? ¿Qué hecho o dato importante aprendiste leyendo este libro?
- Pídale que lleve un récord de sus cuentos y selecciones favoritos, así como de las palabras interesantes que encuentre en los mismos. También, puede llevar un diario con comentarios sobre los libros.

Disfrute de la lectura. ¡Su niño, de seguro, también disfrutará!

Atentamente,

GRADE K: REPRODUCIBLE FICTION BOOKMARKS

Share these bookmarks with your children to remind them of some key features of different fiction genres.

Read Fiction

✓ Look at the cover.

✓ Say the name of the book.

✓ Look at the pictures.

✓ Read the story.

✓ See what happens first.

✓ See what happens last.

Read a Fairy Tale

✓ Say the name of the book.

✓ Flip through the book.

✓ Look for things that are not real.

✓ Read the story.

✓ Think about where the story takes place.

✓ Look for a happy ending.

Read a Poem

✓ Read the name of the poem.

✓ Read the poem aloud.

✓ Hear words that sound the same.

✓ Hear a pattern.

✓ Think about the words.

Read a Fantasy

✓ Look at the cover.

✓ Say the name of the book.

✓ Look at the pictures.

✓ Look for things that could not happen in real life.

MARCADORES DE GÉNERO REPRODUCIBLES

Reparta estos marcadores a sus alumnos para que recuerden algunas de las características más importantes de los géneros de ficción.

Al leer un cuento de ficción

✓ Mira la portada.

✓ Di el nombre del libro.

✓ Mira los dibujos.

✓ Lee el cuento.

✓ Mira qué ocurre primero.

✓ Mira qué ocurre al final.

Al leer un cuento de hadas

✓ Di el nombre del libro.

✓ Hojea el libro.

✓ Busca cosas que no sean reales.

✓ Lee el cuento.

✓ Piensa en dónde ocurre el cuento.

✓ Busca el final feliz.

Al leer un poema

✓ Lee el nombre del poema.

✓ Lee el poema en voz alta.

✓ Pon atención a las palabras que suenen parecido.

✓ Oye el patrón.

✓ Piensa en las palabras.

Al leer un cuento de fantasía

✓ Mira la portada.

✓ Di el nombre del libro.

✓ Mira los dibujos.

✓ Busca cosas que no podrían ocurrir en la vida real.

GRADE 1: REPRODUCIBLE FICTION BOOKMARKS

Share these bookmarks with your children to remind them of some key features of different fiction genres.

Reading Fiction

✓ Look at the cover.

✓ Read the title.

✓ Look at the pictures.

✓ See who is in the story. See what they do.

✓ Read the story.

✓ Think about what happens first, next, last.

Reading a Fairy Tale

✓ Read the title.

✓ Flip through the book.

✓ Look for places, people, and animals that are not real.

✓ Read the story.

✓ Think about where the story takes place.

✓ Think about when the story takes place.

✓ Look for a happy ending.

Reading a Poem

✓ Read the title. Find out what the poem is about.

✓ Read the poem aloud.

✓ Listen for words that rhyme.

✓ Listen for a pattern in the words.

✓ Think about the pictures that the words make in your mind.

Reading Fantasy

✓ Read the title.

✓ Flip through the book.

✓ Look for things that could not happen in real life.

✓ Look for places that could not be real.

✓ Look for animals that act like people and talk in the story.

MARCADORES DE GÉNERO REPRODUCIBLES

Reparta estos marcadores a sus alumnos para que recuerden algunas de las características más importantes de los géneros de ficción.

Al leer un cuento de ficción

- ✓ Mira la portada.
- ✓ Lee el título.
- ✓ Mira los dibujos.
- ✓ Mira quiénes participan en el cuento. Mira qué hacen.
- ✓ Lee el cuento.
- ✓ Piensa en qué pasa primero, al medio y al final.

Al leer un cuento de hadas

- ✓ Lee el título.
- ✓ Hojea el libro.
- ✓ Busca lugares, personas y animales que no sean reales.
- ✓ Lee el cuento.
- ✓ Piensa en dónde ocurre el cuento.
- ✓ Piensa en cuándo ocurre el cuento.
- ✓ Busca el final feliz.

Al leer un poema

- ✓ Lee el título. Descubre de qué trata el poema.
- ✓ Lee el poema en voz alta.
- ✓ Pon atención a las palabras que riman.
- ✓ Busca un patrón en las palabras.
- ✓ Piensa en las cosas que te imaginas al leer.

Al leer un cuento de fantasía

- ✓ Lee el título.
- ✓ Hojea el libro.
- ✓ Busca cosas que no podrían ocurrir en la vida real.
- ✓ Busca lugares que no podrían ser reales.
- ✓ Busca animales que actúen como personas y que hablen.

GRADE 2: REPRODUCIBLE FICTION BOOKMARKS

Share these bookmarks with your children to remind them of some of the key features of different fiction genres.

Quick Clues for Reading Fiction

✓ Look at the cover.

✓ Read the title.

✓ Look for people in the story who are like real people.

✓ Read where the story happens, such as a school or a home.

✓ Find out what people do to fix problems.

Quick Clues for Reading a Fairy Tale

✓ Read the title.

✓ Look at the pictures. Look for places, people, and animals that are not real.

✓ Read the story.

✓ Read to find out where the story takes place.

✓ Think about when the story happens.

✓ Look for a happy ending.

Quick Clues for Reading a Mystery

✓ Read the title to find out what the mystery is.

✓ Read the story. Find out the puzzle or crime. See who wants to solve it.

✓ Look for clues to solve the mystery.

✓ Think about what will happen next.

Quick Clues for Reading a Poem

✓ Read the title. Find out what the poem is about.

✓ Read the poem aloud.

✓ Listen for a pattern in the sentences.

✓ Listen for a pattern in the words.

✓ Think about the pictures the words make in your mind.

Quick Clues for Reading a Fable

✓ Read the title. Look for names of animals.

✓ Read the story. See how the animals or objects talk.

✓ Read the end. Find out what happens to one of the animals.

✓ Think about the lesson learned.

Quick Clues for Reading Fantasy

✓ Look for people, animals, and places that are not real.

✓ Find out if there are animals that talk or people who travel in time.

✓ Find out what the problem is.

✓ Read to see how the problem is solved.

MARCADORES DE GÉNERO REPRODUCIBLES

Reparta estos marcadores a sus alumnos para que recuerden algunas de las características más importantes de los géneros de ficción.

Breves consejos para leer textos de ficción

✓ Mira la portada.

✓ Lee el título.

✓ En el cuento, busca personas que sean como las personas de verdad.

✓ Lee dónde ocurre la historia, por ejemplo, en una escuela o una casa.

✓ Descubre qué hace la gente para resolver los problemas.

Breves consejos para leer un cuento de hadas

✓ Lee el título.

✓ Mira los dibujos. Busca lugares, personas y animales que no sean reales.

✓ Lee el cuento.

✓ Lee para saber dónde ocurre la historia.

✓ Piensa cuándo ocurre la historia.

✓ Busca el final feliz.

Breves consejos para leer un cuento de misterio

✓ Lee el título para saber de qué trata el misterio.

✓ Lee el cuento. Descubre el acertijo o el crimen. Descubre quién quiere resolverlo.

✓ Busca pistas para resolver el misterio.

✓ Piensa qué ocurrirá después.

Breves consejos para leer un poema

✓ Lee el título. Descubre de qué trata el poema.

✓ Lee el poema en voz alta.

✓ Busca un patrón en las oraciones.

✓ Busca un patrón en las palabras.

✓ Piensa en las cosas que te imaginas al leer.

Breves consejos para leer una fábula

✓ Lee el título. Busca nombres de animales.

✓ Lee la historia. Fíjate cómo hablan los animales o los objetos.

✓ Lee el final. Descubre qué le ocurre a uno de los animales.

✓ Piensa en la lección aprendida.

Breves consejos para leer un cuento de fantasía

✓ Busca personas, animales y lugares que no sean reales.

✓ Fíjate si hay animales que hablan o gente que viaja en el tiempo.

✓ Descubre cuál es el problema.

✓ Lee para saber cómo se resuelve el problema.

GRADE 3: REPRODUCIBLE FICTION BOOKMARKS

Share these bookmarks with your students to remind them of some key features of different fiction genres.

Quick Clues for Reading Realistic Fiction

✓ Look at the cover and the title.

✓ Read the story. See if the characters are like real people.

✓ Look for where and when the story happens. See if it's like a real place.

✓ Read where the story happens, such as a school or a home.

✓ Find out what people do to solve their problems.

Quick Clues for Reading a Folktale

✓ Read the title. Think what the story is about.

✓ Read the story. See which characters are good and which are bad.

✓ Find out what the characters' goals are.

✓ Look for things that happen three times.

✓ Find out if the good characters reach their goals in the end. See what happens to the bad characters.

Quick Clues for Reading a Mystery

✓ Read the title to learn what the mystery is.

✓ Read the story to find the puzzle or crime and who wants to solve it.

✓ Look for clues to solve the mystery.

✓ Think about events that are scary and can't be explained.

✓ Look for clues that help you guess what will happen next.

✓ See how the mystery is solved in the end.

Quick Clues for Reading a Poem

✓ Read the title. Think about what the topic of the poem is.

✓ Look at how many lines there are and if they are in groups.

✓ Read the poem aloud.

✓ Listen for a pattern in the words.

✓ Listen for a pattern in the sentences.

✓ Think about the pictures that form in your mind as you read.

Quick Clues for Reading a Play

✓ Read the title.

✓ Find a list of characters in the beginning.

✓ Read each act or part of the play. Note where each act takes place.

✓ Look for the names of characters and the words they say.

✓ Look for words that tell you how the characters speak and move.

Quick Clues for Reading Fantasy

✓ Read the title. Think what it tells you about the story.

✓ Read the story. Look for people, places, and animals that are not real.

✓ Look for animals that may talk and people who may travel in time.

✓ Find out what the problem is.

✓ Read to see how the problem is solved and if magic or magical thinking is used.

MARCADORES DE GÉNERO REPRODUCIBLES

Reparta estos marcadores a sus alumnos para que recuerden algunas de las características más importantes de los géneros de ficción.

Breves consejos para leer ficción realista

✓ Mira la portada y el título.

✓ Lee el cuento. Fíjate si los personajes son como las personas de verdad.

✓ Busca dónde y cuándo ocurre la historia. Piensa si es como un lugar real.

✓ Lee dónde ocurre la historia, por ejemplo, en una escuela o una casa.

✓ Averigua qué hace la gente para resolver los problemas.

Breves consejos para leer un cuento folclórico

✓ Lee el título. Piensa sobre qué trata el cuento.

✓ Lee el cuento. Piensa qué personajes son buenos y cuáles son malos.

✓ Descubre cuáles son las metas de los personajes.

✓ Busca cosas que ocurran tres veces.

✓ Descubre si al final los personajes buenos alcanzan sus metas. Lee qué les ocurre a los personajes malos.

Breves consejos para leer un cuento de misterio

✓ Lee el título para saber de qué trata el misterio.

✓ Lee el cuento para hallar el acertijo o problema y quiénes desean resolverlo.

✓ Busca pistas para resolver el misterio.

✓ Piensa en los eventos aterradores que no se puedan explicar.

✓ Busca pistas para adivinar qué va a ocurrir.

✓ Descubre cómo se resuelve el misterio al final del cuento.

Breves consejos para leer un poema

✓ Lee el título. Piensa cuál es el tema del poema.

✓ Mira cuántas líneas tiene el poema y si están en grupos.

✓ Lee el poema en voz alta.

✓ Busca un patrón en las palabras.

✓ Busca un patrón en las oraciones.

✓ Piensa qué te imaginas al leer el poema.

Breves consejos para leer una obra de teatro

✓ Lee el título.

✓ Busca la lista de personajes al principio de la obra.

✓ Lee todos los actos o partes de la obra. Fíjate dónde ocurre cada acto.

✓ Busca los nombres de los personajes y lo que dicen.

✓ Busca palabras que te indiquen cómo hablan y se mueven los personajes.

Breves consejos para leer un cuento de fantasía

✓ Lee el título. Piensa qué te indica sobre el cuento.

✓ Lee el cuento. Busca personas, lugares y animales que no sean reales.

✓ Busca animales que hablen o personas que viajen en el tiempo.

✓ Descubre cuál es el problema.

✓ Lee para saber cómo se resuelve el problema y si se usó magia para hacerlo.

GRADE 4: REPRODUCIBLE FICTION BOOKMARKS

Share these bookmarks with your students to remind them of some key features of different fiction genres.

Quick Clues for Reading Realistic Fiction

✓ Read the title. Think what the cover shows.

✓ Read the story. Meet the characters and learn about the setting.

✓ Note how characters are like real people with real problems.

✓ Follow the sequence of events. Predict what will happen next.

✓ Find out what people do to solve problems or reach goals.

Quick Clues for Reading a Novel

✓ Read the title and the author's name.

✓ Check how many chapters there are.

✓ Note the setting and the time covered by the story as you read.

✓ Note the main characters and what they are like.

✓ Follow the events, problems, and conflicts in the plot.

✓ Note how problems are solved in the end.

Quick Clues for Reading a Mystery

✓ Read the title to learn what the mystery is.

✓ Note the characters who want to solve the mystery and why.

✓ Look for clues to solve the mystery.

✓ Look for how the author builds suspense.

✓ Look for clues that help you guess what will happen next.

✓ See how the mystery is solved in the end.

Quick Clues for Reading Historical Fiction

✓ Read the title and the author's name.

✓ Note when and where in history the story takes place.

✓ Read the story. Imagine how people lived in this time.

✓ See how characters take part in historical events.

✓ Compare how people in the past solve problems with what people do today.

Quick Clues for Reading a Play

✓ Read the title and the playwright's name.

✓ Read the list of characters' names in the beginning.

✓ Note where each act of the play takes place.

✓ Look for characters' names before the words they say.

✓ Note words that explain how the characters speak and move.

Quick Clues for Reading a Fable

✓ Read the title and the author's name. Aesop is the author of many fables.

✓ Note if the characters are animals.

✓ See if one character tries to trick or outsmart another character.

✓ Decide what the problem is.

✓ See who learns a lesson in the end. Decide what the lesson is.

MARCADORES DE GÉNERO REPRODUCIBLES

Reparta estos marcadores a sus alumnos para que recuerden algunas de las características más importantes de los géneros de ficción.

Breves consejos para leer ficción realista

✓ Lee el título. Piensa qué muestra la portada.

✓ Lee el cuento. Conoce los personajes y el ambiente.

✓ Fíjate que los personajes son como las personas reales y que tienen problemas de verdad.

✓ Sigue la secuencia de sucesos. Predice qué ocurrirá después.

✓ Descubre qué hace la gente para resolver los problemas o alcanzar sus metas.

Breves consejos para leer una novela

✓ Lee el título y el nombre del autor.

✓ Explora cuántos capítulos hay.

✓ Al leer, pon atención al ambiente y a la época de la historia.

✓ Fíjate en los personajes principales y en lo que hacen.

✓ Pon atención a los sucesos, problemas y conflictos de la trama.

✓ Descubre cómo se resuelven los problemas al final.

Breves consejos para leer un cuento de misterio

✓ Lee el título para saber de qué trata el misterio.

✓ Fíjate en los personajes que quieren resolver el misterio y por qué quieren hacerlo.

✓ Busca pistas para resolver el misterio.

✓ Fíjate en cómo el autor crea suspenso.

✓ Busca pistas para adivinar qué ocurrirá después.

✓ Descubre cómo se resuelve el misterio al final.

Breves consejos para leer ficción histórica

✓ Lee el título y el nombre del autor.

✓ Fíjate en qué momento y lugar de la historia ocurre el cuento.

✓ Lee el cuento. Imagina cómo vivía la gente en esa época.

✓ Observa cómo los personajes participan en acontecimientos históricos.

✓ Compara cómo se resolvían los problemas en el pasado y cómo se resuelven hoy en día.

Breves consejos para leer una obra de teatro

✓ Lee el título y el nombre del dramaturgo.

✓ Lee la lista de personajes al principio de la obra.

✓ Fíjate dónde ocurre cada acto de la obra.

✓ Busca los nombres de los personajes antes de sus diálogos.

✓ Pon atención a las palabras que indican cómo hablan y se mueven los personajes.

Breves consejos para leer una fábula

✓ Lee el título y el nombre del autor. Esopo es autor de muchas fábulas.

✓ Fíjate si los personajes son animales.

✓ Piensa si un personaje trata de engañar o burlar a otro.

✓ Descubre cuál es el problema.

✓ Descubre quién aprende una lección al final de la fábula. Decide cuál fue esa lección.

GRADE 5: REPRODUCIBLE FICTION BOOKMARKS

Share these bookmarks with your students to remind them of some key features of different fiction genres.

Quick Clues for Reading Realistic Fiction

✓ Read the title and the author's name.

✓ Look for characters who are as believable as real people.

✓ Note if the problems characters have and the actions they take to solve them seem truthful.

✓ Decide if the outcomes are reasonable. Think about whether this could happen in real life.

✓ Think about the ending and decide if it is satisfactory.

Quick Clues for Reading a Novel

✓ Read the title and the author's name. Learn about the story on the back cover or book jacket.

✓ Note the setting and the time frame the story covers as you read.

✓ Look for major and minor characters and their role in the story.

✓ Follow the sequence of events and conflicts in the plot. Note if there are subplots.

✓ Decide if conflicts are resolved in the end.

Quick Clues for Reading a Mystery

✓ Read the title for a clue to what the mystery is.

✓ Note the characters who want to solve the mystery and why.

✓ Note how suspense builds as characters look for clues.

✓ Look for clues that foreshadow what will happen next.

✓ Find out in the end if the mystery is solved as you thought or if the ending is a surprise.

Quick Clues for Reading Historical Fiction

✓ Read the title and the author's name.

✓ Note when and where in history the story takes place.

✓ Note people's clothing, food, and homes. See what kind of work they do.

✓ See how characters take part in historical events.

✓ Look for how the setting affects what happens to the characters.

Quick Clues for Reading Science Fiction

✓ Read the title and the author's name.

✓ Find out if the story happens in the future and on another planet.

✓ Note details of the world in which the characters live.

✓ Look for scientific ideas that influence the plot.

✓ Read to see how characters solve problems and conflicts in this world.

Quick Clues for Reading a Legend

✓ Read the title to find what hero the story will be about.

✓ Read the story to discover what amazing deeds the hero did.

✓ Decide which deeds are more realistic and might be based on a real person in history.

✓ Note the conflicts and the problems.

✓ Think about what the hero's goal is and if this goal is reached.

MARCADORES DE GÉNERO REPRODUCIBLES

Reparta estos marcadores a sus alumnos para que recuerden algunas de las características más importantes de los géneros de ficción.

Breves consejos para leer ficción realista

✓ Lee el título y el nombre del autor.

✓ Busca personajes que parezcan personas reales.

✓ Determina si los problemas que tienen los personajes y las decisiones que toman para resolverlos parecen verídicos.

✓ Decide si los resultados son razonables. Piensa si esto podría ocurrir en la vida real.

✓ Piensa en el final y determina si es satisfactorio.

Breves consejos para leer una novela

✓ Lee el título y el nombre del autor. Lee la contraportada o sobrecubierta para aprender más del libro.

✓ Mientras lees, fíjate en el ambiente y periodo de tiempo en que ocurre la historia.

✓ Busca los personajes principales y secundarios y su papel en la historia.

✓ Sigue la secuencia de sucesos y los conflictos de la trama. Fíjate si hay historias secundarias.

✓ Decide si al final los conflictos se resuelven o no.

Breves consejos para leer un cuento de misterio

✓ Lee el título para saber de qué trata el misterio.

✓ Fíjate en los personajes que quieren resolver el misterio y por qué quieren hacerlo.

✓ Nota que hay más misterio a medida que los personajes buscan pistas.

✓ Busca pistas que predigan qué sucederá después.

✓ Al final, descubre si el misterio se resolvió como pensabas o si fue una sorpresa.

Breves consejos para leer ficción histórica

✓ Lee el título y el nombre del autor.

✓ Fíjate cuándo y dónde ocurre la historia.

✓ Presta atención a la vestimenta, alimentos y viviendas de la gente. Fíjate en qué trabajan.

✓ Lee cómo los personajes participan en acontecimientos históricos.

✓ Presta atención a cómo el ambiente afecta lo que les ocurre a los personajes.

Breves consejos para leer ciencia ficción

✓ Lee el título y el nombre del autor.

✓ Averigua si la historia ocurre en el futuro o en otro planeta.

✓ Fíjate en los detalles del mundo en que viven los personajes.

✓ Busca ideas científicas que influyan en la trama.

✓ Al leer, descubre cómo los personajes resuelven problemas y conflictos en ese mundo.

Breves consejos para leer una leyenda

✓ Lee el título para descubrir sobre qué héroe tratará la historia.

✓ Lee la historia para descubrir qué hazañas realizó ese héroe.

✓ Decide cuáles hazañas son más realistas y podrían basarse en una persona verdadera.

✓ Pon atención a los conflictos y a los problemas.

✓ Piensa cuál es la meta del héroe y si la alcanza.

GRADE 6: REPRODUCIBLE FICTION BOOKMARKS

Share these bookmarks with your students to remind them of some key features of different fiction genres.

Quick Clues for Reading a Graphic Novel

✓ Read the title and the author's name.

✓ Preview the pictures, or graphic part of the novel, before you start reading.

✓ Find characters' words in the speech balloons.

✓ Look for how characters feel in the illustrations.

✓ Find descriptions of what happens in the text boxes on the illustrations.

✓ Follow the story sequence by moving from panel to panel.

Quick Clues for Reading a Novel

✓ Read the title and the author's name. Learn about the story on the back cover or book jacket.

✓ Decide where and when the story takes place as you begin to read.

✓ Identify the major and minor characters and the problems or conflicts they have.

✓ Follow the rising action in the plot.

✓ Decide where the story climax is and what resolution follows at the end.

Quick Clues for Reading a Poem

✓ Read the title to learn what the poem is about.

✓ Listen for rhyme and/or rhythm as you read.

✓ Determine the emotion the poet expresses.

✓ Decide what kind of poem it is, depending on length, the rhythm, number of lines, and syllables per line.

✓ Pay attention to the images the words create in your mind.

Quick Clues for Reading Historical Fiction

✓ Read the title and the author's name.

✓ Note the historical setting for the story.

✓ Pay attention to details of clothing, food preparation, and transportation to get a sense of the time period.

✓ Note any names of real places and real people in history.

✓ Decide how the setting influences the plot and the characters' actions.

Quick Clues for Reading Science Fiction

✓ Read the title for clues to what the story is about.

✓ Decide what the setting is: another planet, a spaceship, and/or the future.

✓ Note how the setting is different from the world in which you live.

✓ Decide how science or futuristic technology influences the plot.

✓ Follow the plot to identify conflicts and how they are resolved in the end.

Quick Clues for Reading a Myth

✓ Read the title to learn who and what the story is about.

✓ Read the story to decide what natural event or human question might be explained.

✓ Identify the setting and the culture the myth comes from.

✓ Look for human characters who may interact with gods and goddesses or mythical creatures.

✓ Note how conflicts are resolved.

MARCADORES DE GÉNERO REPRODUCIBLES

Reparta estos marcadores a sus alumnos para que recuerden algunas de las características más importantes de los géneros de ficción.

Breves consejos para leer una novela gráfica

✓ Lee el título y el nombre del autor.

✓ Antes de comenzar a leer, revisa las ilustraciones, o parte gráfica de la novela.

✓ Lee lo que dicen los personajes en los globos de diálogo.

✓ Mira las ilustraciones para saber cómo se sienten los personajes.

✓ Lee las descripciones de lo que pasa en las cajas de texto.

✓ Para seguir la secuencia de la historia lee de panel a panel.

Breves consejos para leer una novela

✓ Lee el título y el nombre del autor. Lee la contraportada o sobrecubierta para aprender más sobre el libro.

✓ Mientras lees, fíjate dónde y cuándo ocurre la historia.

✓ Identifica los personajes principales y secundarios y sus problemas o conflictos.

✓ Sigue el desarrollo de la acción en la trama.

✓ Decide cuál es el climax de la historia y cuál es la resolución final.

Breves consejos para leer un poema

✓ Lee el título para saber de qué trata el poema.

✓ Mientras lees, presta atención a la rima o al ritmo.

✓ Determina qué emoción expresa el poeta.

✓ Identifica qué tipo de poema es, de acuerdo al largo, ritmo, número de versos y sílabas por verso.

✓ Presta atención a las imágenes que las palabras crean en tu mente.

Breves consejos para leer ficción histórica

✓ Lee el título y el nombre del autor.

✓ Fíjate en el ambiente histórico del cuento.

✓ Para entender la época, fíjate en detalles como la vestimenta, la preparación de los alimentos y los medios de transporte.

✓ Fíjate en los nombres de lugares y personas verdaderos en la historia.

✓ Decide cómo el ambiente influye en la trama y en las acciones de los personajes.

Breves consejos para leer ciencia ficción

✓ Lee el título para comprender sobre qué trata la historia.

✓ Identifica el ambiente: otro planeta, una nave espacial y/o el futuro.

✓ Fíjate cómo el ambiente es distinto del mundo en que vives.

✓ Decide cómo la ciencia o la tecnología futurista influye en la trama.

✓ Sigue la trama para identificar conflictos y cómo éstos se resuelven al final.

Breves consejos para leer mitos

✓ Lee el título para que sepas sobre quién o qué trata la historia.

✓ Lee la historia para identificar qué evento natural o pregunta se explica.

✓ Identifica el ambiente y la cultura de la cual proviene el mito.

✓ Fíjate en personajes humanos que interactúen con dioses o personajes míticos.

✓ Presta atención a cómo se resuelven los conflictos.

REPRODUCIBLE NONFICTION BOOKMARKS

Share these bookmarks with your students to remind them of some of the key features of nonfiction text.

Quick Clues for Reading Nonfiction

✓ Preview the piece.

✓ Read the title, introduction, and headings to discover the main ideas.

✓ Make a prediction about the subject of the piece.

✓ Pay special attention to bold-faced words and extra graphic features.

✓ Study the graphic aids and read the captions carefully.

Quick Clues for Reading Maps

✓ Read the map title.

✓ Find the symbols.

✓ Look at the map key. Read the labels.

✓ Find the map scale.

✓ Find the compass rose.

Quick Clues for Reading Primary Sources

✓ First, read the title.

✓ Preview the text to learn about the topic.

✓ Read the main article.

✓ Read the primary source material. Ask yourself, "How does this information add to what I know about the topic?"

Quick Clues for Reading Graphs

✓ Read the title of the graph.

✓ Think about the topic.

✓ Look at each part of the graph and read each label.

✓ Think about what information is being represented.

✓ Look at the labels. Think about what the numbers stand for.

✓ For line graphs, use your finger to trace from each dot to the side and the bottom.

Quick Clues for Reading Reference Sources

✓ Look up your topic in the table of contents or index.

✓ Preview the text.

✓ Use the special features as you read.

✓ Think about how the information from the source fits with what you know.

Quick Clues for Reading Magazine Articles

✓ Read the title, deck, and subheadings to learn the main ideas.

✓ Predict what the article will be about.

✓ Notice any special features.

✓ Pay attention to bold-faced words.

✓ Study the graphic aids and read the captions carefully.

MARCADORES DE LIBROS REPRODUCIBLES

Reparta estos marcadores entre sus alumnos para que recuerden algunas de las características más importantes de los textos de no ficción.

Breves consejos para leer textos de no ficción

✓ Hojea el artículo.

✓ Lee el título, la introducción y los encabezamientos para determinar la idea principal.

✓ Haz una predicción sobre el tema del artículo.

✓ Presta especial atención a las palabras en negrita u otras características sobresalientes.

✓ Observa las gráficas y lee los pies de grabado detenidamente.

Breves consejos para leer mapas

✓ Lee el título del mapa.

✓ Busca los símbolos del mapa.

✓ Observa la leyenda del mapa.

✓ Lee los rótulos.

✓ Busca la escala.

✓ Busca la rosa náutica.

Breves consejos para leer fuentes de información

✓ Primero, lee el título.

✓ Haz una lectura preliminar del texto para tener una idea del tema.

✓ Lee el artículo principal.

✓ Mientras lees, pregúntate qué nueva información has aprendido sobre el tema.

Breves consejos para leer gráficas

✓ Lee el título de la gráfica. Piensa sobre el tema.

✓ Observa cada sección de la gráfica y lee cada rótulo.

✓ Piensa en la información que se presenta en la gráfica.

✓ Observa los rótulos. Piensa en qué significan los números que aparecen.

✓ En las gráficas lineales, marca con el dedo las líneas que van de cada punto a las coordenadas.

Breves consejos para leer fuentes de referencia

✓ Busca el tema de interés en la tabla de contenido o en el índice.

✓ Haz una lectura preliminar del texto.

✓ A medida que leas, ten en cuenta características especiales.

✓ Analiza si la información que aparece en esta fuente es la que necesitas.

Breves consejos para leer artículos de revista

✓ Lee el título, la introducción y los subtítulos para determinar la idea principal.

✓ Haz una predicción sobre el tema del artículo.

✓ Observa cualquier característica especial.

✓ Presta atención a las palabras en negrita.

✓ Estudia las gráficas y lee los rótulos detenidamente.

Skills & Strategies Chart: Fiction Focus

Level	Title	Series	Author	Genre	Comprehension Strategies	Phonics and Word Study	Writing Options	Technology
A	Boxes		Avelyn Davidson	Realistic Fiction	Using Illustrations	Telling Sentences	descriptive label	www.artistshelpingchildren.org/boxesartscraftstideaskidsboxprojects.html
A	Helping		Linda Johns	Realistic Fiction	Developing Print Awareness	Initial Sounds	descriptive journal	http://www.atozteacherstuff.com/Tips/Classroom_Jobs/
A	Hop, Skip, and Jump		Janelle Cherrington	Realistic Fiction	Developing Print Awareness	Oral Blending of Sounds	descriptive narrative	http://www.gameskidsplay.net
A	Little Animals		Janet Reed	Fantasy	Understanding Genre: Fantasy	Beginning Consonants	expository descriptive	http://www.kidsrunning.com/
A	My Dog Fluffy		Janelle Cherrington	Informational Text	Using Punctuation	Naming Words	descriptive narrative	http://www.kindnews.org/teacher_zone/lesson_plans.asp
A	My House		Catherine Peters	Informational Text	Recognizing Sequence	Beginning Sounds	descriptive graphic aid	http://www.contractor.edu/buildhouselp/welcome.html
A	Playing		Avelyn Davidson	Realistic Fiction	Recognizing Patterned Text	Pictures and Word Structure	expository narrative	http://www.gameskidsplay.net/
A	Run, Rabbit!		Yael Landman	Realistic Fiction	Using Punctuation	High-Frequency Words	narrative expository	http://www.hsus.org/wildlife/a_closer_look_at_wildlife/rabbits.html
A	Storm, The		Avelyn Davidson	Informational Text	Activating Prior Knowledge	High-Frequency Words	list graphic aid	http://www.nws.noaa.gov/om/reachout/thunderstorm.shtml
A	Time		Avelyn Davidson	Realistic Fiction	Understanding Sequence	Phonogram -ag	descriptive narrative	http://www.time-for-time.com/lesson1.htm
B	Ants Go Home, The		Linda Johns	Fantasy	Understanding Sequence	High-Frequency Words	descriptive expository	http://www.pestworldforkids.org/ants.html
B	Fishing		Janet Reed	Fantasy	Recognizing Story Pattern	Beginning and Ending Sounds	list narrative	http://www.mbayaq.org/lc/kids_place/
B	Getting There		Edwin Johns	Nonfiction	Understanding Photographs	Initial Consonant Sounds	expository descriptive	www.atozkidsstuff.com/tran.html
B	Home Run!		Catherine Peters	Realistic Fiction	Recognizing Setting	Words With Phonogram -it	narrative expository	http://www.theteacherscorner.net/printable-worksheets/seasonal/baseball/index.htm
B	Let's Play		Catherine Peters	Realistic Fiction	Reading Sentences	Words With Consonants	narrative list	www.education.com/reference/article/Ref_Developing_Language/
B	Look at Us		Linda Johns	Realistic Fiction	Identifying Setting	Sentence Structure	descriptive expository	http://www.edheads.org/activities/simple%2Dmachines/
B	My Feet		Janet Reed	Realistic Fiction	Making Predictions	High-Frequency Words	expository list	teachers-subject-guides.suite101.com/article.cfm/kindergarten_physical_education
B	Night Shift	Brain Bank	Ryan Josh	Nonfiction	Recognizing Patterned Text	Naming Words	expository graphic aid	www.teacher.scholastic.com/commclub/index.htm
B	Off to the City		Avelyn Davidson	Fantasy	Identifying Sequence	Words With Short a	narrative poster	www.bicyclinginfo.org/education/children-5to8.cfm
B	Zebras Don't Brush Their Teeth!	Brain Bank	Lynette Evans	Nonfiction	Comparing and Contrasting	Action Words	expository list	www.redcross.org/services/hss/resources/scrubby_bear_personal_hygiene.pdf
C	Big Blue Sea, The	Brain Bank	Janine Scott	Informational Text	Recognizing Patterned Text	Compound Words	descriptive expository	http://www.ceismc.gatech.edu/busyt/bio_marine.shtml
C	Brave Dave and the Dragons		Janet Reed	Fantasy	Making Predictions	Words With Consonants	expository narrative	http://www.educatall.com/page/19/Knights-and-princesses.html

Level	Title	Series	Author	Genre	Comprehension Strategies	Phonics and Word Study	Writing Options	Technology
C	Hide and Seek		Janet Reed	Fantasy	Recognizing Questions	Describing Words	graphic aid, descriptive	www.gameskidsplay.net
C	It's Time to Eat!		Avelyn Davidson	Informational Text	Reading Questions and Answers	Punctuation	expository, descriptive	http://www.sandiegozoo.org/animalbytes/index.html
C	Little Blue Fish		Lynette Evans	Realistic Fiction	Recognizing Setting	Punctuation	narrative, expository	http://www.fi.edu/fellows/fellow8/dec98/intera.html
C	Little Duckling Is Lost		May Nelson	Fantasy	Recognizing Patterned Text	Initial Consonants	descriptive, narrative	http://www.eastvalleywildlife.org/ducks.htm
C	Oak Street Party, The		Catherine Peters	Realistic Fiction	Comparing and Contrasting	Apostrophe *s*	descriptive, list	http://www.crayola.com/lesson-plans/detail/community-celebrations-3-d-timeline-lesson-plan/
C	One Frog, One Fly		Wendy Blaxland	Fantasy	Understanding Genre: Fantasy	Describing Words	narrative, expository	http://www.picadome.fcps.net/lab/curr1/food_chain/default.htm
C	Pass the Pasta, Please!		Linda Johns	Informational Text	Recognizing Punctuation	Initial Consonant Sounds	descriptive, graphic aid	http://www.ilovepasta.org/shapes.html
C	Patterns	Emergent Reader	Samantha Berger, Daniel Moreton	Informational Text	Using Picture Details	Plurals	descriptive, list	http://www.uen.org/themepark/patterns/nature-patterns.shtml
D	After School Fun		May Nelson	Realistic Fiction	Identifying Setting	Initial Consonants	labeling, narrative	http://www.exploratorium.edu/afterschool/index.html
D	Dog Walker, The		Janet Reed	Realistic Fiction	Comparing and Contrasting	Exclamation Points	narrative, description	http://dogplay.com/youth.html
D	Little Red Hen, The		retold by Janelle Cherrington	Traditional Literature	Recognizing Patterned Text	Words With Short Vowels	labeling, descriptive	www.grainchain.com/5-to-7/Where-does-bread-come-from/Default.aspx
D	Little Turtle, The		Vachel Lindsay	Poem	Recognizing Sequence	Words With r-Controlled Vowels	descriptive, list	http://www.sandiegozoo.org/animalbytes/t-turtle.html
D	Noisy Breakfast, The		Ellen Blonder	Fantasy	Recognizing Story Pattern	Words With Short *i*	narrative, graphic aid	http://kidshealth.org/kid/stay_healthy/food/pyramid.html
D	Rainy Day, A		Lynette Evans	Realistic Fiction	Making Predictions	Compound Words	narrative, list	http://www.animalcorner.co.uk
D	Wake Up, Wake Up!		Brian & Rebecca Wildsmith	Humorous Fiction	Recognizing Sentence Pattern	Onomatopoeia	narrative, descriptive	http://www.kidsfarm.com/farm.htm
D	What Do You See? A Book About the Seasons	Brain Bank	Sara Shapiro	Science Nonfiction	Summarizing	Words With Long *e*	labeling, descriptive	http://www.instructorweb.com/lesson/seasons.asp
D	Where in the World?	Brain Bank	May Nelson	Informational Text	Making Predictions	Short Vowels	descriptive, graphic aid	http://www.educationworld.com/a_lesson/archives/state.shtml
D	Who Lives Here?		Janet Reed	Realistic Fiction	Activating Prior Knowledge	Consonant Blends	descriptive, graphic aid	www.ecokidsonline.com/pub/eco_info/topics/canadas_north
E	Flap and Sing: Birds	Investigators	Ian Douglas	Narrative Nonfiction	Sequencing	Describing Words	descriptive, graphic aid	http://www.aviary.org/index.php
E	Fred's Wish for Fish		Yael Landman	Realistic Fiction	Reading Everyday Speech	Words With Digraphs	descriptive, narrative	http://pbskids.org/itsmylife/family/pets/article5.html
E	Fresh Fall Leaves		Betsy Franco	Realistic Fiction	Using Illustrations	Words With -*ing*	narrative, descriptive	http://www.amug.org/~jbpratt/education/mypages/autumnleaves.html
E	I Go With Grandpa		Yael Landman	Realistic Fiction	Comparing and Contrasting	Short Vowel *u*	narrative, descriptive	http://www.instructorweb.com/lesson/seasons.asp
E	Let's Play Soccer		Ian Douglas	Informational Text	Recognizing Patterned Text	Verbs	expository, descriptive	www.education.com/reference/article/Ref_Developing_Language/
E	Living Things	Brain Bank	Dorothy Avery	Science Nonfiction	Understanding Categorizing	Pronouns	expository, graphic aid	www.fi.edu/tfi/units/life/classify/classify.html
E	Magic Pot, The		Laura Smith	Fantasy	Understanding Genre: Fantasy	Words With /ou/	narrative, expository	www.goodcharacter.com/Estopics.html
E	No Snacks, Jack!		Janet Reed	Realistic Fiction	Understanding Cause and Effect	Contractions	narrative, persuasive	www.crayola.com/lesson-plans/detail/happy-healthy-habits-lesson-plan/

Level	Title	Series	Author	Genre	Comprehension Strategies	Phonics and Word Study	Writing Options	Technology
E	Painting		Janine Scott	Realistic Fiction	Analyzing Character	End Punctuation	expository descriptive	www.coe.ufl.edu/courses/eec6304/paint.htm
E	Yard Sale, The		Janelle Cherrington	Realistic Fiction	Making Predictions	Naming Words	labeling narrative	http://www.cambriarecycles.org/Reuse/YardSale.htm
F	Biscuit Visits the Big City		Alyssa Satin Capucilli	Realistic Fiction	Understanding Setting	Words That Describe	narrative expository	http://www.alyssacapucilli.com/
F	Bug, a Bear, and a Boy, A		David McPhail	Fantasy	Distinguishing Fantasy/Reality	Picture Details	narrative descriptive	http://www.edutopia.org/common-ground
F	Country Mouse and the Town Mouse, The		retold by Janet Reed	Traditional Literature/Fable	Understanding Genre: Fable	Reading Punctuation	persuasive narrative	www.learningtogive.org/lessons/unit83/lesson3.html
F	Go Home, Daisy		Barbara Hill	Realistic Fiction	Making Predictions	Action Words	expository descriptive	http://www.petclub.org/lost_pets.htm
F	Goldilocks and the Three Bears		retold by Sara Shapiro	Traditional Literature/Folktale	Reading Dialogue	Words With ou	expository letter	http://www.atozteacherstuff.com/pages/315.shtml
F	How Lizard Lost His Colors		retold by Sara Shapiro	Traditional Literature/Folktale	Understanding Cause and Effect	Words With ow	narrative expository	http://teacher.scholastic.com/writewit/mff/folktalewshop_index.htm
F	Loose Tooth		Lola M. Schaefer	Realistic Fiction	Summarizing	Words With Vowels oo	narrative graphic aid	http://www.ada.org/public/education/teachers/ideas.asp
F	Meg and the Lost Pencil Case		Greg Parasmo	Realistic Fiction	Understanding Problems and Solutions	Suffix -ed	narrative expository	http://www.4h.missouri.edu/go/programs/character/resources/schoolstages.pdf
F	Melt It, Shape It: Glass	Investigators	May Nelson	Narrative Nonfiction	Reading for Information	Consonant Blends	expository descriptive	http://www.glassforever.co.uk/
F	Todd's Teacher		Janelle Cherrington	Realistic Fiction	Understanding Setting	Consonant Blends	narrative expository	www2.scholastic.com/browse/lessonplan.jsp?id=219
G	At the Apple Farm		Rachel Albanese and Laura Smith	Informational Text	Recognizing Story Sequence	Words With Short a	graphic aid narrative	www.usapple.org/consumers/kids
G	Deep Blue Sea, The		Audrey Wood	Realistic Fiction	Understanding Patterned Text	Words With Consonant + le	narrative descriptive	www.audreywood.com/mac_site/auds_jumpstation/aud_jumpstation.htm
G	Gingerbread Man, The		retold by Janelle Cherrington	Traditional Literature	Understanding Plot	Past-Tense Words	narrative expository	http://www.atozteacherstuff.com/Themes/Gingerbread/
G	I Just Forgot	Little Critter	Mercer Mayer	Fantasy	Using Illustrations	Reading Action Words With -ed	letter expository	www.littlecritter.com/
G	In Our Yard		Janet Reed	Realistic Fiction	Summarizing	Words With /ou/	poetry expository	http://www.insectidentification.org/
G	Is This a Moose?		Jenny Armstrong	Science Nonfiction	Comparing and Contrasting	Question Sentences	expository graphic aid	www.nhptv.org/NATUREWORKS/nw4.htm.
G	Justin's New Bike		Barbara Hill	Realistic Fiction	Drawing Conclusions	Action Words With -ing	list expository	http://kidshealth.org/kid/watch/out/bike_safety.html
G	Rabbit's Party		Eve Bunting	Fantasy	Making Inferences	Short Vowels	list narrative	http://teacherlink.ed.usu.edu/TLresources/units/Byrnes-celebrations/bday.html
G	Three Billy Goats Gruff, The		retold by Sara Shapiro	Traditional Literature/Fairy Tale	Recognizing Sequence	Contractions	narrative expository	http://edsitement.neh.gov/view_lesson_plan.asp?id=387#LESSON5
G	Very Silly School, A		Janelle Cherrington	Fantasy	Distinguishing Fantasy from Reality	Words With Short i	description expository	http://pbskids.org/arthur/parentsteachers/activities/acts/imaginary_pets.html?cat=art
H	Aunt Maud's Mittens		Yael Landman	Humorous Fiction	Recognizing Sequence of Events	Multisyllabic Words	narrative list	http://www.atozkidsstuff.com/article15.html
H	Father Who Walked on His Hands, The		based on a story by Margaret Mahy	Realistic Fiction	Using Illustrations	Plurals	expository descriptive	www.khake.com/page64.html
H	Good Morning, Monday		Sheila Keenan	Realistic Fiction	Understanding Setting	Compound Words	expository descriptive	www2.scholastic.com/browse/article.jsp?id=11619

Level	Title	Series	Author	Genre	Comprehension Strategies	Phonics and Word Study	Writing Options	Technology
H	Hop! Spring! Leap! Animals That Jump		Fiona Bayrock	Science Nonfiction	Monitoring Comprehension	Consonant Blends With s	descriptive narrative	www.teachersdomain.org/resource/tdc02.sci.life.colt.move/
H	Little Red Riding Hood		retold by Sara Shapiro	Fairy Tale	Making Inferences	Words With oo	narrative descriptive	http://www.usm.edu/english/fairytales/lrrh/lrrh-home.htm
H	Sammy the Seal		Syd Hoff	Fantasy	Using Punctuation	Dialogue	description narrative	www.lpzoo.org/animals/index.html/
H	Sione's Talo		Lino Nelisi	Traditional Literature/Folktale	Drawing Conclusions	Action Words in Past Tense	descriptive narrative	www.aucklandmuseum.com/site_resources/library/Education/Teachers_Guide/Teacher Resources_Library/Social_Science/SocSci10PacificPath1_1_.pdf
H	Trains		Rachel Albanese	Informational Text	Relating to Personal Experience	Consonant Blends	descriptive narrative	http://www.academickids.com/encyclopedia/index.php/Trains
H	Unusual Show, An		Ellen Blonder	Fantasy	Comparing and Contrasting	Opposites	list expository	www.plcmc.org/Services/Storytimes_to_go!/pdfs/Getting%20Dressed.pdf
H	Why Did the Chicken Cross the Road?		Janet Reed	Fantasy	Making Inferences	Reading Words With /ou/	descriptive persuasive	http://www.moneyinstructor.com
I	Animals at Night	Now I Know	Melvin Berger and Gilda Berger	Informational Text	Understanding Genre: Informational Text	Contractions	narrative expository	http://kindernature.storycounty.com/display.aspx?DocID=2005418944
I	Dolphins and Porpoises	Now I Know	Melvin and Gilda Berger	Informational Text	Using Picture Clues	Consonant Blends	descriptive narrative	www.savethewhales.org/dolphins.html/
I	Fat Cat, The: A Danish Folktale		translated by Jack Kent	Traditional Literature/Folktale	Recognizing Patterned Text	Multisyllabic Words	letter list	http://oaks.nvg.org/danish-folktales.html
I	Mama Zooms		Jane Cowen-Fletcher	Fantasy	Monitoring Comprehension	Compound Words	descriptive narrative	http://primaryschool.suite101.com/article.cfm/easy_ways_to_encourage_imagination
I	Nana's Place		Akimi Gibson	Realistic Fiction	Making Inferences	Dialogue	narrative descriptive	http://www.childrensgrief.net/info.htm
I	Shoo, Fly Guy!		Tedd Arnold	Humorous Fiction	Recognizing Story Sequence	Exclamatory Sentences	narrative expository	http://bugguide.net/node/view/7266
I	Two Crazy Pigs		Karen Berman Nagel	Fantasy	Understanding Compare and Contrast	Words With -ing	graphic aid descriptive	http://teacher.scholastic.com/writeit/humor/teacher/humorwriting.htm
I	Wax Man, The		retold by Olga Loya	Traditional Literature/Folktale	Understanding Cause and Effect	Action Words	narrative expository	http://www.americanfolklore.net/bedtimestories.html
I	We're Going On a Nature Hunt		Steve Metzger	Realistic Fiction	Understanding Sequence	Long i: Consonant + Final e Pattern	descriptive narrative	http://kidsactivities.suite101.com/article.cfm/scavenger_hunting
I	Wheels on the Race Car, The		Alex Zane	Fantasy	Recognizing Setting	Sound Words	persuasive narrative	www.wheelsontheracecar.com/interview.htm
J	Antonio's Music		Joanna Emery	Biography	Visualizing	Irregular Past-Tense Verbs	expository graphic aid	www.classicalarchives.com/bios/vivaldi_bio.html
J	Big, Brown Pot, The		Margaret Mahy	Humorous Fiction	Identifying Cause and Effect	Past-Tense Verbs	narrative descriptive	www.pbs.org/parents/parenthelpers/cooking.html
J	Big Cats	Investigators	Lynette Evans	Narrative Nonfiction	Comparing and Contrasting	Comparatives -er, -est	narrative graphic aid	www.bigcats.com
J	Big Smelly Bear		Britta Teckentrup	Fantasy	Understanding Plot	Words With -ed	list persuasive	http://www.cyh.sa.gov.au/HealthTopics/HealthTopicDetailsKids.aspx?p=335np=289id=2146
J	In the Barrio		Alma Flor Ada	Realistic Fiction	Categorizing Information	Unfamiliar Words	expository descriptive	http://www.sedl.org/scimath/pasopartners/senses/
J	Just Us Women		Jeannette Caines	Realistic Fiction	Making Inferences	Contractions	list narrative	http://www.kent.k12.wa.us/curriculum/tech/K6/5/Roadtrip/unit_planRoadTrip.doc
J	Kenny and the Little Kickers		Claudio Marzollo	Fantasy	Understanding Character	Dialogue	narrative persuasive	http://kidshealth.org/parent/emotions/feelings/self_esteem.html
J	Poppleton Has Fun	Poppleton	Cynthia Rylant	Fantasy	Using Illustrations	Compound Words	letter description	http://atozteacherstuff.com/Themes/Friendship/

Level	Title	Series	Author	Genre	Comprehension Strategies	Phonics and Word Study	Writing Options	Technology
J	Safety in Numbers	Investigators	Lynette Evans	Narrative Nonfiction	Generating Questions	Multiple-Meaning Words	expository narrative	www.sandiegozoo.org/animalbytes/got-ques-tions_groups_list.html
J	Young Cam Jansen and the Spotted Cat Mystery	Young Cam Jansen	David A. Adler	Mystery	Understanding Chapters	Compound Words	narrative list	www.educationworld.com/a_tsl/archives/02-1/les-son036.shtm
K	Allie's Basketball Dream		Barbara E. Barber	Realistic Fiction	Understanding Visualizing	Compound Words	narrative persuasive	http://webtech.kennesaw.edu/reading/alliesdream.htm
K	Andy Shane and the Very Bossy Dolores Starbuckle		Jennifer Richard Jacobson	Realistic Fiction	Recognizing Story Structure	Diphthong ou	narrative list	http://www.bam.gov/sub_yourlife/yourlife_conflict.html
K	Don't Let the Pigeon Stay Up Late!		Mo Willems	Fantasy	Drawing Conclusions	Words With r-Controlled Vowels	narrative expository	www.childrenslit.com/childrenslit/mai_willems_mo.html
K	Frog Prince, The	Hello Reader	Edith H. Tarcov	Traditional Literature/Fairy Tale	Recognizing Sequence	Consonant Blends	descriptive narrative	http://www.suelebeau.com/fairytales.htm
K	Great Gracie Chase, The: Stop that Dog!		Cynthia Rylant	Realistic Fiction	Understanding Cause and Effect	Past Tense With -ed	narrative expository	www.loveyourdog.com
K	Gym Teacher From the Black Lagoon, The	Black Lagoon	Mike Thaler	Fantasy	Recognizing Point of View	Contractions	narrative expository	www.yale.edu/ynhti/curriculum/units/2002/4/02.04.05.x.html
K	Ibis: A True Whale Story		John Himmelman	Fantasy	Identifying Author's Purpose	Multiple-Meaning Words	expository descriptive	www.nightheron.com/trees_activityguideibisthewhale.html
K	Johnny Appleseed		Eva Moore	Traditional Literature/Folktale	Understanding Cause and Effect	r-Controlled Vowels	expository poetry	http://www.appleseed.net
K	On My Way to Buy Eggs		Chih-Yuan Chen	Realistic Fiction	Understanding Figurative Language	Vowel Digraphs	descriptive narrative	http://www.brucevanpatter.com/funstuff.html
K	Three Days on a River in a Red Canoe		Vera B. Williams	Realistic Fiction	Recognizing Point of View	Compound Words	descriptive narrative	http://boatsafe.com/kids/knots.htm
L	Alligator Baby		Robert Munsch	Fantasy	Recognizing Story Pattern	Reading Words With -ed	narrative graphic aid	www.robertmunsch.com
L	Amelia Bedelia Under Construction	Amelia Bedelia	Herman Parish	Realistic Fiction	Understanding Illustrations	Homophones	expository narrative	www.educationworld.com/a_lesson/dailylp/dailylp048.shtml
L	Anansi the Spider: A Tale from the Ashanti		Gerald McDermott	Traditional Literature	Using Illustrations	Words With Long o	list narrative	http://www2.scholastic.com/browse/search?query=folktales
L	Cam Jansen and the Secret Service Mystery	Cam Jansen	David Adler	Realistic Fiction/Mystery	Understanding Plot	Action Verbs	expository list	http://kids.mysterynet.com
L	Miss Nelson Has a Field Day		Harry Allard	Realistic Fiction	Making Predictions	Contractions	descriptive expository	www.ducksters.com/sports/footballrules.php
L	Picking Apples & Pumpkins		Amy & Richard Hutchings	Informational Text	Understanding Compare and Contrast	Compound Words	expository narrative	http://localfoods.about.com/od/searchbyregion/Search_Seasonal_Fruits_Vegetables_By_Region.htm
L	Ricky Ricotta's Mighty Robot vs. the Mecha-Monkeys from Mars		Dav Pilkey	Science Fiction	Drawing Conclusions	Contractions	narrative descriptive	http://spaceplace.nasa.gov/en/kids/
L	Triple Rotten Day, The	It's Robert (#16)	Barbara Seuling	Realistic Fiction	Making Predictions	Multisyllabic Words	narrative persuasive	http://www2.scholastic.com/browse/contributor.jsp?id=2379
L	Worst Day of My Life, The	Little Bill	Bill Cosby	Realistic Fiction	Understanding Plot as Problem and Solution	Compound Words	narrative list	http://www.educationworld.com/a_curr/strategy/strategy019.shtml
L	Young Thurgood Marshall: Fighter for Equality		Eric Carpenter	Biography	Practice Summarizing	Proper Nouns	graphic aid expository	http://brownvboard.org/
M	Alexander, Who's Not (Do you hear me? I mean it!) Going to Move	Alexander	Judith Viorst	Realistic Fiction	Understand Making Inferences	Possessive Words With 's	narrative expository	www.kidslife.com.au/article.asp?ContentID=helping_kids_cope_with_change
M	Case of the Food Fight, The	Jigsaw Jones Mystery (#28)	James Preller	Mystery	Understanding Cause and Effect	Onomatopoeia	descriptive expository	http://www.mysterynet.com/learn/

Level	Title	Series	Author	Genre	Comprehension Strategies	Phonics and Word Study	Writing Options	Technology
M	Dancing With the Indians		Angela Shelf Medearis	Poem	Making Inferences	Inflectional Ending -ing	poetry, descriptive	http://www.awesomelibrary.org/Classroom/Social_Studies/Multicultural/Native_American.html
M	How a House is Built		Gail Gibbons	Informational Text	Understanding Sequence	Context Clues	list, descriptive	www.historyforkids.org/learn/architecture/houses.htm
M	Ivy and Bean and the Ghost That Had to Go	Ivy + Bean (#2)	Annie Barrows	Humorous Fiction	Understanding Text Features	Consonant Blends: s + qu	descriptive, narrative	www.anniebarrows.com/ivyandbean/
M	New Coat for Anna, A		Harriet Ziefert	Historical Fiction	Understanding Historical Context	Context Clues	expository, descriptive	http://www.usmint.gov/kids/timeMachine/
M	Penguin and the Pea, The		Janet Perlman	Fractured Fairy Tale	Understanding Cause and Effect	Words With Suffix -ly	descriptive, narrative	www.britishcouncil.org/learnenglish-central-poems-fairy-tales.htm
M	Stink: The Incredible Shrinking Kid		Megan McDonald	Humorous Fiction	Understanding Puns	Words With Suffixes	graphic-narrative; descriptive	http://www.childdevelopmentinfo.com/parenting/self_esteem.shtml
M	Stuart Goes to School		Sara Pennypacker	Fantasy	Visualizing	Compound Words	expository, narrative	http://kidshealth.org/kid/feeling/home_family/moving.html
M	Vampires Don't Wear Polka Dots	Bailey School Kids (#1)	Debbie Dadey and Marcia Thornton Jones	Fantasy	Making Predictions	Compound Words	narrative, expository	http://www.nea.org/classmanagement/disck021113.html.
N	Alfie the Apostrophe		Moira Rose Donahue	Fantasy	Understanding Main Idea and Details	Words With Apostrophes	descriptive, narrative	http://www.teachingideas.co.uk/english/contents-09writingpunctuationgrammar.htm
N	Fables		Arnold Lobel	Traditional Literature/Fable	Understanding Genre	Words With -ed	graphic aid, persuasive	http://teacher.scholastic.com/writewit/mff/
N	Franny K. Stein, Mad Scientist: Frantastic Voyage	Franny K. Stein (#5)	Jim Benton	Science Fiction	Understanding Plot	Reading Difficult Words	expository, persuasive	http://inventors.about.com/od/kidinventions/ss/kid_inventors_U.htm
N	Lion Dancer: Ernie Wan's Chinese New Year		Kate Waters and Madeline Slovenz-Low	Nonfiction	Generating Questions	Multisyllabic Words	graphic aid, descriptive	http://crafts.kaboose.com/holidays/chinese_new_year.html
N	Mice and Beans		Pam Muñoz Ryan	Fantasy	Distinguishing Fantasy from Reality	Using a Pronunciation Guide	narrative, descriptive	http://www.readwritethink.org/lessons/lesson_view.asp?id=890
N	Our Crazy Class Election	Comic Guy	Tim Roland	Realistic Fiction	Understanding Figurative Language	Idioms	descriptive, persuasive	http://www.kidsvotingusa.org/
N	Spy in the White House, A	Capital Mysteries (#4)	Ron Roy	Mystery	Understanding Idioms	Multiple-Meaning Words	expository, narrative	http://www.yale.edu/ynhti/curriculum/units/1989/4/89.04.06.x.html
N	Suitcase		Mildred Pitts Walter	Realistic Fiction	Understanding Problems and Solutions	Words With the Letter x	narrative, list	ssw.unc.edu/jif/makingchoices/lesson-g4.htm
N	Wonderful Alexander and the Catwings	Catwings	Ursula K. LeGuin	Fantasy	Understanding Theme	Words With -y, -ly	narrative, expository	http://www.ursulakleguin.com
N	Zen Shorts		Jon J. Muth	Traditional Literature/Fable	Understanding Genre: Fable	Words With Prefixes un-, im-	expository, narrative	www.tricycle.com/special-section/bringing-up-buddhists-a-resource-guide
O	Amber Brown Is Green with Envy	Amber Brown	Paula Danziger	Realistic Fiction	Understanding Character	Reading Homophones	descriptive, expository	http://www.edupaperback.org/showauth2.cfm?authid=25
O	Angel Child, Dragon Child		Michele Maria Surat	Realistic Fiction	Understanding Plot	Difficult Words	descriptive, expository	http://www.educationworld.com/a_lesson/lesson/lesson340.shtml
O	Can You Fly High, Wright Brothers?	Science SuperGiants	Melvin Berger and Gilda Berger	Biography	Understanding Sequence	Words With Suffixes		http://www.wright-brothers.org
O	Chocolate Fever		Robert Kimmel Smith	Fiction	Identifying Problem/Solution	Suffixes -less, -ness	expository, graphic aid	http://www.candyusa.org/Chocolate/default.asp
O	Jake Drake, Know-It-All		Andrew Clements	Realistic Fiction	Understanding Story Structure	Reading Words With -ing	list, descriptive	http://www.kidscorner.net/html/sciencefair.php
O	Lost Treasure of the Emerald Eye	Geronimo Stilton (#1)	Geronimo Stilton	Fantasy	Understanding Chapters	Words With Multiple Meanings	narrative, letter	http://www.scholastic.com/titles/geronimostilton
O	Patchwork Quilt, The		Valerie Flournoy	Realistic Fiction	Understanding Character	Diphthongs ou, ow	expository, descriptive	http://www.madison.k12.wi.us/tnl/detectives/kids/KIDS-00032k.html

Level	Title	Series	Author	Genre	Comprehension Strategies	Phonics and Word Study	Writing Options	Technology
O	Pinduli		Janell Cannon	Trickster Tale	Understanding Cause and Effect	Suffixes -y and -ly	descriptive narrative	www.wku.edu/~mary.meredith/student.htm
O	Shark Lady: True Adventures of Eugenie Clark		Ann McGovern	Biography	Understanding Cause and Effect	Reading Compound Words	descriptive expository	www.marinebio.com/MarineBio/MindGames
O	Talented Clementine, The		Sara Pennypacker	Realistic Fiction	Making Predictions	Words With Soft c and Hard c	expository list	www.scholastic.com/titles/abbyhayes/brainwaves/talent.htm
P	Nina, the Pinta, and the Vanishing Treasure, The (Alec Flint Super Sleuth)	Alec Flint Mystery (#1)	Jill Santopolo	Mystery	Understanding Problems and Solutions	Synonyms	narrative expository	http://americanhistory.si.edu/kids/index.cfm
P	Countdown to the Year 1000	Dragon Slayers' Academy (#8)	Kate H. McMullan	Fantasy	Understanding Setting	Unusual Language	expository persuasive	http://www.historyforkids.org/learn/medieval/history/history.htm
P	Da Wild, Da Crazy, Da Vinci (Time Warp Trio)	Time Warp Trio	Jon Scieszka	Science Fiction	Understanding Visualizing	Suffixes	narrative expository	http://www.mos.org/leonardo
P	Helen Keller's Teacher		Margaret Davidson	Biography	Recognizing Setting	Context Clues	list expository	http://www.actionfund.org/ohsay/saysee18.htm
P	Koya DeLaney and the Good Girl Blues		Eloise Greenfield	Realistic Fiction	Understanding Author's Purpose	Challenging Words	narrative persuasive	http://kidshealth.org/parent/emotions/behavior/sportsmanship.html
P	Magic School Bus and the Science Fair Expedition, The	Magic School Bus	Joanna Cole	Science Nonfiction	Generating Questions	Multisyllabic Words	graphic aid expository	http://www.sciencebuddies.org/
P	Mariposa, La		Francisco Jiménez	Realistic Fiction	Making Inferences	Prefixes	narrative expository	http://teacher.scholastic.com/lessonrepro/lessonplans/instructor/science2.htm
P	Talking Eggs, The		Robert D. San Souci	Traditional Literature/Folktale	Understanding Genre: Folktale	Vowel Digraphs	expository narrative	http://www.content.scholastic.com/browse/unitplan
P	Who Stole The Wizard of Oz?		Avi	Mystery	Understanding Point of View	Multisyllabic Words	descriptive narrative	http://www.teachersfirst.com/100books.cfm
P	You Can't See Your Bones with Binoculars		Harriet Ziefert	Informational Text	Using Diagrams	Context Clues	expository narrative	http://www.newtonsapple.tv/TeacherGuide.php?id=1534
Q	Abby Takes a Stand		Patricia McKissack	Historical Fiction	Understanding Sequence	Context Clues	descriptive expository	www.sitins.com/timeline.shtml
Q	Amulet: Book One, The Stonekeeper	Amulet	Kazu Kibuishi	Fantasy/Graphic Novel	Making Predictions	Onomatopoeia	descriptive narrative	http://www.scholastic.com/graphix/
Q	Bunnicula: A Rabbit-Tale of Mystery	Bunnicula	James and Deborah Howe	Fantasy	Identifying Problem/Solution	Understanding Homophones	expository persuasive	http://www.bcplonline.org/kidspage/kids_howe.html
Q	Champ		Marcia Thornton Jones	Realistic Fiction	Understanding Problems and Solutions	Suffixes	narrative expository	http://www.MarciaTJones.com
Q	Just Juice		Karen Hesse	Realistic Fiction	Understanding Theme	Words With Multiple Meanings	expository narrative	http://www.pbs.org/wgbh/misunderstoodminds/
Q	Life and Times of the Peanut, The		Charles Micucci	Informational Text	Using Captions	Context Clues	expository descriptive	http://www.peanut-institute.org/PeanutFAQs.html
Q	Mummies, Pyramids, and Pharaohs		Gail Gibbons	Social Studies Nonfiction	Understanding Steps in a Process	Words With Quotations	expository narrative	http://www.cdli.ca/CITE/egypt_activity.htm
Q	Oggie Cooder	Oggie Cooder (#1)	Sarah Weeks	Realistic Fiction	Understanding Making Predictions	Strong Verbs	graphic aid narrative	http://www.guinnessworldrecords.com.
Q	Punished!		David Lubar	Fantasy	Visualizing	Open Syllables	graphic organizer; narrative	http://www.davidlubar.com/teachers.html
Q	You Be the Detective		Marvin Miller	Realistic Fiction	Understanding Problems/Solutions	Compound Words	descriptive expository	http://kids.mysterynet.com/
R	Achoo! The Most Interesting Book You'll Ever Read About Germs	Mysterious You	Trudee Romanek	Informational Text	Understanding Cause and Effect	Silent Letters	expository narrative	http://kidshealth.org/kid/ill_injure/

Level	Title	Series	Author	Genre	Comprehension Strategies	Phonics and Word Study	Writing Options	Technology
R	Island, The		Gary Paulsen	Realistic Fiction	Understanding Setting	Context Clues	expository descriptive	http://www.trelease-on-reading.com/paulsen.html
R	Julian Rodriguez Episode One: Trash Crisis on Earth	Julian Rodriguez	Alexander Stadler	Fantasy	Understanding Point of View	Suffixes	expository list	http://www.njcu.edu/CILL/vol2/sadow.html.
R	More Than Anything Else		Marie Bradby	Historical Fiction	Understanding Character	Personification	descriptive narrative	http://www.nps.gov/bowa/historyculture/the-great-educator.htm
R	Pocahontas and the Strangers		Clyde Robert Bulla	Fictional Biography	Understanding Compare and Contrast	Reading Suffixes	narrative expository	http://www.americaslibrary.gov/cgi-bin/page.cgi/aa/all/pocahonta
R	Report Card, The		Andrew Clements	Fiction	Understanding Theme	Recognizing Synonyms	expository narrative	http://pbskids.org/itsmylife/school/teststress/index.html
R	Rules		Cynthia Lord	Realistic Fiction	Making Predictions	Personification	expository narrative	http://www.autismsource.org/
R	Trumpet of the Swan, The		E.B. White	Fantasy	Recognizing Compare and Contrast	Reading Suffixes	expository narrative	http://www.webenglishteacher.com/white.html
R	Wackiest White House Pets		Kathryn Gibbs Davis	Informational Text	Visualizing	Diphthongs *ou, ow*	narrative expository	www.presidentialpetmuseum.com/whitehousepets-1.htm
R	When Marian Sang		Pam Muñoz Ryan	Biography	Identifying Problem and Solution	Figurative Language: Metaphor	expository narrative	www.library.upenn.edu/exhibits/rbm/anderson
S	4 Kids in 5E & 1 Crazy Year		Virginia Frances Schwartz	Realistic Fiction	Understanding Character	Figurative Language: Similes	graphic organizer; descriptive	http://www.webenglishteacher.com/creative.html
S	Beethoven Lives Upstairs		Barbara Nichol	Historical Fiction	Identifying Cause and Effect	Suffixes *-er, -or*	letter descriptive	http://www.classicsforkids.com/teachers/lessonplans/beethoven/
S	Bluish		Virginia Hamilton	Realistic Fiction	Drawing Conclusions	Latin Word Roots	descriptive letter	http://kidshealth.org/parent/medical/cancer/cancer_leukemia.html.
S	Dog's Life, A: The Autobiography of a Stray		Ann M. Martin	Fiction	Making Predictions	Word Parts	narrative persuasive	http://www.hsus.org/pets/animal_shelters/
S	Granny Torrelli Makes Soup		Sharon Creech	Realistic Fiction	Understanding Theme	Understanding Idioms	narrative descriptive	http://pbskids.org/itsmylife/friends/friendsfight/article2.html
S	In the Shade of the Nispero Tree		Carmen T. Bernier-Grand	Realistic Fiction	Identifying Plot	Suffixes *-ion, -tion, -ation*	expository letter	www.timeforkids.com/TFK/teachers/aw/wr/main/0,28132,702661,00.html
S	Let It Begin Here!		Dennis Brindell Fradin	Social Studies Nonfiction	Understanding Historical Content	Unfamiliar Words	graphic aid narrative	www.americanrevolution.com.
S	Million Dollar Shot, The		Dan Gutman	Realistic Fiction	Understanding Plot	Reading Multisyllabic Words	descriptive expository	http://pbskids.org/kws/parentsteachers/
S	Puppies, Dogs, and Blue Northers		Gary Paulsen	Autobiography	Visualizing	Synonyms	expository graphic aid	http://www.iditarod.com/teachers/
S	Tru Confessions		Janet Tashjian	Realistic Fiction	Generating Questions	Context Clues	persuasive expository	http://www.educationworld.com/a_lesson/lesson115.shtml
T	10 Deadliest Plants, The	The 10	Angie Littlefield and Jennifer Littlefield	Science Nonfiction	Categorizing Information	Comparative Adjectives	expository persuasive	http://www.kidsgardening.com
T	Amazing Life of Benjamin Franklin, The		James Cross Giblin	Biography	Uncovering Text Structure	Compound Words	narrative expository	www.teachingbenfranklin.org
T	Chasing Vermeer		Blue Balliett	Realistic Fiction/Mystery	Understanding Plot	Context Clues	graphic aid narrative	www.scholastic.com/blueballiett
T	Dirty Tricks (Raven Hill Mysteries #5)	Raven Hill Mysteries (#5)	Emily Rodda	Mystery	Making Inferences	Suffix *-ion*	descriptive graphic aid	http://www.mysterynet.com

Level	Title	Series	Author	Genre	Comprehension Strategies	Phonics and Word Study	Writing Options	Technology
T	Drita, My Homegirl		Jenny Lombard	Realistic Fiction	Comparing and Contrasting	Informal Language	graphic organizer/descriptive; narrative	http://www.nytimes.com/learning/general/specials/kosovo/lessons.html
T	Fair Weather		Richard Peck	Realistic Fiction	Reading Informal Speech	Colloquialisms and Idioms	descriptive letter	http://xroads.virginia.edu/~ma96/WCE/title.html
T	Orphan Train Rider: One Boy's True Story		Andrea Warren	Biography	Identifying Problems and Solutions	Idioms	descriptive narrative	http://www.orphantraindepot.com/
T	Power of Un, The		Nancy Etchemendy	Science Fiction	Understanding Cause and Effect	Prefixes	graphic aid narrative	http://www.pbs.org/wgbh/nova/time/
T	Replay		Sharon Creech	Realistic Fiction	Understanding Theme	Figurative Language	narrative persuasive	http://www2.scholastic.com/browse/collateral.jsp?id=337_type=Contributor_typeId=1811
T	Something Upstairs		Avi	Mystery	Understanding Setting	Difficult Words	expository persuasive	www.kidsreads.com/authors/au-avi.asp
U	Adventures of Marco Polo, The		Russell Freedman	Biography	Understanding Compare and Contrast	Latin Roots	persuasive expository	www.nationalgeographic.com/xpeditions/activities/10/marcopolo.html
U	All of the Above		Shelley Pearsall	Realistic Fiction	Understanding Point of View	Synonyms	narrative expository	http://www.nea.org/neatodayextra/mathfun.html
U	Charlie Bone and the Invisible Boy	Charlie Bone	Jenny Nimmo	Fantasy	Understanding Text Structure	Context Clues	descriptive narrative	http://www.scholastic.com/charliebone/index.htm
U	Creepy Creatures (Goosebumps Graphix)	Goosebumps Graphix (#1)	R.L. Stine	Graphic Novel	Understanding Text Structure	Compound Words	expository narrative	http://www.ncte.org/pubs/chron/highlights/122031.htm
U	Ginger Pye		Eleanor Estes	Realistic Fiction/Mystery	Understanding Characters	Suffixes -er and -est	expository descriptive	http://kcllibrary.lonestar.edu/decade50.html
U	Graduation of Jake Moon, The		Barbara Park	Realistic Fiction	Understanding Point of View	Multisyllabic Words	expository narrative	http://www.alz.org/living_with_alzheimers_just_for_kids_and_teens.asp
U	Hush		Jacqueline Woodson	Realistic Fiction	Understanding Plot Sequence	Suffix -ness	expository narrative	http://www.jacquelinewoodson.com/
U	Nothing But the Truth: A Documentary Novel		Avi	Realistic Fiction	Recognizing Events	Colloquialisms	descriptive narrative	www.jiskha.com/social_studies/psychology/rumors.html
U	Tale of Despereaux, The		Kate DiCamillo	Fantasy	Drawing Conclusions	Synonyms	descriptive poetry	http://edsitement.neh.gov/view_lesson_plan.asp?id=387
U	Tangerine		Edward Bloor	Realistic Fiction	Compare and Contrast	Varying Words With Prefixes and Suffixes	narrative expository	http://www2.scholastic.com/browse/collateral.jsp?id=972
V	10 Most Wondrous Ancient Sites, The	The 10	Carol Drake	Social Studies Nonfiction	Using Compare and Contrast	Multisyllabic Words	descriptive persuasive	http://www.wonderclub.com/AllWorldWonders.html
V	Becoming Naomi León		Pam Muñoz Ryan	Realistic Fiction	Understanding Cause and Effect	Suffixes	descriptive narrative	http://www.uwex.edu/ces/gprg/qandas.html#emotion
V	Birdwing		Rafe Martin	Fantasy	Understanding Problem and Solution	Compound Words	narrative descriptive	www.grimmstories.com
V	Desperate Journey		Jim Murphy	Historical Fiction	Generating Questions	Difficult Words	narrative graphic aid	http://www.laguardiawagnerarchive.lagcc.cuny.edu/eriecanal/
V	Ellis Island	Cornerstones of Freedom	Judith Jango-Cohen	Social Studies Nonfiction	Understanding Main Idea and Details	Root Words	expository narrative	www.ellisisland.org/
V	Fall of the Amazing Zalindas, The (Sherlock Holmes/Baker Street Irregulars)		Tracy Mack and Michael Citrin	Mystery	Understanding Character	Context Clues	narrative expository	http://www.kidsloveamystery.com/
V	Firework-Maker's Daughter, The		Philip Pullman	Fairy Tale	Understanding Character	Similes	expository descriptive	www.readwritethink.org/lessons/lesson_view.asp?id=42

Level	Title	Series	Author	Genre	Comprehension Strategies	Phonics and Word Study	Writing Options	Technology
V	Forty Acres and Maybe a Mule		Harriet Robinet	Historical Fiction	Making Predictions	Synonyms	narrative description	www.digitalhistory.uh.edu/reconstruction/index.html
V	Foster's War		Carolyn Reeder	Historical Fiction	Understanding Problems and Solutions	Understanding Strong Verbs	narrative expository	http://teacher.scholastic.com/pearl/
V	Pictures of Hollis Woods		Patricia Reilly Giff	Realistic Fiction	Understanding Point of View	Figurative Language	graphic aid narrative	http://www.bookbrowse.com/biographies/index.cfm?author_number=1073
W	Blood on the River: James Town 1607		Elisa Carbone	Historical Fiction	Drawing Conclusions	Context Clues		www.historyisfun.org/Jamestown-Settlement.htm
W	Chu Ju's House		Gloria Whelan	Realistic Fiction	Visualizing	Suffix -ous	expository descriptive	www.kn.pacbell.com/wired/China/
W	Guilty By a Hair! (24/7: Science Behind the Scenes)	24/7: Science Behind the Scenes	Anna Prokos	Science Nonfiction	Noticing Details	Multisyllabic Words	expository graphic aid	http://pbskids.org/dragonflytv/show/forensics.html.
W	Harriet Tubman, Secret Agent		Thomas B. Allen	Social Studies Nonfiction	Generating Questions	Synonyms	expository narrative	http://www.pbs.org/wgbh/aia/part4/title.html
W	Home of the Brave		Katherine Applegate	Free Verse	Understanding Problems and Solutions	Idioms	expository narrative	www.pbs.org/wnet/africa/tools/index.html
W	Invention of Hugo Cabret, The		Brian Selznick	Historical Fiction/Graphic Novel	Understanding Plot	Latin Roots	expository descriptive	http://www.theinventionofhugocabret.com/intro_flash.htm
W	Lightning Thief, The	Percy Jackson (#1)	Rick Riordan	Fantasy	Understanding Visualization	Root Words	persuasive expository	http://www.mythweb.com
W	Lights, Camera, Amalee	Amalee	Dar Williams	Realistic Fiction	Comparing and Contrasting	Prefixes en-, em-	narrative expository	http://www.worldwildlife.org/species/
W	Out From Boneville (Bone)	Bone (#1)	Jeff Smith	Graphic Novel	Understanding Point of View	Nonstandard Spelling	expository narrative	http://www.education-world.com/a_curr/profdev/profdev105.shtml/
W	Tunnels		Roderick Gordon and Brian Williams	Fantasy	Comparing and Contrasting	Colorful Adjectives	narrative expository	http://www2.scholastic.com/browse/collection.jsp?id=300
X	Antarctica: Journeys to the South Pole		Walter Dean Myers	Informational Text	Understanding Text Structure	Understanding Synonyms	narrative expository	http://www.pbs.org/wgbh/nova/shackleton/
X	Break With Charity, A: A Story About the Salem Witch Trials		Ann Rinaldi	Historical Fiction	Understanding Character	Affixes	narrative expository	http://www.law.umkc.edu/faculty/projects/ftrials/salem/salem.htm
X	Fight for Freedom: The American Revolutionary War		Benson Bobrick	Social Studies Nonfiction	Understanding Cause and Effect	Using Context Clues	persuasive expository	http://www.ushistory.org/march/index.html
X	Four Pictures by Emily Carr		Nicolas Debon	Biography/Graphic Format	Making Inferences	Compound Words	narrative expository	www.emilycarr.ca
X	Girl Named Disaster, A		Nancy Farmer	Novel	Visualizing	Similes	poem expository	http://www.pbs.org/wnet/africa/index.html
X	Millicent Min, Girl Genius		Lisa Yee	Realistic Fiction	Understanding Genre	Multiple-Meaning Words	descriptive narrative	http://www.quotationspage.com/subjects/friendship/
X	Somewhere in the Darkness		Walter Dean Myers	Realistic Fiction	Making Predictions	Recognizing Colloquialisms	expository narrative	http://www.readingrockets.org/books/interviews/myersw
X	Storm Thief		Chris Wooding	Science Fiction	Understanding Plot	Antonyms	narrative descriptive	http://www2.ku.edu/_sfcenter/young_SF.htm
X	Usborne Book of Scientists, The: From Archimedes to Einstein		Struan Reid and Patricia Fara	Informational Text	Understanding Cause and Effect	Greek Prefixes tele-, micro-	expository	http://www.intute.ac.uk/sciences/cgi-bin/browse.pl?id=246
X	When Hitler Stole Pink Rabbit		Judith Kerr	Historical Fiction	Identifying Problem/Solution	Adverbs	descriptive graphic aid	http://www.ushmm.org/education
Y	Artemis Fowl (Book 1)	Artemis Fowl (#1)	Eoin Colfer	Fantasy	Identifying Plot	Prefixes com-, con-	expository descriptive	http://edsitement.neh.gov/view_lesson_plan.asp?id=387

Level	Title	Series	Author	Genre	Comprehension Strategies	Phonics and Word Study	Writing Options	Technology
Y	Boy Who Dared, The		Susan Campbell Bartoletti	Historical Fiction	Understanding Theme	Context Clues	narrative persuasive	http://fcit.usf.edu/HOLOCAUST/TIMELINE/timeline.htm
Y	Geronimo: A Novel		Joseph Bruchac	Historical Fiction	Evaluating Author's Purpose	Similes and Metaphors	expository narrative	http://www.indigenouspeople.net/geronimo.htm
Y	Get On Out of Here, Philip Hall		Bette Greene	Realistic Fiction	Identifying Point of View	Suffixes -ation and -ion	letter descriptive	www.activehealthykids.ca/Ophea/Ophea.net/student-youth-leader-ship.cfm
Y	Heroes of the Holocaust: True Stories of Rescues by Teens		Allan Zullo and Mara Bovsun	Social Studies Nonfiction	Understanding Historical Context	Common and Proper Nouns	narrative expository	http://www.adl.org/hidden
Y	Jumping Tree, The		René Saldaña, Jr.	Realistic Fiction	Understanding Character	Context Clues	expository graphic aid	http://nydiabenitez.tripod.com/id24.html
Y	Larklight		Philip Reeve	Science Fiction	Understanding Setting	Metaphors	expository graphic aid	http://www.pbs.org/empires/victoria/ and http://www.victorians.org.uk/
Y	Pemba's Song: A Ghost Story		Marilyn Nelson and Tonya C. Hegamin	Mystery	Understanding Problem and Solution	Colloquialisms	poem graphic aid	http://www.poetryoutloud.org/poems/poet.html?id=80669
Y	Vlad the Impaler: The Real Count Dracula	Wicked History, A	Enid Goldberg and Norman Itzkowitz	Biography	Understanding Historical Context	Context Clues	narrative graphic aid	www.donlinke.com/drakula/vlad.htm
Y	Yearling, The		Marjorie Kinnan Rawlings	Novel	Understanding Structure	Personification	narrative descriptive	www.cah.ucf.edu/crosscreek/rawling1.php
Z	An American Plague		Jim Murphy	Social Studies Nonfiction	Understanding Cause and Effect	Root Words and Affixes	expository narrative	www.philadelphiahistory.org/akm/lessons/yellowFever
Z	Best Ghost Stories Ever, The	Scholastic Classic	Christopher Krovatin	Fiction	Understanding Cause and Effect	Multisyllabic Words	expository narrative	http://people.howstuffworks.com/ghost-stories.htm
Z	Detective Stories		Philip Pullman, editor	Mystery	Drawing Conclusions	Understanding Slang	expository narrative	www.springfieldlibrary.org/stacks/advis.html
Z	Finding My Hat		John Son	Realistic Fiction	Making Inferences	Suffixes	narrative expository	http://www.pbs.org/hiddenkorea/index.htm
Z	Harry Potter and the Deathly Hallows	Harry Potter	J. K. Rowling	Novel	Understanding Chapters	Context Clues	descriptive narrative	http://curriculalessons.suite101.com/article.cfm/harry_potter_lesson_plan
Z	Jane Eyre	Scholastic Classic	Charlotte Brontë	Novel	Understanding Theme	Context Clues	expository persuasive	http://www.haworth-village.org.uk/brontes/charlotte/charlotte.asp
Z	Malcolm X: By Any Means Necessary		Walter Dean Myers	Biography	Identifying Main Idea and Details	Multisyllabic Words	expository persuasive	http://www.cmgww.com/historic/malcolm/about/bio.htm
Z	Stormbreaker (Alex Rider)	Alex Rider Adventure (#1)	Anthony Horowitz	Mystery	Understanding Character	Difficult Words	persuasive narrative	http://www.anthonyhorowitz.com/alexrider/
Z	Time Machine, The		H. G. Wells	Science Fiction	Understanding a Frame Story	Figurative Language: Paradox	narrative descriptive	http://www.mentorplace.org/wnet/Future.htm
Z	Toning the Sweep		Angela Johnson	Realistic Fiction	Understanding Point of View	Strong Verbs	expository narrative	http://www.pbs.org/wnet/aaworld/timeline/civil_01.html

Skills & Strategies Chart: Content Areas

Level	Title	Content Area/Topic	Comprehension Strategies	Phonics and Word Study	Text Feature	Writing Options	Technology
A	1, 2, 3 in the Box	Math/counting 1–5	Recognizing Punctuation	Recognizing Words With -og	Book Cover	Expository Expository	www.math.com/teachers.html
	Elephants Like To …	Life Science/elephants	Reading Action Words	Reading High-Frequency Words	Photographs	Expository Expository	www.sandiegozoo.org
	Flowers Have Colors	Earth and Space Science/colors	Using Adjectives	Using Beginning Sounds	Book Cover	Expository Graphic Aids	www.crayola.com
	I See Bugs!	Life Science/animals, colors	Compare and Contrast	Recognizing Words With -ug	Index	Descriptive Expository	www.nwf.org/kids
	Numbers All Around	Math/counting 1–12	Using Picture Details	Reading Numerals	Photographs	Expository Expository	www.math.com/teachers.html
	On a Boat	Social Studies/boats	Recognizing Patterned Text	Reading High-Frequency Words	Photographs	Expository Expository	www.scholastic.com
	School Day	Social Studies/school rules	Recognizing Setting	Using Beginning Sounds	Book Cover	Descriptive Expository	www.scholastic.com
	We Play Together	Social Studies/rules, working together	Understanding Genre: Photo Essay	Using Beginning Sounds	Photographs	Expository Expository	www.gameskidsplay.net
	We Read	Social Studies/reading	Recognizing Patterned Text	Listening for Syllables	Book Cover	Expository Expository	www.readroom.com
	We Write	Social Studies/writing	Developing Print Awareness	Reading Plurals	Lists	Expository Persuasive	www.scholastic.com
B	Can We Go?	Social Studies/traffic safety	Recognizing Questions	Reading Words With -an	Question and Answer Format	Expository Expository	www.kidshealth.org/kid/watch/
	Can You See The Rabbit?	Life Science/animals	Compare and Contrast	Reading High-Frequency Words	Photographs	Expository Expository	www.nwf.org/kids
	From Sheep to Sweater	Social Studies/manufacturing	Making Predictions	Reading Words With /s/	Photographs	Expository Descriptive	www.animaland.org/
	How to Make a Wind Sock	Earth Science/wind	Following Directions	Recognizing Plural Words	Diagrams	Expository Descriptive	http://sln.fi.edu/tfi/units/energy/windguide.html
	I See Flags	Math/shapes	Compare and Contrast	Using Beginning Sounds	Captions	Descriptive Descriptive	www.cwflags.com/fotw/flags/
	Look-and-Find Shapes	Math/shapes	Using Picture Details	Reading High-Frequency Words	N/A	Expository Graphic Aid	www.scholastic.com/earlylearner/age5/learning/shapeup.htm
	We Live Here	Social Studies/homes	Recognizing Setting	Reading High-Frequency Words	Photographs	Expository Narrative	www.storiestogrowby.com
	What's the Weather?	Earth and Space Science/weather	Using Picture Details	Using Beginning Sounds	Illustrator's Name	Expository Descriptive	www.teacher.scholastic.com/activities/wwatch/
	Who Hid?	Life Science/animals	Attending to and Uncovering Text Structure	Reading Words With -id	Photographic Illustrations	Descriptive Expository	http://science.howstuffworks.com/animal-camouflage1.htm
	Whose Bones?	Life Science/skeletons	Compare and Contrast	Reading Words With Short i	Title Page	Expository Expository	www.enchantedlearning.com/themes/skeleton.shtml

Level	Title	Content Area/Topic	Comprehension Strategies	Phonics and Word Study	Text Feature	Writing Options	Technology
C	Fun With Simple Machines	Physical Science/simple machines	Understanding Concepts	Using Punctuation	N/A	Descriptive Expository	http://edheads.org/activities/simple-machines/index.htm
	How Will I Get to Grandma's House?	Social Studies/transportation	Making Predictions	Recognizing Questions	Book Cover	Expository Descriptive	www.kids.gov
	A Kitten Is a Baby Cat	Life Science/animal babies	Activating Prior Knowledge	Using Picture Clues	N/A	Expository Expository	www.aspca.org
	My Scrapbook	Social Studies/family	Recognizing Language Patterns in Text	Reading Synonyms	Labels	Expository Descriptive	www.scholastic.com/familymatters/parentguides/holiday/memories.htm
	On the Farm	Social Studies/farming	Recognizing Story Sequence	Reading Unfamiliar Words	Title Page	Descriptive Expository	www.oznet.ksu.edu/wheatpage/
	Please, Thank You	Social Studies/manners	Recognizing Questions	Using Beginning Sounds	N/A	Narrative Descriptive	www.songsforteaching.com
	Signs	Social Studies/signs	Using Photographs	Reading Words With s-Blends	Title Page	Descriptive Persuasive	www.nysgtsc.state.ny.us/kidssign.htm
	We Like Summer!	Earth and Space Science/seasons	Recognizing Patterned Text	Reading Season Words	N/A	Descriptive Expository	www.brainpop.com/science/weather/seasons/index.weml
	What Time Is It?	Math/telling time	Recognizing Story Sequence	Reading Words With a-e	Inset Illustrations	Narrative Expository	http://www.kidsolr.com/earlychildhood/basicskillsa.html
	Where Are They?	Math/counting 1–10	Recognizing Punctuation	Reading Plurals	Book Cover	Descriptive Expository	www.math.com/teachers.html
D	Animals in Art	Social Studies/art	Activating Prior Knowledge	Reading Words With Short i	Illustrations	Descriptive Expository	www.metmuseum.org
	Clifford Can	Math/counting 1–10	Visualizing	Reading Words With -an	N/A	Narrative Descriptive	www.math.com/teachers.html
	Feel Better	Life Science/health	Recognizing Patterned Text	Recognizing Verbs	Title Page	Descriptive Expository	www.kidshealth.org
	How Many Ducks?	Math/subtraction	Understanding Concepts	Reading Rhyming Words	N/A	Narrative Expository	www.math.com/teachers.html
	I Need a Little Help	Social Studies/social development	Relating to Personal Experience	Reading Words With Long e	About the Author and Illustrator	Persuasive Narrative	www.lessonplanspage.com/SSHelping23.htm
	The Little Red Hen	Literature/folk tales	Recognizing Patterned Text	Recognizing Verbs	N/A	Expository Narrative	www.storiestogrowby.com
	Look at These Trees	Life Science/trees	Compare and Contrast	Consonant Blends	For More Information	Descriptive Graphic Aid	www.domtar.com/arbre/english/start.htm
	Then and Now	History/inventions	Compare and Contrast	Reading High-Frequency Words	For More Information	Expository Descriptive	www.enchantedlearning.com/inventors/
	We Need the Sun	Earth and Space Science/sun	Reading Questions and Answers	Reading High-Frequency Words	N/A	Expository Expository	www.kidsgardening.com
	Where Does Food Grow?	Social Studies/food production	Relating to Personal Experience	Recognizing Verbs	Book Cover	Descriptive Graphic Aid	www.oznet.ksu.edu/wheatpage/
E	All Around Our Country	Geography/United States	Using Illustrations	Reading Words With Long Vowels	N/A	Descriptive Graphic Aid	www.usgs.gov/
	Animal Moms and Dads	Life Science/animals	Compare and Contrast	Reading Words With Short Vowels	Book Cover	Expository Descriptive	www.nwf.org/
	Cat in the Bag	Math/Counting 1–10	Recognizing Patterned Text	Reading Words With Short a	About the Author and Illustrator	Expository Narrative	www.aspca.org
	City Life and Country Life	Social Studies/culture	Compare and Contrast	Reading Words With r-Controlled Vowels	N/A	Expository Expository	www.nps.gov/
	Hello, Doctor!	Life Science/health	Activating and Applying Prior Knowledge	Using Context	N/A	Expository Descriptive	www.kidshealth.org/kid/
	Let's Go to a Fair	Social Studies/community	Using Photographs	Reading Words With /ou/	Index	Descriptive Expository	www.mda.state.mi.us/kids/countyfair/index.html
	Let's Go to a Museum	Social Studies/art	Compare and Contrast	Recognizing Verbs With -ing	Index	Descriptive Narrative	www.metmuseum.org
	On the Job	Social Studies/careers	Drawing Conclusions	Reading Words With Consonant Blends	Book Cover	Descriptive Graphic Aid	www.bls.gov/k12/html/edu_over.htm
	School Long Ago	History/school	Relating to Personal Experience	Recognizing Past and Present Tense	Italic Words	Descriptive Expository	www.oldbethpage.org
	What Do Artists Use?	Social Studies/art	Recognizing Patterned Text	Reading Words With Consonant Digraphs	For More Information	Descriptive Expository	www.crayola.com

Skills & Strategies Chart: Leveled Bookroom Content Areas

Level	Title	Content Area/Topic	Comprehension Strategies	Phonics and Word Study	Text Feature	Writing Options	Technology
F	Animal Pals	Life Science/"helper" birds	Recognizing Sentence Patterns	Reading Words With Short Vowels	Photographs	Descriptive / Graphic Aid	www.nwf.org/
	Ellen Ochoa	Social Studies/astronauts	Making Inferences	Reading Words With Long a	Table of Contents	Descriptive / Expository	www.jsc.nasa.gov/Bios/astrobio.html
	How Does Your Salad Grow?	Life Science/plants	Making Inferences	Reading Unfamiliar Words	Photographs	Poetry / Graphic Aid	www.teacher.scholastic.com/lessonrepro/k_2theme/outdoors.htm
	I Can Play Soccer	Social Studies/sports	Reading for Information	Reading Words With -ing	Glossary	Descriptive / Expository	www.scholastic.com/titles/abbyhayes/soccer.htm
	I Like Cheese	Life Science/nutrition	Activating and Applying Prior Knowledge	Reading Adjectives	To Find Out More	Graphic Aid / Descriptive	www.nutritionexplorations.org
	I'm a Seed	Life Science/plants	Compare and Contrast	Recognizing Contractions	Book Cover	Narrative / Expository	www.kidsgardening.com
	My Goldfish	Life Science/animals	Summarizing	Reading Words With l-Blends	Index	Descriptive / Narrative	www.avma.org/care4pets
	Storms	Earth and Space Science/weather	Recognizing Cause and Effect	Reading Words With r-Controlled Vowels	For More Information	Graphic Aid / Narrative	www.teacher.scholastic.com/activities/wwatch/
	Watch Me Plant a Garden	Life Science/plants	Recognizing Sequence of Events	Reading Words With Long e	Table of Contents	Descriptive / Expository	www.kidsgardening.com
	What Can I Buy?	Math/counting money	Synthesizing	Reading Compound Words	Illustrations	Narrative / Expository	www.scholastic.com
G	Find the Wild Animal	Life Science/animal camouflage	Recognizing Questions	Reading Verbs	Table of Contents	Descriptive / Expository	www.teacher.scholastic.com/dirtrep/animal/animal/
	From Seed to Pumpkin	Life Science/plants	Making Predictions	Reading Words With Consonant Blends	Glossary	Poetry / Graphic Aid	www.scholastic.com/lessonrepro/k_2theme/outdoors.htm
	How Big? How Much?	Math/measurement	Relating to Personal Experience	Recognizing Punctuation	Illustrations	Expository / Expository	www.nist.gov/public_affairs/kids/morenist.htm
	It's a Good Thing There are Insects	Life Science/animals	Reading for Information	Reading Multisyllabic Words	Picture Glossary	Expository / Descriptive	www.enature.com
	Made with Glass	Physical Science/matter	Recognizing Sequence	Reading Verbs	N/A	Expository / Descriptive	www.glassline.net
	Make a Leaf Rubbing	Social Studies/art	Activating Prior Knowledge	Reading Words With Long a	Illustrations	Expository / Descriptive	www.teacher.scholastic.com/lessonrepro/lessonplans/ect/curric0697.htm
	Math at the Store	Math/counting and money	Making Inferences	Reading Words With Long a	Glossary	Expository / Descriptive	www.usmint.gov
	The Secret Code	Social Studies/communication	Recognizing Sequence of Events	Recognizing Pronouns	Braille Chart	Expository / Narrative	www.afb.org/braillebug
	Tic-Tac-Toe, Three in a Row	Math/logic	Generating Questions	Reading Directional Words	Problems/Activities	Poetry / Narrative	www.teacher.scholastic.com/annie/
	Tracks in the Sand	Life Science/animal tracks	Summarize	Reading High-Frequency Words	Photographs	Narrative / Descriptive	www.wildkingdom.com/kids_zone/tracks/

Level	Title	Content Area/Topic	Comprehension Strategies	Phonics and Word Study	Text Feature	Writing Options	Technology
H	The 100th Day	Math/counting	Recognizing Setting	Reading Pronouns	Book Cover	Narrative / Descriptive	www.math.com/teachers.html
	Colin Powell	Social Studies/famous Americans	Recognizing Main Idea and Details	Reading Words With Long e	Index	Expository / Graphic Aid	www.whitehouse.gov/
	A Day with a Mechanic	Social Studies/community workers	Reading for Information	Reading Words With oo	Index	Descriptive / Persuasive	www.bls.gov/k12/html/edu_over.htm
	A Day with Air Traffic Controllers	Social Studies/community workers	Summarizing	Reading Words With r-Controlled Vowels	Glossary	Expository / Descriptive	www.nasm.si.edu
	From Acorn to Oak Tree	Life Science/plants	Recognizing Sequence of Events	Reading Words With oo	Table of Contents	Persuasive / Descriptive	www.kidsgardening.com
	George Washington	American History/famous Americans	Recognizing Cause and Effect	Reading Words With Long e	Table of Contents	Persuasive / Descriptive	www.whitehouse.gov/history/presidents/
	I Am Planet Earth	Earth and Space Science/Earth	Understanding Theme	Reading Words With r-Controlled Vowels	Diagrams	Expository / Persuasive	www.nasa.gov/audience/forkids/home/index.html
	Monster Money	Math/money	Summarizing	Reading Rhyming Words	Problems/Activities	Expository / Descriptive	www.usmint.gov/kids/
	School in Colonial America	Social Studies/life long ago	Generating Questions	Reading Words With -ed	Table of Contents	Expository / Expository	www.history.org
	The Wheat We Eat	Social Studies/food production	Summarizing	Reading Words With -ed	Captions	Expository / Expository	www.ncagr.com/cyber/kidswrld/nutrition
I	The Apple Pie Tree	Science/plants	Understanding Comparisons	Reading Words With -ch	Recipe	Expository / Descriptive	www.domtar.com/arbre/english/start.htm
	Beetles	Life Science/insects	Reading for Information	Reading Words With Long e	Table of Contents	Descriptive / Persuasive	www.teacher.scholastic.com/researchtools/articlearchives/bugs/
	Choosing Eyeglasses with Mrs. Koutris	Social Studies/community workers	Recognizing Problems and Solutions	Reading Possessive Words	Meet the Author and Photographer	Narrative / Expository	http://bhpr.hrsa.gov/kidscareers/studentsk5.htm
	A Flag for All	American History/national symbols	Understanding Plot	Reading Words With l-Blends	About the Author and Illustrator	Expository / Descriptive	www.usflag.org
	A House Spider's Life	Life Science/spiders	Recognizing Sequence of Events	Reading Suffixes	Glossary	Expository / Descriptive	www.americanhumane.org/kids/spiders.htm
	How Many Ants?	Math/counting	Attending to Text Structure	Reading Words That End In y	Diagrams	Expository / Narrative	www.storyplace.org
	Looking Through a Telescope	Science and Technology/telescopes	Summarizing	Reading Consonant Blends	Index	Expository / Narrative	www.teacher.scholastic.com/researchtools/articlearchives/space/
	Presidents' Day	American History/presidents' day	Generating Questions	Reading Words With -ern	Calendar	Expository / Persuasive	www.americanhistory.si.edu
	Where Do Puddles Go?	Physical Science/water cycle	Making Inferences	Reading Multisyllabic Words	Diagrams	Graphic Aid / Narrative	http://ga.water.usgs.gov/edu
	Shadows	Earth and Space Science/shadows	Using Picture Details	Reading Compound Words	Phonetic Pronunciations	Narrative / Expository	www.scholastic.com
J	Bart's Amazing Charts	Math/graphs	Identifying Problems/Solutions	Reading Multisyllabic Words	Bar Graphs	Descriptive / Graphic Aid	http://nces.ed.gov/nceskids/graphing
	An Earthworm's Life	Life Science/animal life cycles	Reading for Information	Reading Words With r-Controlled Vowels	Italic Words	Expository / Descriptive	http://yucky.kids.discovery.com/flash/worm
	Field Mouse and the Dinosaur Named Sue	Earth Science/dinosaurs	Recognizing Setting	Reading Multisyllabic Words	Specialized Vocabulary	Graphic Aid / Narrative	www.fieldmuseum.org/sue/
	Germs! Germs! Germs!	Life Science/health	Understanding Cause/Effect	Reading Compound Words	Title Page	Narrative / Expository	http://kidshealth.org/kid/talk/qa/germs.html
	Giant Pandas: Gifts From China	Life Science/animals	Generating Questions	Reading Words With Long i	Index	Descriptive / Expository	www.nationalzoo.si.edu/animals/giantpandas/
	Harriet Tubman	Social Studies/famous Americans	Understanding Story Grammar	Reviewing Words With Consonant Blends	Italic Words	Expository / Descriptive	www.harriettubman.com
	How Do Your Lungs Work?	Life Science/health	Reading for Information	Reading Multisyllabic Words	Diagrams	Persuasive / Expository	http://kidshealth.org/kid/index.jsp
	Inside an Ant Colony	Life Science/animal life cycles	Reading for Information	Understanding Plurals	Index	Narrative / Expository	www.antcolony.org
	Thunder and Lightning	Earth Science/weather	Generating Questions	Reading Words With r-Controlled Vowels	Captions	Expository / Persuasive	www.wildweather.com
	We Need Directions	Social Studies/maps	Reading for Information	Reading Words With Final e	Maps	Expository / Narrative	www.teacher.scholastic.com/fieldtrp/socstu/maps.htm

Leveled Bookroom Content Areas Skills & Strategies Chart

Level	Title	Content Area/Topic	Comprehension Strategies	Phonics and Word Study	Text Feature	Writing Options	Technology
K	The 512 Ants on Sullivan Street	Math/doubling	Recognizing Setting	Reading Base Words	Number Chart	Poetry / Narrative	www.teacher.scholastic.com/annie/
	The Best Way to Play (Little Bill #2)	Social Studies/values	Understanding Character	Reading Contractions and Possessives	About the Author and Illustrator	Narrative / Expository	www.nickjr.com/kids/html_site/little_bill/
	The Earth Is Mostly Ocean	Earth Science/oceans	Summarize	Understanding Suffixes	Index	Descriptive / Expository	www.pbs.org/wgbh/nova/abyss/life/
	Fluff and Feathers, Spikes and Skin	Life Science/animals	Reading for Information	Reading Multisyllabic Words	N/A	Descriptive / Expository	www.animaland.org
	A Girl Named Helen Keller	Social Studies/famous Americans	Recognizing Point of View	Reading Irregular Past-Tense Verbs	One-Hand Manual Alphabet	Descriptive / Narrative	www.handspeak.com
	The Mississippi River	Geography/rivers	Reading for Information	Understanding Common and Proper Nouns	Captions	Descriptive / Expository	http://nationalgeographic.com/geographyaction/rivers
	Plants that Eat Animals	Life Science/plants	Cause and Effect	Reading Compound Words	Picture Glossary	Expository / Graphic Aid	www.airlieeducation.org/carnivorous_plants2.htm
	Sounds All Around	Physical Science/sound	Recognizing Main Ideas	Reading Sound Words	Lists	Descriptive / Expository	www.kidshealth.org/kid/body/ear_noSW.html
	Under the Ground	Science and Technology/machines	Generating Questions	Reading Words With Final e	Index	Expository / Graphic Aid	www.transitmuseumeducation.org
	Veterans Day	Social Studies/national holidays	Recognizing Main Idea	Reading Words With -ed	Picture Glossary	Expository / Descriptive	www.patriotism.org/veterans_day
L	Antarctica	Geography/antarctica	Categorizing Information	Understanding Common and Proper Nouns	Index	Persuasive / Descriptive	www.nationalgeographic.com/maps
	Bats	Life Science/animals	Reading for Information	Reading Unfamiliar Words	Photographs	Descriptive / Narrative	www.nwf.org/kids
	Chomp! A Book About Sharks	Life Science/animals	Understanding Chapters	Reading Words With r-Controlled Vowels	Boldface Text	Expository / Persuasive	www.pbs.org/wgbh/nova/sharks
	Flies Are Fascinating	Life Science/insects	Compare and Contrast	Reading Compound Words	Index	Expository / Descriptive	www.enature.com
	The Grapes of Math	Math/logic and problem solving	Making Inferences	Recognizing Contractions	Answer Key	Expository / Expository	www.justriddlesandmore.com/math.html
	In 1492	Social Studies/United States history	Recognizing Main Idea and Details	Reading Words With -ed	Background Notes	Descriptive / Persuasive	www.infoplease.com/spot/columbusday1.html
	Japan	Social Studies/Japan	Attending to and Uncovering Text Structure	Reading Compound Words	Captions	Expository / Descriptive	http://gme.grolier.com
	Solar System	Earth and Space Science/solar system	Categorize Information	Reading Difficult Words	Charts	Expository / Descriptive	www.teacher.scholastic.com/researchtools/articlearchives/space/
	Tell Me Why Planes Have Wings	Physical Science/flight	Understanding Cause/Effect	Reading Multisyllabic Words	Table of Contents	Expository / Narrative	www.exploratorium.edu
	Tyrannosaurus rex	Earth and Space Science/dinosaurs	Using Illustrations	Reading Words With -ed	Time Lines	Expository / Persuasive	www.zoomdinosaurs.com

Level	Title	Content Area/Topic	Comprehension Strategies	Phonics and Word Study	Text Feature	Writing Options	Technology
M	A. Lincoln and Me	History/famous Americans	Understanding Character	Reading Compound Words	Illustrations	Descriptive Persuasive	www.teacher.scholastic.com/fieldtrp/socstu/lincoln.htm
	Five True Horse Stories	Life Science/animals	Activating Prior Knowledge	Reading Compound Words	Table of Contents	Expository Narrative	www.animaland.org
	Helping Paws: Dogs That Serve	Social Studies/working dogs	Categorizing Information	Understanding Suffixes	Boldface Subheadings	Persuasive Narrative	www.nfb.org
	I Hate English!	Social Studies/cultures	Compare and Contrast	Understanding Homophones	Unconventional Paragraph Format	Descriptive Expository	www.nychinatown.com
	The Journey of a Butterfly	Life Science/insects	Recognizing Main Idea	Using Context Clues	Maps	Expository Narrative	www.enature.com
	Save the Rain Forests	Earth Science/rain forests	Understanding Figurative Language	Reading Words With /ou/	Maps	Expository Persuasive	www.enchantedlearning.com/subjects/rainforest
	Sound, Heat & Light: Energy At Work	Physical Science/energy	Summarize	Recognize Variations of Words	Labels	Graphic Aid Expository	www.energyquest.ca.gov/index.html
	Tell Me How Much It Weighs	Math/weights and measurements	Thinking Aloud	Reading Words With Silent gh	Table of Contents	Expository Expository	www.scholastic.com
	Turtles Take Their Time	Life Science/turtles	Generating Questions	Using Context Clues	Photographs	Descriptive Narrative	www.nwf.org/kids
	What If You'd Met ... Beethoven?	Social Studies/music	Summarizing	Reading Words With -ing	Maps	Descriptive Graphic Aid	www.playmusic.org
N	Becoming a Citizen	Social Studies/citizenship	Understanding Chapters	Reading Multisyllabic Words	Captions	Expository Narrative	http://usgovinfo.about.com/blinstst.htm
	Constellations	Earth and Space Science/stars	Understanding Chapters	Reading Words With Consonant Blends	Captions	Expository Narrative	www.astro.wisc.edu/~dolan/constellations
	Hawks on the Clock	Science and Technology/animal helpers	Recognizing Main Idea and Details	Reading Words With Consonant /j/ g	Maps	Persuasive Narrative	www.wcs.org
	Let's Find Out About Money	Math/money	Understanding Concepts	Reading Words With -ing	Labels	Expository Descriptive	www.usmint.gov
	Measuring Penny	Math/measurement	Understanding Charts	Reading Words With s-Blends	Graphs	Expository Narrative	www.teacher.scholastic.com/maven/
	Special Olympics	Social Studies/people with disabilities	Summarizing	Reading Words With -ed	Bulleted List	Descriptive Persuasive	www.specialolympics.com
	Staying Healthy: Sleep and Rest	Life Science/health	Understanding Cause and Effect	Reading Words With s-Blends	Boldface Words	Descriptive Expository	www.sleepfoundation.org/children/childrenand sleep.cfm
	Tell Me How Far It Is	Math/measurement	Understanding Informational Texts	Reading Words With Vowel Digraphs	Numbered List	Graphic Aid Persuasive	www.math.com/teachers.html
	Wild Weather: Blizzards!	Earth Science/weather	Using Illustrations	Reading Words With -ed	Bulleted List	Descriptive Descriptive	www.nws.noaa.gov
	Working at a TV Station	Social Studies/community workers	Main Idea/Supporting Details	Reading Compound Words	Appendix	Expository Expository	www.cbs4.com
O	Abraham Lincoln: Road to the White House	Social Studies/famous Americans	Compare/Contrast	Understanding Compound Words	Index	Expository	http://teacher.scholastic.com/fieldtrp/socstu/lincoln.htm
	The Amazing Book of Mammal Records	Life Science/mammals	Main Idea/Details	Reading Words With -ing	Inset Text	Persuasive	www.earthlife.net/mammals/welcome.html
	Getting to Know the U.S. Presidents: James Monroe	Social Studies/famous Americans	Summarizing	Reading Plurals	Illustrations	Descriptive	www.whitehouse.gov/history/presidents
	Growing Crystals	Earth Science/common crystals	Compare/Contrast	Reading Multisyllabic Words	Reference Section	Descriptive	www.smithsonianeducation.org/educators/lesson_plans/minerals/index.html
	Mount St. Helens National Volcanic Monument	Earth Science/volcanoes	Summarizing	Recognizing Homophones	Maps	Letter	www.fema.gov/kids/volcano.htm
	A Million Fish... More or Less	Math/numbers, mathematical reasoning	Recognizing Genre: Tall Tales	Using Context Clues	Related Activities	Expository	www.americanfolklore.net/tt.html
	Plant Life	Life Science/plants	Using Picture Details	Reading Suffixes	Cross-Section Diagram	Expository	www.urbanext.uiuc.edu/gpe/index.html
	Rosa Parks: Freedom Rider	Social Studies/Rosa Parks, civil rights	Understanding Genre: Biography	Reading Suffixes	Predictable Format	Graphic Aid	www.rosaparks.org
	Squanto, Friend of the Pilgrims	Social Studies/Native Americans	Using Historical Context	Understanding Compound Words	Table of Contents	Letter	www.nativeamericans/Squanto.htm
	Stargazers	Earth and Space Science/stars	Understanding Cause/Effect	Words With Multiple Meanings	Labels	Graphic Aid	http://starchild.gsfc.nasa.gov

Leveled Bookroom Content Areas Skills & Strategies Chart

Level	Title	Content Area/ Topic	Comprehension Strategies	Phonics and Word Study	Text Feature	Writing Options	Technology
P	Eat Your Vegetables! Drink Your Milk!	Life Science/nutrition	Understanding Cause/Effect	Reading Suffixes	Charts	Expository	www.americanheart.org/presenter.jhtml?identifier=3028660
	A Drop of Water	Earth Science/properties of water	Summarizing	Reading Suffixes	Photographs	Graphic Aid	http://ga.water.usgs.gov/edu
	Getting to Know the U.S. Presidents: Andrew Jackson	Social Studies/famous Americans	Monitoring Comprehension	Reading Verbs	Captions	Graphic Aid	www.whitehouse.gov/history/presidents
	Heroes of the Revolution	Social Studies/Revolutionary War	Compare/Contrast	Recognizing Antonyms	Time Line	Expository	www.pbs.org/ktca/liberty
	Magic School Bus: Lost in the Solar System	Space Science/space exploration	Drawing Conclusions	Words With Multiple Meanings	Author's Style	Letter	www.windows.ucar.edu
	Sir Cumference and the Sword in the Cone	Math/solid shapes, measurement, algebra	Understanding Plot	Figurative Language	Additional Information	Expository	www.cut-the-knot.org/ geometry.shtml
	Snakes	Life Science/snakes	Categorizing Information	Understanding Compound Words	Photographs	Expository	www.pbs.org/wnet/nature/lesson_plans/reptiles2.html
	Where Have All the Pandas Gone?	Life Science/endangered species	Recognizing Setting	Understanding Compound Words	Question and Answer Format	Graphic Aid	www.fws.gov/endangered
	What Makes You Cough, Sneeze, Burp, Hiccup, Blink, Yawn, Sweat, and Shiver?	Life Science/health	Cause/Effect	Reading Words with -ing	Illustrations	Expository	www.kidshealth.org
	Wilma Unlimited	Social Studies/famous Americans	Making Predictions	Adjectives	Illustrations	Graphic Aid	www.lkwpl.org/wiohio/rudo-wil.htm
Q	All About Sharks	Life Science/sharks	Noting Details	Commas and Colons	Diagrams	Expository	www.sharks.org
	All About Turtles	Life Science/turtles	Compare/Contrast	Roots	Captions	Expository	http://animaldiversity.ummz.umich.edu/site/index.html
	Can You Believe? Hurricanes	Earth Science/hurricanes	Understanding Cause/ Effect	Figurative Language: Similes	Charts	Expository	www.fema.gov/kids/hurr.htm
	Copper	Physical Science/copper; elements	Main Idea/Details	Inflectional Endings	Glossary	Graphic Aid	www.nwma.org/education/copper_facts.htm
	Cut Down To Size At High Noon	Math/understanding scale drawings	Recognizing Setting	Words With Multiple Meanings	Diagrams	Expository	www.redkid.net/monsterpro.html
	If You Lived at the Time of the Great San Francisco Earthquake	Social Studies/1906 San Francisco earthquake	Understanding Cause/Effect	Words With Multiple Meanings	Question and Answer Format	Descriptive	www.archives.gov/exhibits/sf-earthquake-and-fire
	If You Lived with the Indians of the Northwest Coast	Social Studies/Northwest Coast Indians	Main Idea/Details	Understanding Compound Words	Question and Answer Format	Narrative	http://content.lib.washington.edu/aipnw/
	In Their Own Words: Paul Revere	Social Studies/famous Americans	Making Inferences	Understanding Compound Words	Index	Expository	www.paulreverehouse.org
	The Magic School Bus: Food Chain Frenzy	Life Science/food chains	Understanding Sequence	Adjectives that Compare	Question and Answer Format	Graphic Aid	www.nwf.org/gardenforwildlife/
	Oxygen	Physical Science/elements	Understanding Cause/Effect	Proper Nouns	Index	Expository	http://periodic.lanl.gov/elements/8.html

Level	Title	Content Area/Topic	Comprehension Strategies	Phonics and Word Study	Text Feature	Writing Options	Technology
R	Allergies	Life Science/health	Understanding Cause/Effect	Reading Prefixes	Sidebars	Expository	www.aaaai.org/patients/just4kids/science
	Can't You Make them Behave, King George?	Social Studies/American Revolution	Recognizing Reality/Fantasy	Using Picture Clues	Author's Notes	Expository	www.americanrevolution.com/KingGeorge3rd.htm
	Food Chains	Life Science/food chains	Compare/Contrast	Greek and Latin Prefixes	Flow Charts	Graphic Aid	www.enchantedlearning.com/subjects/foodchain
	Getting to Know the U.S. Presidents: George Washington	Social Studies/famous Americans	Main Idea/Details	Words With Multiple Meanings	Captions	Expository	www.mountvernon.org/learn/meet_george/index.cfm
	Getting to Know the U.S. Presidents: John Quincy Adams	Social Studies/famous Americans	Summarizing	Denotation/Connotation	Illustrations	Expository	www.presidentsusa.net/jqadams.html
	Getting to Know the U.S. Presidents: Thomas Jefferson	Social Studies/famous Americans	Understanding Cause/Effect	Reading Suffixes	Illustrations	Expository	www.whitehouse.gov
	The Great Fire	Social Studies/disasters in America	Understanding Sequence	Understanding Compound Words	Maps	Interview	www.chicagohs.org/fire
	O, Say Can You See?	Social Studies/U.S. symbols	Reading for Information	Recognizing Synonyms	Table of Contents	Graphic Aid	www.brownielocks.com/patrioticsymbols.html
	Octopuses, Squids, and Cuttlefish	Life Science/aquatic animals	Generating Questions	Understanding Context Clues	Glossary	Graphic Aid	www.thecephalopodpage.org
	Where Was Patrick Henry on the 29th of May?	Social Studies/famous Americans	Understanding Sequence	Reading Action Verbs	Illustrations	Expository	www.history.org/Almanack/people/bios/biohen.cfm
S	Abraham Lincoln	Social Studies/famous Americans	Drawing Conclusions	Roots	Headings	Expository	www.pbs.org/wgbh/amex/lincolns
	Cuts, Scrapes, Scabs and Scars	Life Science/health	Summarizing	Adjectives	Sidebars	Expository	www.kidshealth.org/kid
	The Civil Rights Movement in America	Social Studies/civil rights movement	Understanding Cause/Effect	Reading Multisyllabic Words	Sidebars	Expository	www.civilrightsteaching.org/About/about.htm
	In Their Own Words: Christopher Columbus	Social Studies/famous Americans	Understanding Cause/Effect	Reading Suffixes	Maps	Graphic Aid	www.ibiblio.org/expo/1492.exhibit/c-Columbus/columbus.html
	Light and Color	Physical Science/light and color	Understanding Cause/Effect	Recognizing Antonyms	Diagrams	Expository	www.thetech.org/exhibits/online/color
	In Their Own Words: Thomas Edison	Social Studies/famous Americans	Summarizing	Adverbs	Captions	Expository	www.nps.gov/edis
	Valley Forge	Social Studies/American Revolution	Making Predictions	Understanding Compound Words	Time Line	Expository	www.ushistory.org/valleyforge/
	Wacky Trees	Life Science/trees	Noting Details	Reading Prefixes	Sidebars	Graphic Aid	www.units.muohio.edu/dragonfly/trees.htmlx
	The Water Cycle	Earth Science/water cycle	Understanding Cause/Effect	Using Context Clues	Boldface Print	Expository	www.epa.gov/water/kids.html
	What's Your Angle, Pythagorus?	Math/Pythagorean Theorem	Recognizing Reality/Fantasy	Denotation/Connotation	Historical Note	Expository	www.pbs.org/wgbh/nova/proof/puzzle/use.html
T	Black Holes	Earth and Space Science/space	Monitoring Comprehension	Using Context Clues	Diagrams with Keys	Expository	www.nasa.gov
	Enemies of Slavery	Social Studies/slavery	Summarizing	Reading Prefixes	Headings	Expository	http://xroads.virginia.edu/~hyper/wpa/wpahome.html
	Land Predators	Life Science/predatory animals	Summarizing	Understanding Compound Words	Graphic Aids	Expository	www.sw-center.org/swcbd/programs/predator/
	Life in the Rainforests	Life Science/biomes	Noting Details	Recognizing Synonyms	Sidebars	Persuasive	www.srl.caltech.edu/personnel/krubal/rainforest/serve_home.html
	Lightning	Earth Science/weather	Understanding Cause/Effect	Words With Multiple Meanings	Photographs	Expository	www.lightningsafety.noaa.gov/teachers.htm
	Lost Star: The Story of Amelia Earhart	Social Studies/famous Americans	Drawing Conclusions	Words With Multiple Meanings	Index	Expository	www.ameliaearhartmuseum.org/bio1.htm
	A Picture of Freedom: The Diary of Clotee, a Slave Girl	Social Studies/slavery in the U.S.	Understanding Historical Context	Words With Multiple Meanings	Predictable Format	Letter	www.pbs.org/wgbh/aia/home.html
	Seahorses, Pipefishes, and Their Kin	Life Science/ocean life	Compare/Contrast	Understanding Compound Words	Predictable Format	Expository	www.sheddaquarium.org/SEA/fact_sheets.cfm?id=89
	Volcanoes	Earth Science/volcanoes	Summarizing	Reading Vivid Verbs	Glossary	Graphic Aid	http://interactive2.usgs.gov/learningweb/explorer/
	Volcanoes and Earthquakes	Earth Science/natural hazards	Visualizing	Recognizing Synonyms	Cross-Section Diagram	Expository	http://interactive2.usgs.gov/learningweb

Leveled Bookroom Content Areas
Skills & Strategies Chart

Level	Title	Content Area/Topic	Comprehension Strategies	Phonics and Word Study	Text Feature	Writing Options	Technology
U	African-Americans in the Thirteen Colonies	Social Studies/African-Americans in the 18th century	Using Picture Details	Reading Suffixes	Illustrations	Expository	www.pbs.org/wgbh/aia/home.html
	Count to A Million	Math/counting and numbers	Recognizing Patterned Text	Reading Main and Helping Verbs	Predictable Format	Graphic Aid	http://education.jlab.org/placevalue/index.html
	The Challenger Disaster	Earth and Space Science/space shuttle	Understanding Cause/Effect	Reading Prefixes and Suffixes	Time Line	Expository	www.nasa.gov
	The Truth About Great White Sharks	Science/great white sharks	Compare/Contrast	Reading Multisyllabic Words	Index	Graphic Aid	www.nationalgeographic.com/kids/creature_feature/0206/sharks2.html
	The Life and Death of Stars	Earth and Space Science/stars	Recognizing Fact/Opinion	Reading Multisyllabic Words	Time Line	Expository	http://hurricanes.nasa.gov/universe/science/stars.html
	Remember the Ladies	Social Studies/women in U.S. history	Compare/Contrast	Reading Multisyllabic Words	Predictable Format	Expository	www.wic.org/misc/history.htm; www.lkwdpl.org/WIHOHIO/figures.htm
	September 11th, 2001	Social Studies/terrorist attacks on September 11, 2001	Understanding Cause/Effect	Denotation/Connotation	Sidebars	Expository	http://americanhistory.si.edu/september11/
	The Story of Harriet Tubman: Freedom Train	Social Studies/famous Americans	Recognizing Setting	Recognizing Colloquialisms	Table of Contents	Expository	www.americaslibrary.gov/cgi-bin/page.cgi/aa/tubman
	Under the Ocean	Earth Science/ocean life	Categorizing Information	Using Context Clues	Headings/Subheadings	Expository	www.onr.navy.mil/focus/ocean/life/default.htm
	The Watsons Go to Birmingham—1963	Social Studies/civil rights movement	Making Inferences	Figurative Language	Epilogue	Expository	www.americaslibrary.gov
V	African Americans in the 13 Colonies	Social Studies/African Americans in the Old West	Main Idea/Details	Reading Multisyllabic Words	Time Line	Evaluative	www.buffalosoldiermuseum.com/kids.html
	The Battle of the Alamo	Social Studies/the Alamo	Summarizing	Recognizing Synonyms	Maps	Persuasive	www.thealamo.org/
	The Boston Tea Party	Social Studies/Boston Tea Party	Understanding Cause/Effect	Reading Quotations	Glossary	Expository	www.boston-tea-party.org
	The California Gold Rush	Social Studies/the gold rush	Summarizing	Reading Suffixes	Maps	Expository	www.museumca.org/goldrush
	Color Me Dark	Social Studies/culture	Making Inferences	Figurative Language: Similes	Predictable Format	Expository	http://memory.loc.gov/ammem/aaohtml/aohome.html
	The Declaration of Independence	Social Studies/national documents	Generating Questions	Compound Sentences	Time Line	Expository	www.ushistory.org/declaration
	Escape to Freedom	U.S. History/famous Americans	Understanding Genre: Drama	Figurative Language	Introduction	Graphic Aid	www.webenglishteacher.com/douglass.html
	An Extraodinary Life: The Story of a Monarch Butterfly	Life Science/monarch butterfly	Understanding Sequence	Understanding Compound Words	Maps	Descriptive	www.monarchwatch.org/
	What a Great Idea! Inventions that Changed the World	Physical Science/inventions	Summarizing	Reading Prefixes	Introduction	Graphic Aid	http://memory.loc.gov/learn/features/science/learn_more.html
	Women's Right to Vote	Social Studies/women's rights	Compare/Contrast	Consonant plus -le	Sidebars	Persuasive	www.pbs.org/stantonanthony/index.html

Level	Title	Content Area/Topic	Comprehension Strategies	Phonics and Word Study	Text Feature	Writing Options	Technology
W	Adam of the Road	Social Studies/Medieval England	Understanding Character	Reading Strong Verbs	Illustrations	Expository	www.kathimitchell.com/middleages.htm
	Daniel's Story	Social Studies/Holocaust	Understanding Point of View	Reading Dialogue and Quotations	Maps	Graphic Aid	www.ushmm.org/education/foreducators/
	Dear Dr. Bell... Your Friend, Helen Keller	Social Studies/famous Americans	Summarizing	Denotation/Connotation	Captions	Letter	www.afb.org/braillebug/helen_keller_bio.asp
	Extraordinary Women Scientists	Science/women in science	Understanding Sequence	Understanding Compound Words	Bibliography	Expository	www.astr.ua.edu/4000WS/4000WS.html
	Extraordinary Young People	Social Studies/extraordinary young people	Understanding Genre: Biography	Adjectives	Index	Descriptive	www.amazing-kids.org/
	G is for Googol	Math/numbers, mathematical reasoning	Using Picture Details	Reading Multisyllabic Words	Sidebars	Expository	www.teachers.ash.org.au/jeather
	A Grand Canyon Journey	Earth Science/geology and Grand Canyon	Understanding Sequence	Using Context Clues	Cross-Sections Diagram	Narrative	www.nps.gov/grca/
	The Journal of James Edmond Pease	Social Studies/civil war	Visualizing	Figurative Language: Simile	Predictable Format	Expository	www.pbs.org/civilwar
	Portraits of African-American Heroes	Social Studies/famous Americans	Understanding Genre: Biography	Reading Multisyllabic Words	Predictable Format	Expository	www.si.edu/resource/faq/nmah/afroam.htm
	Standing Tall: The Stories of Ten Hispanic Americans	Social Studies/Hispanic Americans	Understanding Sequence	Words With Multiple Meanings	Index	Expository	www.cr.nps.gov/nr/feature/hispanic
X	Black Eagles: African Americans in Aviation	Social Studies/African Americans in aviation	Understanding Sequence	Reading Past-Tense Verbs	Photographs	Descriptive	http://teacher.scholastic.com/space/mae_jemison/
	The Forgotten Heroes: The Story of the Buffalo Soldiers	Social Studies/Buffalo Soldiers	Evaluating Author's Purpose	Recognizing Synonyms	Introduction/Epilogue	Descriptive	www.cmohs.org
	The Glory Field	Social Studies/African Americans	Understanding Character	Using Context Clues	Diagrams	Descriptive	www.si.edu/resource/faq/nmah/afroam.htm
	The Great Depression	Social Studies/Great Depression	Summarizing	Reading Multiple Affixes	Photographs	Letter	www.digitalhistory.uh.edu/learning_history
	Katarina	Social Studies/Holocaust	Drawing Conclusions	Using Context Clues	Prologue	Graphic Aid	http://fcit.usf.edu/HOLOCAUST/people/CHILDREN.htm
	The Librarian Who Measured the Earth	Math/mathematical reasoning	Understanding Character	Using Context Clues	Bibliography	Expository	www.livius.org
	Nelson Mandela	Social Studies/human rights	Making Inferences	Denotation/Connotation	Index	Expository	www.anc.org.za/people/mandela
	Not Guilty	Social Studies/Justice System	Making Predictions	Reading Multisyllabic Words	Further Reading	Persuasive	http://pbskids.org/wayback/fair/tp.html
	Up Before Daybreak: Cotton and People in America	Social Studies/children in history	Main Idea/Details	Denotation/Connotation	Table of Contents	Graphic Aid	www.historyplace.com
Y	Within Reach: My Everest Story	Social Studies/famous Americans	Recognizing Fact/Opinion	Words With Multiple Meanings	Predictable Format	Expository	www.pbs.org/wgbh/nova/everest
	Air Raid—Pearl Harbor!	Social Studies/World War II	Visualizing	Reading Prefixes	Maps	Expository	http://content.scholastic.com/browse/article.jsp?id=7656
	Favorite Greek Myths	Social Studies/Greek mythology	Summarizing	Reading Strong Verbs	Introduction	Expository	www.historyforkids.org/learn/greeks/religion/
	Hana's Suitcase	Social Studies/Holocaust	Understanding Sequence	Understanding Compound Words	Introduction and Afterword	Graphic Aid	http://greekrelig.htm
	In Their Own Words: Davy Crockett	Social Studies/famous Americans	Understanding Sequence	Figurative Language	Headings	Expository	www.bsu.edu/classes/cantu/crockett.htm
	Indian Chiefs	Social Studies/Native Americans	Paraphrasing	Recognizing Synonyms	Photographs	Expository	www.cccoe.net/tribes/studres.htm
	Isaac Newton	Science/famous scientists	Understanding Character	Dashes, Parentheses	Bibliography	Expository	www.newton.cam.ac.uk/newton.html
	Leonardo daVinci	Science/famous scientists	Understanding Genre: Biography	Reading Suffixes	Bibliography	Persuasive	www.mos.org/leonardo/
	New Kids in Town	Social Studies/immigration	Understanding Character	Reading Prefixes and Suffixes	Source Notes	Expository	www.immigrationmuseumofnewamericans.org
	Stars and Planets	Science/stars and planets	Main Idea/Details	Greek and Latin Roots	Index	Persuasive	www.nasa.gov
	The Wright Brothers: How They Invented the Airplane	Social Studies/inventions	Main Idea/Details	Greek and Latin Roots	For Further Reading	Graphic Aid	http://wright.nasa.gov/

Leveled Bookroom Content Areas
Skills & Strategies Chart

Level	Title	Content Area/ Topic	Comprehension Strategies	Phonics and Word Study	Text Feature	Writing Options	Technology
Z	Bat 6	Social Studies/war's aftermath	Understanding Character	Using Context Clues	Predictable Format	Expository	www.pbs/org/childofcamp
	Beyond Belief: Strange, True Mysteries of the Unknown	Social Studies/unexplained phenomena	Visualizing	Reading Prefixes	Table of Contents	Narrative	www.pbs.org/wgbh/nova/lochness/legend.html
	The Disaster of the Hindenburg	Social Studies/disasters	Summarizing	Understanding Compound Words	Diagrams	Expository	www.airships.net
	Flight #116 Is Down!	Social Studies/disasters	Recognizing Setting	Reading Multisyllabic Words	Predictable Format	Narrative	www.fema.gov/kids/
	The Greatest: Muhammad Ali	Social Studies/famous Americans	Main Idea/Details	Reading Suffixes	Time Line	Narrative	www.ali.com
	Guys Write for Guys Read	Social Studies/personal development	Visualizing	Recognizing Homophones	Table of Contents	Narrative	www.guysread.com
	Memories of Vietnam: War in the First Person	Social Studies/Vietnam War	Making Inferences	Using Context Clues	Question Format	Expository	www.pbs.org/battlefieldvietnam/
	To Be a Slave	Social Studies/American slavery	Summarizing	Understanding Compound Words	Bibliography	Persuasive	http://memory.loc.gov/ammem/ndlpedu/lessons/psources/slavery.html
	We Shall Not Be Moved: The Women's Factor Strike of 1909	Social Studies/Women's Rights	Monitoring Comprehension	Reading Action Verbs with Direct Objects	Epilogue	Expository	www.ashp.cuny.edu/video/heaven/fuprising.html
	When Plague Strikes: The Black Death, Smallpox, AIDS	Social Studies/plagues	Main Idea/Details	Reading Multisyllabic Words	Index	Graphic Aid	www.cdc.gov/ncidod/dvbid/plague/

Skills & Strategies Chart: Nonfiction Focus

Level	Title	Genre	Comprehension Strategies	Phonics and Word-Solving Strategies	Writing Options	Technology	Web Site Sponsor
A	Big and Little	Science Nonfiction	Understanding Concepts	Listening For Syllables / Recognizing Phonogram -ig	Descriptive / Descriptive	www.math.com/teachers.html	Math.com
	Games	Social Studies Nonfiction	Recognizing Patterned Text	Using Context / Using Beginning Sounds	Expository / Expository	www.gameskidsplay.net	Games Kids Play
	I Can, We Can	Social Studies Nonfiction	Identifying Main Idea	Reading Action Words / Recognizing Pronouns I and We	Descriptive / Graphic Aid	www.scholastic.com	Scholastic
	In the Woods	Fantasy	Recognizing Story Sequence	Recognizing Rhyming Words / Reading Words With -og	Narrative / Descriptive	www.storiestogrowby.com	Whootie Owl's Stories to Grow By
	Kittens	Concept Book: Counting	Recognizing Punctuation	Reading High-Frequency Words / Reading Numerals	Narrative / Descriptive	www.animaland.org	American Society for the Prevention of Cruelty to Animals
	Let's Go!	Concept Book: Transportation	Understanding Genre: Photo Essay	Reading High-Frequency Words / Understanding Contractions	Descriptive / Expository	education.dot.gov/k5/gamk5.htm	"Transportation Wonderland" from the U.S. Department of Transportation
	My Color	Concept Book: Color	Using Adjectives	Reading High-Frequency Words / Using Beginning Sounds	Descriptive / Descriptive	www.nwf.org/kids	National Wildlife Federation
	School	Social Studies Nonfiction	Developing Print Awareness	Reading High-Frequency Words / Reading Plurals	Narrative / Expository	www.scholastic.com	Scholastic
	We Can!	Realistic Fiction	Recognizing Setting	Reading High-Frequency Words / Recognizing Phonogram-an	Narrative / Graphic Aid	www.scholastic.com	Scholastic
	What Bears Like	Science Nonfiction	Using Picture Details	Using Context / Using Beginning Sounds	Descriptive / Expository	www.nwf.org/kids	National Wildlife Federation
B	Baby Animals Learn	Science Nonfiction	Comparing/Contrasting	Reading Words With Consonant Blends / Matching Same Sounds	Descriptive / Persuasive	www.sandiegozoo.org	San Diego Zoo
	Carrots	Science Nonfiction	Recognizing Setting	Reading Unfamiliar Words / Matching Same Sounds	Expository / Descriptive	www.kidsgardening.com	National Gardening Association
	Goldilocks	Folktale	Making Predictions	Recognizing Punctuation / Reading Plural Words	Descriptive / Narrative	www.storiestogrowby.com	Whootie Owl's Stories to Grow By
	Hop In!	Fantasy	Distinguishing Fantasy/Reality	Reading Words With Short Vowels / Using Punctuation	Persuasive / Narrative	www.scholastic.com	Scholastic
	Kites	Concept Book: Colors	Using Illustrations	Reading Compound Words / Reading Rhyming Words	Descriptive / Narrative	www.kites.org/zoo	The Virtual Kite Zoo
	Two Can Do It!	Social Studies Nonfiction	Understanding Concepts	Reading Unfamiliar Words / Recognizing Homophones	Descriptive / Descriptive	www.scholastic.com	Scholastic
	Water	Science Nonfiction	Comparing/Contrasting	Using Beginning Sounds / Reading Compound Words	Descriptive / Descriptive	ga.water.usgs.gov/edu	"Water Science for Schools" from the U.S. Geological Survey
	We Are Painting	Concept Book: Counting	Understanding Concepts	Reading Color Words / Reading Plurals	Descriptive / Narrative	www.crayola.com	Crayola
	We Like to Play!	Realistic Fiction	Recognizing Setting	Reading Action Words / Reading High-Frequency Words	Descriptive / Narrative	www.scholastic.com	Scholastic
	What Am I?	Concept Book: Shapes	Recognizing Questions	Understanding Rebuses / Reading High-Frequency Words	Descriptive / Descriptive	www.math.com/teachers.html	Math.com
C	At Work	Science Nonfiction	Using Illustrations	Reading Words That Look Similar / Reading Plurals	Expository / Descriptive	www.animaland.org	American Society for the Prevention of Cruelty to Animals
	Bugs!	Science Nonfiction	Reading Questions and Answers	Reading Number Words / Reading Compound Words	Descriptive / Persuasive	www.nwf.org/kids	National Wildlife Federation
	Frog Egg to Robin	Science Nonfiction	Understanding Concepts	Reading Plurals / Matching Same Sounds	Descriptive / Expository	www.aviary.org	The National Aviary
	How Many Can Play?	Concept Book	Recognizing Patterned Text	Reading Compound Words / Reading Unfamiliar Words	Descriptive / Expository	www.jumpingforjoy.org/games.html	Jumping For Joy
	I Can Run	Concept Book: Actions	Recognizing Patterned Text	Reading Words With Consonant Blends / Using Punctuation	Narrative / Expository	www.scholastic.com	Scholastic
	I See Fish	Science Nonfiction	Comparing/Contrasting	Reading High-Frequency Words / Recognizing Questions	Descriptive / Persuasive	www.aqua.org	National Aquarium in Baltimore
	It's a Party	Concept Book: Celebrations	Using Photographs	Reading Contractions / Matching Same Sounds	Descriptive / Descriptive	www.kidsparties.com/traditions.htm	"Birthday Traditions From Around the World" from Kids Parties Connection

Level	Title	Genre	Comprehension Strategies	Phonics and Word-Solving Strategies	Writing Options	Technology	Web Site Sponsor
	Joshua James Likes Trucks	Concept Book	Making Predictions	Matching Same Sounds / Using Context	Descriptive / Descriptive	www.scholastic.com	Scholastic
	Pancakes, Crackers, and Pizza: A Book About Shapes	Concept Book: Shapes	Reading Long Sentences	Reading Food Words / Reading Compound Words	Descriptive / Narrative	www.math.com/teachers.html	Math.com
	Rain	Concept Book: Colors	Recognizing Story Sequence	Reading Compound Words / Reading Color Words	Narrative / Descriptive	ga.water.usgs.gov/edu	"Water Science for Schools" from the U.S. Geological Survey
D	Footprints In the Snow	Science Nonfiction	Relating to Personal Experiences	Recognizing Verbs / Using Punctuation	Expository / Descriptive	www.nwf.org/kids	National Wildlife Federation
	I Know Karate	Informational Fiction	Using Illustrations	Recognizing Verbs / Reading High-Frequency Words	Descriptive / Descriptive	www.scholastic.com	Scholastic
	Nests, Nests, Nests	Science Nonfiction	Comparing/Contrasting	Reading Words With Consonant Blends / Reading Plurals	Descriptive / Descriptive	www.aviary.org	The National Aviary
	One Happy Classroom	Concept Book: Counting	Recognizing Story Pattern	Working With Word Parts / Reading Compound Words	Descriptive	www.scholastic.com	Scholastic
	Paul the Pitcher	Realistic Fiction	Understanding Concepts	Reading Words With Short i / Reading Words That Are Opposites	Descriptive / Descriptive	www.kidsdomain.com/sports/baseball	"Baseball Fun" from Kids Domain
	Rain! Rain!	Informational Fiction	Recognizing Story Sequence	Reading Rhyming Words / Reading High-Frequency Words	Narrative / Descriptive	ga.water.usgs.gov/edu	"Water Science for Schools" from the U.S. Geological Survey
	Ten Cats Have Hats	Concept Book: Counting	Recognizing Sentence Pattern	Reading Rhyming Words / Reading Number Words	Narrative / Narrative	www.math.com/teachers.html	Math.com
	Too Many Balloons	Concept Book: Colors	Reading Environmental Print	Matching Same Sounds / Reading Plurals	Descriptive / Descriptive	www.crayola.com	Crayola
	Where Do Birds Live?	Science Nonfiction	Understanding Concepts	Using Beginning Sounds / Listening for Vowel Sounds	Expository / Expository	www.sandiegozoo.org	San Diego Zoo
	Who Am I?	Concept Book: Jobs	Using Illustrations	Reading Words With -er / Reading Compound Words	Descriptive / Descriptive	www.bls.gov/k12/html/edu_over.htm	The Bureau of Labor Statistics' Career information
E	Animal Babies	Science Nonfiction	Recognizing Patterned Text	Reading Contractions / Reading Words With Long e	Expository / Poetry	www.animaland.org	American Society for the Prevention of Cruelty to Animals
	A Box Can Be Many Things	Realistic Fiction	Reading Everyday Speech	Reading Unfamiliar Words / Reading Words With /ou/	Descriptive / Poetry	www.scholastic.com	Scholastic
	A Buzz Is Part of a Bee	Concept Book	Using Illustrations	Reading Rhyming Words / Reading Words With Consonant Digraphs	Graphic Aid / Expository	gears.tucson.ars.ag.gov	Carl Hayden Bee Research Center
	Clay Art with Gloria Elliott	Nonfiction	Understanding Setting	Reading Words With Long a / Reading Plurals	Descriptive / Expository	www.handsoncrafts.org	Hands on Crafts
	I Can See	Concept Book: Letters	Comparing/Contrasting	Reading Words With Short a / Matching Same Sounds	Descriptive / Descriptive	www.scholastic.com	Scholastic
	Just Like Me	Realistic Fiction	Using Illustrations	Using Common Spelling Patterns / Matching Same Sounds	Descriptive / Narrative	www.grolier.com	Grolier
	Look! I Can Read!	Realistic Fiction	Recognizing Questions	Reading Compound Words / Recognizing Rhyming Words	Descriptive / Persuasive	www.readroom.com	The Reading Room
	Polar Babies	Science Nonfiction	Understanding Character	Using Punctuation / Reading Words With Short i	Descriptive / Narrative	www.nwf.org/kids	National Wildlife Federation
	Up, Up, and Away: The Story of Amelia Earhart	Biography	Understanding Character	Reading Words With -ed / Reading Words With Consonant Blends	Expository / Expository	www.nationalaviation.org	National Aviation Hall of Fame
	The Voyage of Mae Jemison	Biography	Recognizing Story Sequence	Reading Words With -ing and -ed / Reading Words That Look Similar	Descriptive / Expository	www.nasa.gov/kids.html	NASA "Just For Kids"
F	Amy Loves the Snow	Realistic Fiction	Recognizing Setting	Reading Compound Words / Recognizing Contractions and Possessives	Expository / Narrative	www.wildwildweather.com	Dan's Wild Wild Weather Page
	Cookie's Week	Concept Book: Days of the Week	Understanding Cause/Effect	Reading Compound Words / Reading Words With r-Controlled Vowels	Expository / Narrative	www.animaland.org	American Society for the Prevention of Cruelty to Animals
	Firehouse Sal	Informational Fiction	Making Predictions	Reading Number Words / Reading Words With Consonant Blends	Expository / Graphic Aid	www.nfpa.org/sparky	"Sparky the Fire Dog" web site from The National Fire Protection Association
	Frog's Lunch	Informational Fiction	Reading Dialogue	Reading Words With -ing and -ed / Reading Words With Consonant Blends	Expository / Narrative	www.exploratorium.edu/frogs	The Exploratorium's Frogs Exhibition
	Harry's House	Informational Fiction	Drawing Conclusions	Distinguishing Between Nouns and Verbs / Recognizing Contractions and Possessives	Expository / Expository	www.animaland.org	American Society for the Prevention of Cruelty to Animals
	I Am Fire	Science Nonfiction	Relating to Personal Experiences	Reading Words With Long i / Reading Unfamiliar Words	Expository / Expository	www.nfpa.org/sparky	"Sparky the Fire Dog" web site from The National Fire Protection Association
	Is This You?	Concept Book: How-to	Using Illustrations	Reading High-Frequency Words / Reading Words With Long a and Long e	Expository / Expository	www.scholastic.com	Scholastic

Level	Title	Genre	Comprehension Strategies	Phonics and Word-Solving Strategies	Writing Options	Technology	Web Site Sponsor
	Pizza Party!	Realistic Fiction	Understanding Story Development	Reading Rhyming Words / Reading Action Words	Expository / Narrative	www.kidfood.org	Kid Food CyberClub
	Shine, Sun!	Informational Fiction	Recognizing Setting	Reading Words With Digraphs / Reading High-Frequency Words	Expository / Graphic Aid	www.americansun.org	American Sun Protection Association
	Soccer Camel	Realistic Fiction	Making Inferences	Reading Rhyming Words / Reading Verbs	Narrative / Narrative	www.soccerjr.com	Soccer Jr. Magazine
G	The Class Trip	Realistic Fiction	Relating to Personal Experiences	Reading Verbs / Reading Words With Consonant Blends	Descriptive / Expository	www.sandiegozoo.org	San Diego Zoo
	Dinosaurs	Science Nonfiction	Comparing/Contrasting	Using Context / Using Picture Details	Descriptive / Graphic Aid	www.amnh.org	American Museum of Natural History
	The Great Race	Fantasy	Reading Dialogue	Reading Words With oo / Reading Sound Words	Expository / Narrative	www.scholastic.com	Scholastic
	Make It Move!	Science Nonfiction	Recognizing Questions	Reading Pronouns / Blending Words	Descriptive / Graphic Aid	www.mos.org	Boston Museum of Science
	Pele: The King of Soccer	Biography	Making Inferences	Reading Words With -ed / Reading Words With Short i	Graphic Aid / Descriptive	www.soccerjr.com	Soccer Jr. Magazine
	Sam the Garbage Hound	Realistic Fiction	Comparing/Contrasting	Reading Words With g / Reading Adjectives	Narrative / Graphic Aid	www.animaland.org	American Society for the Prevention of Cruelty to Animals
	Sometimes Things Change	Science Nonfiction	Making Predictions	Reading Words With Consonant Blends / Reading High-Frequency Words	Descriptive / Expository	ga.water.usgs.gov/edu	"Water Science for Schools" from the U.S. Geological Survey
	Teddy Bear for Sale	Fantasy	Making Inferences	Reading Directional Words / Recognizing Verbs	Narrative / Descriptive	www.theodoreroosevelt.org	Theodore Roosevelt Association
	Wait, Skates!	Realistic Fiction	Recognizing Story Sequence	Reading Words With Long a / Reading Punctuation	Narrative / Narrative	www.grolier.com	Grolier
	Why Can't I Fly?	Fantasy	Recognizing Plot	Reading Words With Long i / Reading Rhyming Words	Poetry / Narrative	www.animalsoftherainforest.com	The Jason Project
H	Caps, Hats, Socks, and Mittens: A Book About the Four Seasons	Concept Book: Seasons	Making Inferences	Reading Words With s-Blends / Understanding Figurative Language	Descriptive / Narrative	kids.earth.nasa.gov	"For Kids only - Earth Science Enterprise" from NASA
	Come! Sit! Speak!	Realistic Fiction	Recognizing Setting	Reading Words With Long o / Reading Difficult Words	Descriptive / Graphic Aid	www.howtoloveyourdog.com	How to Love Your Dog: A Kid's Guide to Dog Care
	Danny and the Dinosaur Go to Camp	Fantasy	Distinguishing Fantasy/Reality	Reading Words With Long o / Reading Unfamiliar Words	Narrative / Descriptive	www.amnh.org	American Museum of Natural History
	It's Spring!	Informational Fiction	Summarizing	Reading Words With ow / Recognizing Synonyms	Poetry / Narrative	www.favoritepoem.org	The Favorite Poem Project
	A Kiss for Little Bear	Fantasy	Understanding Character	Reading Words With Long e / Reading Pronouns	Graphic Aid / Persuasive	www.scholastic.com	Scholastic
	My Pigs	Nonfiction	Recognizing Main Idea	Reading Words With Long i / Reading Plural Words	Graphic Aid / Expository	www.animaland.org	American Society for the Prevention of Cruelty to Animals
	Plane Rides	Nonfiction	Understanding Story Sequence	Reading Words With Long i and Long a / Reading Compound Words	Expository / Descriptive	www.nasm.si.edu	National Air and Space Museum
	The Very Big Potato	Folktale	Recognizing Cause/Effect	Reading Contractions / Reading Words With Long i	Persuasive / Narrative	www.kidsgardening.com	National Gardening Association
	What Will the Weather Be Like Today?	Science Nonfiction	Understanding Figurative Language	Reading Words With r-Blends / Reading Multisyllabic Words	Expository / Descriptive	www.wildwildweather.com	Dan's Wild Wild Weather Page
	When I First Came to This Land	Historical Fiction	Understanding Poetic Language	Using Common Spelling Patterns / Reading Words With r-Controlled Vowels	Persuasive / Descriptive	www.favoritepoem.org	The Favorite Poem Project
I	All Tuttus Should be Pink	Realistic Fiction	Understanding Theme	Reading Words With Long e / Understanding Plurals	Expository / Narrative	www.abt.org	American Ballet Theatre
	A Day with a Mail Carrier	Social Studies Nonfiction	Summarizing	Reading Words With Long a / Reading 'Unfamiliar Words	Expository / Persuasive	www.si.edu/postal	National Postal Museum
	A Day with Firefighters	Social Studies Nonfiction	Making Inferences	Reading Words With Long o / Using Common Spelling Patterns	Expository / Descriptive	www.nfpa.org/sparky	"Sparky the Fire Dog" web site from The National Fire Protection Association
	The Elves and the Shoemaker	Fairy Tale	Understanding Plot	Reading Words With -ed / Reading Contractions and Possessives	Expository / Narrative	www.storiestogrowby.com	Whootie Owl's Stories to Grow By
	Goldilocks and the Three Bears	Fairy Tale	Understanding Cause/Effect	Recognizing Synonyms / Reading Homophones	Expository / Narrative	www.storiestogrowby.com	Whootie Owl's Stories to Grow By
	I Am a Rock	Science Nonfiction	Reading for Information	Reading Multisyllabic Words / Reading Words With -er	Graphic Aid / Descriptive	www.usgs.gov/education	U.S. Geological Survey
	Messy Bessey's Family Reunion	Realistic Fiction	Recognizing Setting	Reading Words That Rhyme / Reading Compound Words	Expository / Narrative	www.scholastic.com	Scholastic

Level	Title	Genre	Comprehension Strategies	Phonics and Word-Solving Strategies	Writing Options	Technology	Web Site Sponsor
	Red-Eyed Tree Frog	Science Nonfiction	Reading for Information	Reading Words With Long e / Reading Words With Blends	Narrative / Expository	www.animalsoftherainforest.com	The Jason Project
	The Sun's Family of Planets	Science Nonfiction	Understanding Concepts	Reading Unfamiliar Words / Reading Words With -est	Graphic Aid / Narrative	www.nasa.gov/kids.html	NASA "Just For Kids"
	We Just Moved!	Fiction	Relating to Personal Experiences	Reading Compound Words / Reading Words With r-Controlled Vowels	Narrative / Descriptive	www.castles.org	Castles of the World
J	Bear Shadow	Fantasy	Identifying Problems/Solutions	Recognizing Base Words / Recognizing Irregular Past-Tense Verbs	Narrative / Persuasive	www.exploratorium.edu	The Exploratorium
	Henry and Mudge and the Long Weekend	Realistic Fiction	Understanding Character	Recognizing Base Words / Understanding Similes	Narrative / Expository	www.howtoloveyourdog.com	How to Love Your Dog: A Kid's Guide to Dog Care
	How Kittens Grow	Science Nonfiction	Understanding Cause/Effect	Reading Words With Long a / Reading Words With Suffixes	Expository / Poetry	www.animaland.org	American Society for the Prevention of Cruelty to Animals
	Jack Plays the Violin	Realistic Fiction	Making Predictions	Reading Words With Consonant Blends / Understanding Multiple Meaning Words	Graphic Aid / Narrative	www.playmusic.org	American Symphony Orchestra League
	Looking at Maps and Globes	Social Studies Nonfiction	Using Maps and Globes	Reading Words With Consonant l/j/g / Understanding Common and Proper Nouns	Graphic Aid / Descriptive	www.nationalgeographic.com/maps	National Geographic Maps and Geography
	Me on the Map	Social Studies Nonfiction	Using Maps and Charts	Understanding Common and Proper Nouns / Reading Words With s-Blends	Graphic Aid / Expository	www.mapquest.com	MapQuest
	My Life	Autobiography	Comparing/Contrasting	Reading Multisyllabic Words / Understanding Plurals	Expository / Narrative	www.scholastic.com/kids	Scholastic
	On the Lake	Informational Fiction	Making Inferences	Using Context / Recognizing Homophones	Expository / Descriptive	www.boatsafe.com/kids	International Marine Educators, Inc.
	Poppleton Everyday	Fantasy	Understanding Sequence	Reading Compound Words / Recognizing Contractions and Possessives	Narrative / Descriptive	www.scholastic.com	Scholastic
	The Sword in the Stone	Legend	Understanding Plot	Reading Words With Silent Letters / Reading Words With Long i	Narrative / Expository	www.2020site.org/kingarthur	"King Arthur's Legends" from 2020site.org
K	All About Things People Do	Social Studies Nonfiction	Reading for Information	Reading Words With Suffixes / Reading Multisyllabic Words	Expository / Descriptive	www.bls.gov/k12/html/edu_over.htm	The Bureau of Labor Statistics' Career Information
	The Blue Mittens	Realistic Fiction	Comparing/Contrasting	Reading Words With Finale / Recognizing Homophones	Descriptive / Poetry	www.scholastic.com	Scholastic
	Chickens Aren't the Only Ones	Science Nonfiction	Comparing/Contrasting	Recognizing Contractions and Possessives / Reading Multisyllabic Words	Descriptive / Graphic Aid	www.enature.com	Enature
	The Day Jimmy's Boa Ate the Wash	Fantasy	Understanding Cause/Effect	Reading Informal Speech / Reading Words With -ed, -ing	Expository / Graphic Aid	www.animaland.org	American Society for the Prevention of Cruelty to Animals
	Ming Lo Moves the Mountain	Folktale	Understanding Character	Recognizing Base Words / Understanding Irregular Past-Tense Verbs	Graphic Aid / Poetry	www.storiestogrowby.com	Whootie Owl's Stories to Grow By
	Our Flag	Social Studies Nonfiction	Understanding Cause/Effect	Understanding Common and Proper Nouns / Recognizing Synonyms	Descriptive / Descriptive	americanhistory.si.edu	National Museum of American History
	Penguins	Science Nonfiction	Recognizing Setting	Reading Words With Suffixes / Understanding Plurals	Expository / Graphic Aid	www.nwf.org/kids	National Wildlife Federation
	A Place for Grace	Informational Fiction	Identifying Problems/Solution	Reading Words With -ed / Reading Words With -ly	Expository / Graphic Aid	www.handspeak.com	HandSpeak: A Sign Language Dictionary Online
	Shipwreck Saturday	Realistic Fiction	Understanding Point of View	Reading Words With Final e / Understanding Figurative Language	Narrative / Narrative	www.enchantedlearning.com/crafts/origami	"KinderCrafts" from EnchantedLearning.com
	What Magnets Can Do	Science Nonfiction	Making Predictions	Reading Compound Words / Reading Variations of Words	Descriptive / Descriptive	www.exploratorium.edu	The Exploratorium
L	Animal Tracks	Science Nonfiction	Categorizing Information	Reading Words With Suffixes / Reading Words With -ing	Narrative / Expository	www.nwf.org/kids	Natural Wildlife Federation
	Apatosaurus	Science Nonfiction	Reading for Information	Reading Unfamiliar Words / Understanding Suffixes	Expository / Expository	www.amnh.org	American Museum of Natural History
	The Big "M"	Informational Fiction	Making Predictions	Reading Difficult Words / Reading Words With -ed	Narrative / Narrative	www.metmuseum.org	The Metropolitan Museum of Art
	Cam Jansen and the Mystery of the Babe Ruth Baseball	Mystery	Understanding Character	Using Context / Reading Number Words	Graphic Aid / Narrative	kids.mysterynet.com	MysteryNet's Kids Mysteries
	The Mud Pony	Folktale	Making Predictions	Reading Contractions / Reading Compound Words	Narrative / Narrative	www.nmai.si.edu	National Museum of the American Indian
	Play Ball, Amelia Bedelia	Fiction	Comparing/Contrasting	Understanding Idiomatic Expressions / Reading Dialogue	Expository / Narrative	www.kidsdomain.com/sports/baseball	"Baseball Fun" from Kids Domain
	Rain Forest	Science Nonfiction	Using Maps and Diagrams	Reading Multisyllabic Words / Reading Words With r-Controlled Vowels	Persuasive / Expository	www.ran.org	Rainforest Action Network

Level	Title	Genre	Comprehension Strategies	Phonics and Word-Solving Strategies	Writing Options	Technology	Web Site Sponsor
	Solve It!	Mystery	Making Inferences	Reading Informal Speech / Understanding Homophones	Persuasive / Persuasive	kids.mysterynet.com	MysteryNet's Kids Mysteries
	Spiders	Science Nonfiction	Categorizing Information	Reading Plurals and Possessives / Reading Multisyllabic Words	Expository / Poetry	www.enature.com	Enature
M	This Is My House	Social Studies Nonfiction	Comparing/Contrasting	Understanding Plurals / Reading Difficult Words	Descriptive / Descriptive	www.whyy.org/aie	The Foundation For Architecture's Architecture in Education Program
	At 1600 Pennsylvania Avenue	Social Studies Nonfiction	Categorizing Information	Reading Words With r-Controlled Vowels / Recognizing Proper Nouns and Titles	Graphic Aid / Expository	www.whitehouse.gov	The White House
	Boom!	Science Nonfiction	Using Diagrams	Reading Words With /oo/ / Identifying Open and Closed Syllables	Poetry / Graphic Aid	www.usgs.gov	U.S. Geological Survey
	Buddy: The First Seeing Eye Dog	Nonfiction	Understanding Chapters	Reading Words With -ed / Recognizing Contractions	Descriptive / Narrative	www.nfb.org	National Federation of the Blind
	California or Bust!	Historical Fiction	Understanding Setting	Reading Words With Prefixes / Using Context	Expository / Expository	www.americaslibrary.gov	"America's Story" from the Library of Congress
	Firefighters	Social Studies Nonfiction	Recognizing Main Idea/Details	Identifying Open Syllables / Reading Words With Finale	Expository / Descriptive	www.nfpa.org/sparky	"Sparky the Fire Dog" web site from The National Fire Protection Association
	Gung Hay Fat Choy	Social Studies Nonfiction	Reading for Information	Recognizing Variations of Words / Recognizing Homophones	Descriptive / Descriptive	www.camia.org	The Chinese American Museum
	Jungle Jack Hanna's Safari Adventure	Nonfiction	Summarizing	Reading Compound Words / Recognizing Strong Verbs	Expository / Expository	www.nwf.org/kids	National Wildlife Federation
	The Littles Go Exploring	Fantasy	Understanding Character	Reading Words With -ly / Reading Informal Speech	Graphic Aid / Descriptive	www.scholastic.com	Scholastic
	Nine True Dolphin Stories	Science Nonfiction	Relating to Personal Experience	Reading Compound Words / Reading Specialized Vocabulary	Expository / Graphic Aid	www.wcs.org	Wildlife Conservation Society
	Yellowstone National Park	Science Nonfiction	Understanding Informational Texts	Recognizing Variations of Words / Recognizing Plurals	Graphic Aid / Descriptive	www.nps.gov/yell	Yellowstone National Park
N	Amber Brown Is Feeling Blue	Realistic Fiction	Understanding Character / Understanding Point of View	Reading Words With -y, -ly	Expository / Persuasive	www.scholastic.com	Scholastic
	Catwings Return	Fantasy	Making Inferences / Understanding Sequence	Reading Compound Words	Expository / Descriptive	www.scholastic.com	Scholastic
	The Corn Husk Doll	Informational Fiction	Reading for Information / Using Diagrams	Reading Contractions	Expository / Graphic Aid	www.nmai.si.edu	National Museum of the American Indian
	A Dinosaur Named Sue: The Find of the Century	Science Nonfiction	Summarizing / Recognizing Setting	Reading Words With -ed	Expository / Graphic Aid	www.fieldmuseum.org	The Field Museum of Natural History
	Do Tornadoes Really Twist? Questions and Answers About Tornadoes and Hurricanes	Science Nonfiction	Categorizing Information / Comparing/Contrasting	Reading Words With s-Blends	Descriptive / Expository	www.noaa.gov	National Oceanic and Atmospheric Administration
	Endangered Animals	Science Nonfiction	Recognizing Cause/Effect / Understanding Chapters	Reading Difficult Words	Expository / Persuasive	www.wcs.org	Wildlife Conservation Society
	The Garden on Green Street	Realistic Fiction	Understanding Plot / Understanding Sequence	Reading Words With -ing	Graphic Aid / Persuasive	www.kidsgardening.com	National Gardening Association
	How Is a Crayon Made?	Nonfiction	Understanding Concepts / Relating to Personal Experience	Reading Words With Prefixes	Descriptive / Graphic Aid	www.crayola.com	Crayola
	Lily and Miss Liberty	Historical Fiction	Identifying Problems/Solutions / Understanding Historical Context	Understanding Plural	Descriptive / Descriptive	www.nps.gov/stli	Statue of Liberty National Monument
	Louis Braille: The Boy Who Invented Books for the Blind	Biography	Understanding Point of View / Story Development	Reading Words With ff/gh	Descriptive / Descriptive	www.nfb.org	National Federation of the Blind
O	The Animal Shelter Mystery	Mystery	Understanding Story Development / Making Predictions	Reading Words With Long a and Long e	Persuasive / Narrative	www.scholastic.com	Scholastic
	Desert Life	Science Nonfiction	Summarizing / Recognizing Setting	Reading Words With Diphthong oi, oy	Expository / Descriptive	www.nps.gov/sagu	Saguaro National Park
	Donner Party: A Diary of a Survivor	Social Studies Nonfiction	Reading for Information / Using Diagrams	Reading Contractions	Narrative / Descriptive	www.historyplace.com	The History Place
	Flossie & the Fox	Fantasy	Understanding Plot / Understanding Genre: Fantasy	Using Context	Narrative / Narrative	www.storiestogrowby.com	Whootie Owl's Stories to Grow By
	I Wonder Why Snakes Shed Their Skins and Other Questions About Reptiles	Science Nonfiction	Categorizing Information / Recognizing Cause/Effect	Reading Suffixes	Expository / Descriptive	www.enature.com	Enature
	The Kids Invention Book	Nonfiction	Understanding Concepts / Relating to Personal Experiences	Reading Multisyllabic Words	Graphic Aid / Narrative	www.sln.org	The Science Learning Network
	Look What Came From Mexico	Social Studies Nonfiction	Understanding Chapters / Comparing/Contrasting	Reading Suffixes	Expository / Descriptive	www.mexonline.com/culture.htm	Mexico Art and Culture Directory

Level	Title	Genre	Comprehension Strategies	Phonics and Word-Solving Strategies	Writing Options	Technology	Web Site Sponsor
	Miss Rumphius	Fiction	Making Inferences Understanding Character	Reading Difficult Words	Descriptive Graphic Aid	www.kidsgardening.com	National Gardening Association
	A Picture Book of Sojourner Truth	Biography	Using Historical Context Understanding Genre: Biography	Recognizing Colloquialisms	Expository Expository	www.americaslibrary.gov	"America's Story" from the Library of Congress
	Where There Was Smoke	Social Studies Nonfiction	Identifying Problems/Solutions Making Predictions	Using Context	Persuasive Expository	www.nps.gov	National Park Service
P	26 Fairmount Avenue	Autobiography	Relating to Personal Experiences Understanding Chapters	Reading Multisyllabic Words	Narrative Descriptive	www.owl.english.perdue.edu	The Purdue University Online Writing Lab
	The Drum Beats On	Social Studies Nonfiction	Understanding Theme Making Inferences	Reading Words With -ing	Descriptive Expository	www.nmai.si.edu	National Museum of the American Indian
	The Eagle Has Landed	Social Studies Nonfiction	Understanding Sequence Understanding Historical Context	Reading Words With Suffixes	Graphic Aid Persuasive	www.nasm.edu	National Air and Space Museum
	Encyclopedia Brown Carries On	Mystery	Understanding Genre: Mystery Summarizing	Reading Unfamiliar Words	Narrative Descriptive	kids.mysterynet.com	MysteryNet's Kids Mysteries
	In the Rain Forest	Science Nonfiction	Recognizing Setting Understanding Point of View	Reading Unfamiliar Words	Persuasive Expository	www.ran.org	Rainforest Action Network
	The Magic School Bus Inside a Beehive	Science Nonfiction	Reading for Information Understanding Plot	Reading Informal Speech	Graphic Aid Descriptive	www.enature.com	Enature
	The Real McCoy: The Life of an African-American Inventor	Biography	Understanding Historical Context Understanding Character	Reading Compound Words	Descriptive Narrative	www.inventorsmuseum.com	Inventors Museum
	Shoebag	Fantasy	Evaluating Author's Purpose Understanding Story Development	Reading Unfamiliar Words	Persuasive Descriptive	www.scholastic.com	Scholastic
	Weather	Science Nonfiction	Summarizing Categorizing Information	Reading Words With Vowel Digraphs	Descriptive Persuasive	www.wildwildweather.com	Dan's Wild Wild Weather Page
	A Whale is Not a Fish and Other Animal Mix-ups	Science Nonfiction	Comparing/Contrasting Understanding Concepts	Understanding Plurals	Expository Descriptive	www.nwf.org/kids	National Wildlife Federation
Q	Adventures of the Shark Lady: Eugenie Clark Around the World	Biography	Summarizing Categorizing Information	Understanding Plurals	Graphic Aid Descriptive	www.aqua.org	National Aquarium In Baltimore
	American Tall Tales	Tall Tale	Understanding Sequence Understanding Exaggeration	Understanding Figurative Language	Descriptive Narrative	www.americaslibrary.gov	"America's Story" from the Library of Congress
	Animals of Long Ago	Science Nonfiction	Categorizing Information Understanding Chapters	Using Context	Graphic Aid Expository	www.amnh.org	American Museum of Natural History
	Exploring the Titanic	Social Studies Nonfiction	Recognizing Cause/Effect Comparing/Contrasting	Reading Words With Prefixes	Expository Narrative	www.encyclopedia-titanica.org	Encyclopedia Titanica
	Favorite Medieval Tales	Legend	Understanding Plot Understanding Character	Reading Suffixes	Narrative Expository	www.learner.org/exhibits/middleages	Learner.org
	Folktales from China	Folktale	Making Inferences Understanding Character	Reading Multisyllabic Words	Narrative Narrative	www.camla.org	The Chinese American Museum
	Help! I'm Trapped in the First Day of Summer Camp	Fantasy	Understanding Genre: Fantasy Making Predictions	Recognizing Colloquialisms	Narrative Narrative	www.scholastic.com	Scholastic
	...If You Lived With the Cherokee	Social Studies Nonfiction	Recognizing Cause/Effect Summarizing	Reading Unusual Language	Expository Narrative	www.nmai.si.edu	National Museum of the American Indian
R	Mary on Horseback Three Mountain Stories	Biography	Identifying Problems/Solutions Recognizing Setting	Reading Dialect	Narrative Graphic Aid	frontiernursing.org	Frontier Nursing Service
	Native American Art	Social Studies Nonfiction	Making Inferences Using Captions	Identifying Open Syllables	Descriptive Expository	www.nmai.si.edu	National Museum of the American Indian
	And Then What Happened, Paul Revere?	Biography	Reading for Information Understanding Character	Reading Historical Language	Graphic Aid Graphic Aid	www.paulreverehouse.org	The Paul Revere House
	Brian's Winter	Realistic Fiction	Recognizing Setting Making Predictions	Reading Words With Suffixes	Narrative Poetry	www.nps.gov	National Park Service
	Draw Me a Story	Biography	Understanding Chapters Understanding Character	Recognizing Possessives	Expository Expository	www.scholastic.com	Scholastic
	A Jar of Dreams	Historical Fiction	Understanding Theme Understanding Point of View	Reading Word Variations	Descriptive Poetry	americanhistory.si.edu/perfectunion	"A More Perfect Union: Japanese Americans and the U.S. Constitution" from Smithsonian
	Journey to Ellis Island: How My Father Came to America	Social Studies Nonfiction	Understanding Sequence Understanding Historical Context	Reading Words With Consonant + -le	Persuasive Expository	www.ellisisland.org	Ellis Island
	The Last Princess: The Story of Princess Ka'iulani of Hawai'i	Biography	Comparing/Contrasting Understanding Historical Context	Identifying Word Parts	Descriptive Narrative	www.hawaiianhistory.org	Hawaiian Historical Society
	Lewis and Clark	Social Studies Nonfiction	Making Inferences Using Primary Sources	Reading Historical Language	Narrative Graphic Aid	americanhistory.si.edu	National Museum of American History

Skills & Strategies Chart: Nonfiction Focus   175

Level	Title	Genre	Comprehension Strategies	Phonics and Word-Solving Strategies	Writing Options	Technology	Web Site Sponsor
	Listening to Crickets: A Story about Rachel Carson	Biography	Understanding Chapters; Identifying Problems/Solutions	Reading Words With Suffixes	Graphic Aid; Descriptive	www.rachelcarson.org	Rachel Carson.org
	Pigs Might Fly	Fantasy	Understanding Point of View; Summarizing	Reading Unusual Language	Descriptive; Narrative	www.scholastic.com	Scholastic
	The Tortoise Shell & Other African Stories	Folktale	Comparing/Contrasting; Understanding Metaphors and Similes	Reading Difficult Words	Narrative; Expository	www.storiestogrowby.com	Whootie Owl's Stories to Grow By
S	Ben and Me	Informational Fiction	Understanding Cause/Effect; Understanding Historical Context	Using Context	Expository; Narrative	www.inventorsmuseum.com	Inventors Museum
	Bessie Coleman	Biography	Understanding Chapters; Understanding Historical Context	Recognizing Variations of Words	Expository; Persuasive	www.firstflight.org	The First Flight Society
	The Broccoli Tapes	Realistic Fiction	Making Predictions; Understanding Character	Distinguishing Homonyms	Narrative; Graphic Aid	www.scholastic.com	Scholastic
	The Chicago Fire	Social Studies Nonfiction	Summarizing; Understanding Sequence	Reading Compound Words	Descriptive; Expository	www.nfpa.org	National Fire Protection Association
	Earthquake! A Story of Old San Francisco	Historical Fiction	Recognizing Setting; Understanding Point of View	Reading Words With Prefixes	Narrative; Graphic Aid	www.historyplace.com	The History Place
	Eureka! It's Television!	Science Nonfiction	Identifying Problems/Solutions; Using Diagrams	Reading Difficult Words	Descriptive; Persuasive	www.mtr.org	The Museum of Television & Radio
	In the Line of Fire: Eight Women War Spies	Biography	Understanding Cause/Effect; Summarizing	Understanding Plurals	Narrative; Expository	www.nwhp.org	National Women's History Project
	In the Year of the Boar and Jackie Robinson	Historical Fiction	Evaluating Author's Purpose; Understanding Theme	Reading Difficult Words	Narrative; Expository	www.baseballhalloffame.org	The National Baseball Hall of Fame
	Salsa Stories	Realistic Fiction	Understanding Point of View; Relating to Personal Experience	Understanding Colloquialisms	Descriptive; Descriptive	www.elmuseo.org	El Museo del Barrio
	The Star Fisher	Historical Fiction	Making Inferences; Understanding Long Sentences	Recognizing Synonyms	Expository; Expository	www.camla.org	The Chinese American Museum
T	The Big Lie: A True Story	Autobiography	Comparing/Contrasting; Understanding Historical Context	Using Context	Narrative; Narrative	www.ushmm.org	U.S. Holocaust Memorial Museum
	The Girl Who Chased Away Sorrow: The Diary of Sarah Nita, a Navajo Girl	Historical Fiction	Making Inferences; Using Maps and Graphic Aids	Reading Words With Consonant + -le	Expository; Persuasive	www.nmai.si.edu	National Museum of the American Indian
	Bonanza Girl	Historical Fiction	Recognizing Setting; Understanding Point of View	Reading Unusual Language	Persuasive; Descriptive	www.pbs.org/goldrush	Public Broadcasting Service
	Sleepers, Wake	Science Fiction	Making Predictions; Understanding Genre: Science Fiction	Reading Multisyllabic Words	Narrative; Persuasive	www.nasa.gov	National Aeronautics and Space Administration (NASA)
	Sounder	Realistic Fiction	Understanding Character; Relating to Personal Experience	Reading Informal Speech	Narrative; Descriptive	www.americaslibrary.gov	"America's Story" from the Library of Congress
	The Story of Levi's	Biography	Understanding Sequence; Identifying Problems/Solutions	Understanding Compound Words	Narrative; Graphic Aid	www.americaslibrary.gov	"America's Story" from the Library of Congress
	The Tall Tale of John Henry	Tall Tale	Recognizing Cause/Effect; Understanding Theme	Recognizing Colloquialisms	Narrative; Narrative	www.nrhs.com	National Railway Historical Society
	Under the Royal Palms: A Childhood in Cuba	Autobiography	Understanding Genre: Autobiography; Understanding Long Sentences	Recognizing Variations of Words	Expository; Narrative	www.almaada.com	Alma Flor Ada's web site
	Volcano: The Eruption and Healing of Mount St. Helens	Science Nonfiction	Summarizing; Using Diagrams	Reading Words With -ing	Expository; Expository	www.usgs.gov	U.S. Geological Survey
	Where Are the Wolves?	Science Nonfiction	Categorizing Information; Understanding Cause/Effect	Understanding Plurals	Expository; Narrative	www.wolf.org	International Wolf Center
U	First Ladies: Women Who Called the White House Home	Biography	Categorizing Information; Understanding Historical Context	Reading Multisyllabic Words	Expository; Persuasive	www.whitehouse.gov	The White House
	Geysers: When Earth Roars	Science Nonfiction	Reading for Information; Using Diagrams	Reading Words With Suffixes	Expository; Narrative	www.yellowstone.net/geysers	Yellowstone National Park
	Golden Games	Social Studies Nonfiction	Understanding Sequence; Understanding Genre: Nonfiction	Reading Words With Suffixes	Expository; Expository	www.olympic.org	International Olympic Committee
	Great Explorations	Biography	Understanding Main Idea/Details; Categorizing Information	Reading Multisyllabic Words	Expository; Narrative	www.historyplace.com	The History Place
	Hoang Anh: A Vietnamese-American Boy	Biography	Comparing/Contrasting; Summarizing	Understanding Compound Words	Narrative; Graphic Aid	www.pbs.org/kcet/newamericans	The New Americans web exhibition from PBS
	An Indian Winter	Social Studies Nonfiction	Understanding Point of View; Using Illustrations	Recognizing Synonyms	Expository; Narrative	www.nmai.si.edu	National Museum of the American Indian

Level	Title	Genre	Comprehension Strategies	Phonics and Word-Solving Strategies	Writing Options	Technology	Web Site Sponsor
	Midnight Magic	Mystery	Recognizing Setting / Understanding Theme	Using Context Clues	Narrative / Descriptive	www.avi-writer.com	Avi's web site
	The Secret Garden	Fiction	Understanding Character / Understanding Plot	Reading Unusual Language	Narrative / Narrative	www.scholastic.com	Scholastic
	Sir Arthur	Biography	Making Inferences / Recognizing Cause/Effect	Understanding Plurals	Narrative / Expository	www.fbi.gov	Federal Bureau of Investigation
	The Story of My Life	Autobiography	Relating to Personal Experiences / Understanding Figurative Language	Using Context	Descriptive / Expository	www.greatwomen.org	National Women's Hall of Fame
V	1000 Facts About Space	Science Nonfiction	Evaluating Author's Purpose / Reading for Information	Reading Multisyllabic Words	Expository / Narrative	www.nasa.gov	National Aeronautics and Space Administration (NASA)
	Alice In Wonderland	Fantasy	Understanding Genre: Fantasy / Recognizing Setting	Reading Unusual Language	Descriptive / Narrative	www.lewiscarroll.org/carroll.html	Lewis Carroll Society of North America
	Eleanor Roosevelt	Biography	Summarizing / Understanding Historical Context	Reading Words With -ed	Graphic Aid / Expository	www.un.org	United Nations
	Get on Board: The Story of the Underground Railroad	Social Studies Nonfiction	Recognizing Setting / Using a Time Line	Reading Words With Suffixes	Expository / Narrative	www.undergroundrailroad.org	National Underground Railroad Freedom Center
	Harry Potter and the Chamber of Secrets	Fantasy	Making Predictions / Understanding Theme	Reading Compound Words	Descriptive / Descriptive	www.scholastic.com/harrypotter	Scholastic
	How I Came to Be a Writer	Autobiography	Evaluating Author's Purpose / Understanding Genre: Autobiography	Using Common Spelling Patterns	Expository / Persuasive	owl.english.purdue.edu	The Purdue University Online Writing Lab
	The Music of Dolphins	Fiction	Making Inferences / Understanding Character	Working With Word Parts	Descriptive / Descriptive	www.scholastic.com	Scholastic
	Old Yeller	Realistic Fiction	Making Predictions / Understanding Plot	Recognizing Colloquialisms	Expository / Narrative	www.americaslibrary.gov	"America's Story" from the Library of Congress
	The True Confessions of Charlotte Doyle	Historical Fiction	Understanding Point of View / Understanding Diagrams	Using Context	Narrative / Narrative	www.historyplace.com	The History Place
	Under Wraps	Social Studies Nonfiction	Recognizing Main Idea/Details / Comparing/Contrasting	Reading Words With Greek or Latin Roots	Expository / Expository	www.virtual-egypt.com	Virtual-Egypt.com
W	Buried in Ice: The Mystery of a Lost Arctic Expedition	Social Studies Nonfiction	Identifying Problems/Solutions / Using Graphic Aids	Understanding Denotation and Connotation	Expository / Narrative	www.amnh.org	American Museum of Natural History
	Dive! My Adventures In the Deep Frontier	Science Nonfiction	Recognizing Main Idea/Details / Understanding Genre: Science Nonfiction	Identifying Open and Closed Syllables	Expository / Expository	www.aqua.org	National Aquarium in Baltimore
	The First Woman Doctor	Biography	Identifying Problems/Solutions / Summarizing	Reading Words With Consonant + le, -al, -el	Expository / Poetry	www.greatwomen.org	National Women's Hall of Fame
	From Rags to Riches	Biography	Understanding Character / Making Inferences	Recognizing Common and Proper Nouns	Descriptive / Poetry	www.s9.com/biography	Biographical Dictionary
	The Moon Bridge	Historical Fiction	Understanding Character / Recognizing Setting	Understanding Punctuation	Expository / Persuasive	americanhistory.si.edu/perfectunion	"A More Perfect Union: Japanese Americans and the U.S. Constitution" from Smithsonian
	Our World of Mysteries: Fascinating Facts About the Planet Earth	Science Nonfiction	Making Predictions / Recognizing Cause/Effect	Understanding Compound Words	Expository / Descriptive	www.archaeology.org	Archaeology Magazine
	The Phantom Tollbooth	Fantasy	Understanding Plot / Understanding Genre: Fantasy	Using Common Spelling Patterns	Descriptive / Narrative	www.scholastic.com	Scholastic
	Sea Otter Rescue: The Aftermath of an Oil Spill	Science Nonfiction	Evaluating Author's Purpose / Understanding Sequence	Reading Unfamiliar Words	Expository / Persuasive	www.wcs.org	Wildlife Conservation Society
	Through My Eyes	Autobiography	Recognizing Cause/Effect / Understanding Genre: Autobiography	Recognizing Variations of Words	Poetry / Expository	www.civilrights.org	The Leadership Conference on Civil Rights
	You Want Women to Vote, Lizzie Stanton?	Biography	Summarizing / Recognizing Main Idea/Details	Recognizing Antonyms	Persuasive / Descriptive	www.nwhp.org	National Women's History Project
X	Anne Frank: Beyond the Diary	Biography	Summarizing / Using Maps	Recognizing Synonyms	Narrative / Descriptive	www.ushmm.org	U.S. Holocaust Memorial Museum
	At Her Majesty's Request: An African Princess In Victorian England	Biography	Identifying Facts/Opinions / Drawing Conclusions	Understanding Homophones	Narrative / Descriptive	www.pbs.org/empires/victoria	"Queen Victoria's Empire" from PBS
	Bully for You, Teddy Roosevelt!	Biography	Sequencing / Recognizing Cause/Effect	Understanding Compound Words	Expository / Persuasive	www.theodoreroosevelt.org	Theodore Roosevelt Association
	Call It Courage	Fiction	Understanding Character / Relating to Personal Experiences	Reading Words With Suffixes	Graphic Aid / Narrative	pvs.hawaii.org	Polynesian Voyaging Society

Level	Title	Genre	Comprehension Strategies	Phonics and Word-Solving Strategies	Writing Options	Technology	Web Site Sponsor
	Children of the Wild West	Social Studies Nonfiction	Summarizing; Identifying Problems/Solutions	Using Context	Narrative; Graphic Aid	americanhistory.si.edu	National Museum of American History
	M.C. Higgins, the Great	Realistic Fiction	Making Inferences; Understanding Theme	Recognizing Dialect	Expository; Expository	www.osmre.gov	U.S. Office of Surface Mining
	One More River to Cross: The Stories of Twelve Black Americans	Biography	Comparing/Contrasting; Understanding Genre: Biography	Understanding Variations of Words	Graphic Aid; Persuasive	www.s9.com/biography	Biographical Dictionary
	Out of the Dust	Historical Fiction	Recognizing Setting; Understanding Point of View	Understanding Compound Words	Poetry; Narrative	www.scholastic.com	Scholastic
X	Sarah Bishop	Historical Fiction	Understanding Character; Understanding Plot	Reading Unfamiliar Words	Narrative; Persuasive	www.historyplace.com	The History Place
	Summer of Fire: Yellowstone 1988	Nonfiction	Categorizing Information; Recognizing Cause/Effect	Using Common Spelling Patterns	Expository; Persuasive	www.nps.gov	National Park Service
Y	Blizzard!	Social Studies Nonfiction	Paraphrasing; Understanding Historical Context	Understanding Strong Verbs	Expository; Graphic Aid	www.noaa.gov	National Oceanic and Atmospheric Administration
	Castle	Social Studies Nonfiction	Identifying Problems/Solutions; Understanding Sequence	Using Context	Expository; Expository	www.castles.org	Castles of the World
	The Colorado River	Social Studies Nonfiction	Recognizing Setting; Understanding Genre: Nonfiction	Understanding Compound Words	Persuasive; Graphic Aid	www.usgs.gov	U.S. Geological Survey
	The Day Martin Luther King, Jr., Was Shot: A Photo History of the Civil Rights Movement	Social Studies Nonfiction	Drawing Conclusions; Understanding Concepts	Understanding Punctuation	Graphic Aid; Expository	www.civilrights.org	The Leadership Conference on Civil Rights
	I Am an American: A True Story of Japanese Internment	Biography	Identifying Cause/Effect; Relating to Personal Experiences	Reading Words With Prefixes and Suffixes	Graphic Aid; Narrative	americanhistory.si.edu/perfectunion	"A More Perfect Union: Japanese Americans and the U.S. Constitution" from Smithsonian
	My Brother Sam Is Dead	Historical Fiction	Understanding Character; Understanding Point of View	Distinguishing Between Direct and Indirect Quotations	Narrative; Expository	americanhistory.si.edu	National Museum of American History
	Restless Spirit: The Life and Work of Dorothea Lange	Biography	Genre: Biography; Understanding Character	Working With Vowel Patterns	Narrative; Descriptive	www.photographymuseum.com	The American Museum of Photography
	Seeing Earth From Space	Science Nonfiction	Recognizing Main Idea/Details; Using Illustrations in Informational Texts	Reading Words With Prefixes	Expository; Persuasive	earth.jsc.nasa.gov	"Earth from Space" from NASA
	Tales Mummies Tell	Social Studies Nonfiction	Identifying Main Idea/Details; Making Predictions	Reading Words With Greek and Latin Roots	Narrative; Graphic Aid	www.virtual-egypt.com	Virtual-Egypt.com
	Tales of Real Escape	Biography	Understanding Genre: News Report; Understanding Story Development	Reading Words With Prefixes	Expository; Descriptive	www.nps.gov/alcatraz	Alcatraz Island
Z	Black Beauty	Fiction	Understanding Point of View; Understanding Sequence	Reading Difficult Words	Narrative; Persuasive	www.aspca.org	American Society for the Prevention of Cruelty to Animals
	City: A Story of Roman Planning and Construction	Social Studies Nonfiction	Understanding Steps in a Process; Using Diagrams	Using Context	Persuasive; Descriptive	www.planning.org	American Planning Association
	The Day the Women Got the Vote: A Photo History of the Women's Rights Movement	Social Studies Nonfiction	Categorizing Information; Recognizing Cause/Effect	Reading Words With Suffixes	Graphic Aid; Persuasive	www.nwhp.org	National Women's History Project
	Great Escapes of World War II	Social Studies Nonfiction	Comparing/Contrasting; Identifying Facts/Opinions	Recognizing Variations of Words	Expository; Descriptive	www.historyplace.com	The History Place
	The History of Emigration from China & Southeast Asia	Social Studies Nonfiction	Comparing/Contrasting; Using Maps	Reading Words With Prefixes	Expository; Expository	www.camla.org	The Chinese American Museum
	The Adventures of Tom Sawyer	Fiction	Understanding Character; Making Predictions	Using Context	Narrative; Play	www.scholastic.com	Scholastic
	Treasure Island	Fiction	Understanding Plot; Understanding Chapters	Using Context	Expository; Narrative	www.nationalgeographic.com/pirates	"Pirates!" from National Geographic
	Triumph on Everest: A Photobiography of Sir Edmund Hillary	Social Studies Nonfiction	Summarizing; Understanding Main Idea/Details	Reading Words With -ed	Expository; Expository	www.nationalgeographic.com	National Geographic
	We Shall Not Be Moved: The Women's Factory Strike of 1909	Social Studies Nonfiction	Identifying Problems/Solutions; Understanding Main Idea/Details	Reading Words With Suffixes	Persuasive; Narrative	www.dol.gov	U.S. Department of Labor
	Where the River Runs: A Portrait of a Refugee Family	Biography	Recognizing Cause/Effect; Comparing/Contrasting	Reading Figurative Language	Descriptive; Expository	www.pbs.org/kcet/newamericans	The New Americans web exhibition from PBS

Skills & Strategies Chart: Additional 6-Packs

Level	Title	Series	Author	Genre	Comprehension Strategy	Phonics and Word Study	Writing Options
A	I Can See		Klein, Adria	Informational Text	Reading for Information	Using Print Clues	description
A	I Like		Pinnell, Gay	Realistic Fiction	Recognizing Story Sequence	Reading Action Words	descriptive expository
A	Lunch		Pinnell, Gay	Realistic Fiction	Recognizing Story Pattern	Matching High-Frequency Words	description
A	My Cats		Robinson, Eileen	Realistic Fiction	Recognizing Story Pattern	Blending Simple Words	description
A	What Do Insects Do?	Emergent Reader	Canizares, Susan; Chanko, Pamela	Realistic Fiction	Reading for Information	Using Context	description
B	Hats Around the World		Charlesworth, Liza	Informational Text	Comparing and Contrasting	Reading Words with Consonant Blends	description
B	Lunch at the Zoo	Reading Discovery	Blaxland, Wendy; Brimage, C.	Informational Text	Making Predictions	Reading Naming Words for Animals	expository
B	Making Mountains	Reading Discovery	Gosset, Rachel; Ballinger, Margaret	Realistic Fiction	Understanding Characters' Feelings	Reading Unfamiliar Words	narrative
B	Who Lives in a Tree?	Emergent Reader	Canizares, Susan; Moreton, Daniel	Informational Text	Making Inferences	Reading Compound Words	expository
B	Who Lives in the Arctic?	Emergent Reader	Canizares, Susan; Chanko, Pamela	Informational Text	Using Picture Clues	Reading Plural Nouns	list
C	Bo and Peter	WiggleWorks	Franco, Betsy	Informational Text	Understanding Story Pattern	Reading Words with Consonant Blends	expository
C	Boots		Schreiber, Anne; Doughty, Arbo	Realistic Fiction	Understanding Story Development	Reading Unfamiliar Words	narrative
C	I Went Walking		Williams, Sue	Informational Text	Recognizing Patterned Text	Short Vowels	expository
C	Swing, Swing, Swing	WiggleWorks	Tuchman, G.; Dieterichs, S.	Fantasy	Understanding Story Development	Reading Contractions	narrative song
C	What Has Stripes?	Reading Discovery	Ballinger, Margaret	Informational Text	Using Illustrations	Reading Words with Consonant Blends	description
D	Don't Be Late		Gibson, Akimi	Realistic Fiction	Recognizing Story Pattern	Using a Rhyming Pattern	poem
D	I Love Mud and Mud Loves Me		Stephens, Vicki	Realistic Fiction	Recalling Story Details	Using Known Word Parts	play
D	I'm Hungry	Reading Discovery	Tuer, Judy	Realistic Fiction	Exploring Characters	Using Word Parts	list
D	Not Enough Water	Reading Discovery	Armstrong, Shane; Hartley, Susan	Realistic Fiction	Making Predictions	Using Context Clues	descriptive
D	Winter Is Here!		Weinberger, Kimberly	Informational Text	Discussing Setting	Focusing on Unfamiliar Words	descriptive poem
E	Ball Game, The	My First Hello Reader #4	Packard, David	Realistic Fiction	Recognizing Characters' Feelings	Using Known Words	descriptive
E	Collections	Reading Discovery	Ballinger, Margaret; Gosset, Rachel	Realistic Fiction	Understanding Theme and Character	Reading Compound Words	list
E	Five Little Monkeys Jumping on the Bed		Christelow, Eileen	Traditional Literature	Identifying Sequence of Events	Inflected Ending ed	poem
E	Just a Seed	Reading Discovery	Blaxland, Wendy	Informational Text	Understanding Sequence of Events	Reading Words with a Suffix	expository
E	Tree Can Be…, A	WiggleWorks	Nayer, Judy	Informational Text	Understanding Setting	Reading Words that Rhyme	poem
F	"What is That?" Said the Cat	Hello Reader	Maccarone, Grace	Fantasy	Understanding Plot	Reading Words with Consonant Blends	poem
F	Bread Bread Bread		Morris, Ann	Informational Text	Understanding Format	Reading Words with a Suffix	list
F	Itchy, Itchy Chicken Pox	Hello Reader	Maccarone, Grace	Realistic Fiction	Making Inferences	Reading Unfamiliar Words	narrative
F	Miss Mary Mack		Hoberman, Mary Ann	Traditional Literature	Recognizing Problem and Solution	Inflected Ending ed	Poem
F	Shoveling Snow	WiggleWorks	Cummings, Pat	Realistic Fiction	Recognizing Story Sequence	Reading Words with a Suffix	sequential narrative
G	All About You		Anholt, Catherine & Laurence	Informational Text	Making Categories	Reading Compound Words	list
G	Carrot Seed, The		Krauss, Ruth	Fantasy	Identifying Sequence of Events	Consonant Blends	expository
G	Each Peach Pear Plum		Ahlberg, Allan & Janet	Traditional Literature	Noting Details	Long i as in spy	sequential description
G	How Have I Grown?		Reid, Mary	Realistic Fiction	Comparing and Contrasting	Working with Word Parts	description
G	My Friends		Gomi, Taro	Fantasy	Exploring Picture Details	Working with Final /ch/	descriptive expository

Skills & Strategies Chart: Additional 6-Packs 179

Skills & Strategies Chart: Additional 6-Packs

Level	Title	Series	Author	Genre	Comprehension Strategy	Phonics and Word Study	Writing Options
H	ABC I Like Me!		Carlson, Nancy	Fantasy	Integrating Prior Knowledge	Consonant Blends	
H	George Shrinks		Joyce, William	Fantasy	Distinguishing between Fantasy and Reality	Reading Action Words	instructions
H	Look-Alike Animals		Bernard, Robin	Informational Text	Comparing and Contrasting	Reading Words with a Suffix	descriptive narrative
H	Ten, Nine, Eight		Bang, Molly	Realistic Fiction	Making Predictions	Digraphs	descriptive list
H	Whose Mouse Are You?		Kraus, Robert	Fantasy	Recognizing Text Pattern	Reading Possessive Words with 's	
I	Apples and Pumpkins		Rockwell, Ann	Realistic Fiction	Finding Story Information in Illustrations	Reading Compound Words	descriptive narrative
I	Leo the Late Bloomer		Kraus, Robert	Fantasy	Making Inferences	Dipthong oo	expository
I	Little Mouse, the Red Ripe Strawberry, and the Big Hungry Bear, The		Wood, Audrey; Wood, Don	Fantasy	Understanding Concepts	Reading Words with r- Controlled Vowels	descriptive narrative
I	Noisy Nora		Wells, Rosemary	Fantasy	Making Predictions	Reading Unfamiliar Words	poem
I	This Is the Place for Me		Cole, Joanna	Fantasy	Using Illustrations	Reading words with Long o	narrative
J	Bear's Bargain		Asch, Frank	Fantasy	Understanding Problems and Solutions	Reading Words with a Suffix	narrative
J	City Mouse–Country Mouse		Wallner, John	Traditional Literature	Understanding Plot and Setting	Using Known Words	graphic aid
J	Fox and His Friends		Marshall, Edward	Fantasy	Understanding Sequence of Events	Reading Contractions	play expository
J	Insects	Reading Discovery	MacLulich, Carolyn	Informational Text	Understanding Theme	Reading Words Parts	
J	Magic Fish, The		Rylant, Cynthia	Traditional Literature	Making Predictions	Finding Common Elements in Words	poem narrative
K	Bedtime for Frances		Hoban, Russell	Fantasy	Reading Dialogue	Recognizing Base Words	narrative
K	Blind Men and the Elephant, The	Hello Reader - Level 3	Backstein, Karen	Traditional Literature	Making Inferences	Using Context Clues	descriptive
K	Bremen-town Musicians, The		Gross, Ruth Below	Traditional Literature	Making Predictions	Reading Words with ou and ow	descriptive letter
K	Frog and Toad are Friends		Lobel, Arnold	Fantasy	Identifying Problem and Solution	Reviewing Final e	letter descriptive/narrative
K	Jamaica's Find		Havill, Juanita	Realistic Fiction	Understanding a Character's Feelings	Reading Two-Syllable Words	play
L	Alexander and the Wind-Up Mouse		Lionni, Leo	Fantasy	Understanding Compare and Contrast	Using Structural Analysis to Read Compound Words	descriptive
L	Big Al		Yoshi, Andrew C.	Fantasy	Making Inferences	Reading Words with -ed	narrative
L	Happy Birthday, Martin Luther King		Marzollo, Jean	Biography	Summarizing	Reading Words with -ed	expository
L	Horrible Harry in Room 2B		Kline, Suzy	Realistic Fiction	Drawing Conclusions	Homophones	expository
L	Miss Nelson Is Missing!		Allard, Harry	Realistic Fiction	Making Inferences	Inflected Ending s	description
M	Art Lesson, The		DePaola, Tomie	Realistic Fiction	Summarizing	Prepositions	description
M	Aunt Flossie's Hats		Howard, Elizabeth	Realistic Fiction	Identifying Main Idea and Details	Adjectives	description
M	Chair for My Mother, A		Williams, Vera B.	Realistic Fiction	Summarizing the Story	Understanding Difficult Words	expository
M	Cloudy with a Chance of Meatballs		Barrett, Judi	Fantasy	Learning about Genre	Analyzing Compound Words	graphic aid/descriptive
M	George Washington's Mother		Fritz, Jean	Informational Text	Recognizing the Characteristics of a Biography	Using Known Word Parts	descriptive poem

Skills & Strategies Chart: Additional 6-Packs

Level	Title	Series	Author	Genre	Comprehension Strategy	Phonics and Word Study	Writing Options
N	Amber Brown Is Not a Crayon		Danziger, Paula	Realistic Fiction	Understanding Character	Using Context Clues	expository
N	Donavan's Word Jar		DeGross, Monalisa	Realistic Fiction	Recognizing Story Structure	Pronoun	expository list
N	Popcorn Book, The		DePaola, Tomie	Informational Text	Understanding Sequence	Using Picture and Context Clues	narrative
N	Rumpelstiltskin		Zelinsky, Paul O.	Traditional Literature	Exploring Illustrations	Understanding Word Meaning	song narrative
N	Stories Julian Tells, The		Cameron, Ann	Realistic Fiction	Making Inferences	Adjectives	descriptive narrative
O	Borreguita and the Coyote		Aardema, Verna	TL	Understanding the Main Idea	Reading Unfamiliar Words	graphic aid/expository
O	Boxcar Children #1, The	Boxcar Children #1	Chandler, Gertrude Warner	Realistic Fiction	Solving Problems	Using Context Clues	descriptive graphic aid
O	Class President		Hurwitz, Johanna	Realistic Fiction	Drawing Conclusions	Past Tense Verbs	descriptive narrative
O	King's Equal, The		Paterson, Katherine	Traditional Literature	Understanding Reality and Fantasy	Suffix -ful	descriptive narrative
O	Legend of the Bluebonnet, The		DePaola, Tomie	Traditional Literature	Solving Problems	Reading Unfamiliar Words	expository/descriptive
P	If You Lived in Colonial Times		McGovern, Ann	Informational Text	Comparing and Contrasting	Reading Period Speech	playgraphic aid
P	Magic School Bus® Inside the Earth, The	Magic School Bus, The	Cole, Joanna; Degen, Bruce	Fantasy	Recognizing Main Idea and Details	Using the Appendix	graphic aid descriptive
P	Riding Freedom		Ryan, Pam Munoz	Historical Fiction	Identifying Problem and Solution	Adjectives	expository
P	Stone Fox		Gardiner, John Reynolds	Realistic Fiction	Making Predictions	Multisyllabic Words	descriptive narrative
P	Wild Weather: Hurricanes!	Hello Reader Science	Hopping, Lorraine	Informational Text	Remembering Facts and Details	Looking for Direct Definitions	graphic aid expository
Q	Dear Mr. Henshaw		Cleary, Beverly	Realistic Fiction	Making Inferences	Syllabication: Consonant + le	descriptive letter
Q	Homer Price		McCloskey, Robert	Realistic Fiction	Drawing Conclusions	Root Words	descriptive narrative
Q	I Have a Dream		Davidson, Margaret	B	Making Inferences	Reading Difficult Words	expository
Q	Tales of a Fourth Grade Nothing		Blume, Judy	Realistic Fiction	Visualizing	Consonant Doubling	descriptive narrative
Q	True Story of the Three Little Pigs, The		Scieszka, Jon	Traditional Literature	Understanding Point of View	Using Context Clues	descriptive persuasive

Skills & Strategies Chart: Additional 6-Packs

Level	Title	Series	Author	Genre	Comprehension Strategy	Phonics and Word Study	Writing Options
R	Adventures of Spider, The		Arkhurst, Joyce C.	Traditional Literature	Making Inferences	Reading Difficult Words	descriptive
R	Can It Rain Cats and Dogs?	Scholastic Q & A	Berger, Melvin & Gilda	Informational Text	Identifying Cause and Effect	Latin and Greek Roots	expository
R	Great Kapok Tree, The		Cherry, Lynne	Informational Text	Exploring Theme	Using Structural Analysis	play
R	Library Card, The		Spinelli, Jerry	Realistic Fiction	Making Inferences	Figurative Language: Metaphors	narrative
R	Sarah, Plain and Tall		MacLachlan, Patricia	Historical Fiction	Comparing and Contrasting	Past Tense Verbs	descriptive letter
S	Gold Cadillac		Taylor, Mildred D.	Historical Fiction	Summarizing	Compound Words	expository
S	Great Gilly Hopkins, The		Paterson, Katherine	Realistic Fiction	Exploring Character Development	Adjectives	descriptive letter
S	Lon Po Po		Young, Ed	Traditional Literature	Making Predictions	Using Context Clues	narrative play
S	Rough-Face Girl, The		Martin, Rafe; Shannon, David	Traditional Literature	Recognizing Genre: Fairy Tales	Understanding Connotations	descriptive/graphic aid
S	Sideways Arithmetic from Wayside School		Sachar, Louis	Informational Text	Drawing Conclusions	Questions Marks	persuasive letter
T	Bridge to Terabithia*		Paterson, Katherine	Realistic Fiction	Problem/Solution	Open Syllables	descriptive persuasive
T	Dear Levi: Letters from the Overland Trail		Woodruff, Elvira	Historical Fiction	Exploring Setting	Suffix -ly	descriptive letter
T	George vs. George		Schanzer, Rosalyn	Informational Text	Recognizing Cause and Effect	Adjectives	descriptive letter
T	Ripley's Incredible Insects		Gilcow, Louise	Informational Text	Comparing and Contrasting	Multisyllabic Words	expository
T	Steal Away		Armstrong, Jennifer	Realistic Fiction	Understanding Characters	Using Context Clues	letter
U	Bud, Not Buddy		Curtis, Christopher Paul	Realistic Fiction	Recognizing Story Structure	Prefix -un	descriptive letter
U	Ella Enchanted		Carson Levine, Gail	Fantasy	Problem/Solution	Consonant + le Syllables	narrative persuasive/letter
U	Julie of the Wolves		George, Jean Craighead	Realistic Fiction	Exploring Setting	Antonyms	descriptive letter
U	Knots in My Yo-Yo String		Spinelli, Jerry	Biography	Summarizing	Compound Words	descriptive expository
U	Rosa Parks: My Story		Parks, Rosa	Biography	Identifying Main Idea and Details	Context Clues	expository list

Skills & Strategies Chart: Additional 6-Packs

Level	Title	Series	Author	Genre	Comprehension Strategy	Phonics and Word Study	Writing Options
V	Esperanza Rising		Ryan, Pam Munoz	Historical Fiction	Exploring Character Development	Antonyms	descriptive narrative
V	Golden Goblet, The		McGraw, Eloise Jarvis	Realistic Fiction	Problem/Solution	Open Syllables	narrative letter
V	Long Way from Chicago, A		Peck, Richard	Historical Fiction	Cause/Effect	Closed Syllables	expository narrative
V	Rascal		North, Sterling	Historical Fiction	Exploring Setting	Prefix re–	persuasive
V	Stealing Home		Denenberg, Barry	Biography	Identifying Cause and Effect	Multisyllabic Words	expository
W	Around the World in a Hundred Years		Fritz, Jean	Informational Text	Categorizing Information	Final e Syllables	expository/graphic aid narrative
W	Crispin: Cross of Lead		Avi	Historical Fiction	Exploring Character Development	Adverbs	narrative
W	Roll of Thunder, Hear My Cry		Taylor, Mildred D	Historical Fiction	Plot	Common and Proper Nouns	persuasive letter
W	Slam!*		Myers, Walter Dean	Realistic Fiction	Exploring Setting	Figurative Language: Similes	descriptive narrative
W	Walk Two Moons		Creech, Sharon	Realistic Fiction	Sequence	Vowel Digraphs	expository narrative
X	Any Small Goodness*		Johnston, Tony	Realistic Fiction	Clarifying Story Ideas	Figurative Language: Similes	descriptive narrative
X	Childtimes		Greenfield, Eloise; Little, Lessie Jones	Biography	Setting	Common Spelling Patterns	play
X	Cleopatra		Green, Robert	Biography	Genre: Biography	Unfamiliar Words	graphic aid/expository narrative
X	Jackie's Nine		Robinson, Sharon	Biography	Comparing and Contrasting	Antonyms	expository
X	Memories of Anne Frank		Gold, Alison Leslie	Biography	Identifying Cause and Effect	Open Syllables	expository
Y	Bull Run		Fleischman, Paul	Historical Fiction	Main Idea/Details	Closed Syllables	narrative play
Y	Call of the Wild, The	Scholastic Jr. Classic	London, Jack	Realistic Fiction	Compare/Contrast	Vowel Digraphs	graphic aid expository
Y	Philip Hall Likes Me. I Reckon Maybe		Greene, Bette	Realistic Fiction	Draw Conclusions	Open and Closed Syllables	narrative graphic aid
Y	Sacajawea		Bruchac, Joseph	Biography	Problem/Solution	Silent Final e	graphic aid descriptive
Y	White Fang		London, Jack	Realistic Fiction	Exploring Character Development	Short Vowels	descriptive letter
Z	Adventures of Huckleberry Finn, The	Apple Classic	Twain, Mark	Historical Fiction	Exploring Character Development	Context Clues	descriptive narrative
Z	Circuit, The		Francisco, Jimenez	Historical Fiction	Compare/Contrast	r-Controlled Vowel Syllables	graphic aid/narrative letter
	Louis Armstrong*	Impact Biography	Brown, Sandford	Biography	Draw Conclusions	Vowel Digraphs	descriptive expository
	Raven and Other Poems, The	Scholastic Classic	Poe, Edgar Allen	Poem	Making Inferences	Syllables with Vowel and Silent e	expository descriptive
	Red Scarf Girl		Jiang, Ji Li	Biography	Problem/Solution	Vowel Digraphs	expository

GUIDED READING RESEARCH BASE

Essential Element	Key Ideas—National Reading Panel
Phonemic Awareness Instruction in Guided Reading • Children use their beginning connections between letters and sounds to check on their reading. They notice mismatches. They use letter-sound information to know how words begin. • Teachers prompt children to make their reading "look right."	"Phonemic awareness instruction is not a complete reading program; it cannot guarantee the reading and writing success of your students. Long lasting effects depend on the effectiveness of the whole curriculum." (3, p. 9) "Phonemic awareness instruction does not need to consume long periods of time to be effective. In these analyses, programs lasting less than 20 hours were more effective than longer programs." (2, p. 2–6) "In addition to teaching phonemic awareness skills with letters, it is important for teachers to help children make the connection between the skills taught and their application to reading and writing tasks." (2, p. 2–33)
Phonics Instruction in Guided Reading • Teachers select texts that, along with high-frequency words that are available to students, offer opportunities to use phonics skills. • As they introduce texts, support reading, and revisit the text after reading, teachers bring students' attention to features of words and strategies for decoding words. • Students apply word solving strategies to reading continuous texts. • Teachers explicitly demonstrate how to take words apart and apply phonics principles to new words students meet in continuous text. • Teachers explicitly teach phonics principles through word work after the text is read. Word work sessions are connected to a phonics continuum. • Teachers prompt students to use phonics skills to take words apart while reading.	"Children need opportunities to use what they have learned in problem solving unfamiliar words that they encounter within continuous text. They use word solving strategies to take words apart while keeping the meaning in mind." (3, p. 18) "Reading words accurately and automatically enables children to focus on the meaning of text." (3) "Programs should acknowledge that systematic phonics instruction is a means to an end. Some phonics programs focus primarily on teaching children a large number of letter-sound relationships. These programs often do not allot enough instructional time to help children learn how to put this knowledge to use in reading actual words, sentences, and texts. Although children need to be taught the major consonant and vowel letter-sound relationships, they also need ample reading and writing activities that allow them to practice this knowledge." (3, p. 17)
Fluency Instruction in Guided Reading • Texts are selected to be within students' control so that they know most of the words and can read fluently (with teaching). • The teacher introduces the text to support comprehension and connections to language. • Teachers draw students' attention to elements of words that will help them recognize or solve them rapidly.	"If text is read in a laborious and inefficient manner, it will be difficult for the child to remember what has been read and to relate the ideas expressed in the text to his or her background knowledge." (1, p. 22) "Repeated and monitored oral reading improves reading fluency and overall reading achievement." (3, p. 11) "It is important to provide students with instruction and practice in fluency as they read connected text." (3, p. 23) "Word recognition is a necessary but not sufficient condition for fluent reading." (3, p. 30) "Fluency is not a stage of development at which readers can read all words quickly and easily. Fluency changes, depending on what readers are reading, their familiarity with the words, and the amount of their practice with reading text." (3, p. 23)

• Teachers help students to understand and use the language patterns that may be found in written text. • Students use word recognition and comprehending strategies in an orchestrated way while reading or rereading a text silently or orally. • Teachers provide explicit demonstrations and instruction in reading fluency. • Teachers prompt for fluency when students are reading aloud. • Students engage in repeated oral readings to work for fluency.	"By listening to good models of fluent reading, students learn how a reader's voice can help written text make sense." (3, p. 26) "Fluency develops as a result of many opportunities to practice reading with a high degree of success. Therefore, your students should practice orally rereading text that is reasonably easy for them—that is, text containing mostly words that they know or can decode easily." (3, p. 27)
Vocabulary Instruction in Guided Reading • Texts are selected so that students know most of the words but there are a few new words to provide opportunities for learning. • The teacher introduces the text to support comprehension, with specific attention to concepts and words. • Students read the text silently or orally with teacher support. • After reading, students and teacher discuss the meaning of the text, with further discussion of word meanings if needed. • The teacher teaches processing strategies, which may include both word recognition and how to determine word meanings. • Students may extend the meaning of the text through writing, which often includes attention to vocabulary. • The teacher provides 1–2 minutes of pre-planned word work which helps students attend to word parts and word meanings (affixes, word structure, homophones, synonyms, etc.).	"Extended instruction that promotes active engagement with vocabulary improves word learning." (3, p. 36) "Teaching specific words before reading helps both vocabulary learning and reading comprehension." (3, p. 36) "Repeated exposure to vocabulary in many contexts aids word learning." (3, p. 36) "Conversations about books help children to learn new words and concepts and to relate them to their prior knowledge and experience." (3, p. 35) "… the larger the reader's vocabulary (either oral or print), the easier it is to make sense of the text." (1, p. 13) "… children often hear adults repeat words several times. They also may hear adults use new and interesting words. The more oral language experiences children have, the more word meanings they learn." (3, p. 35)
Comprehension Instruction in Guided Reading • Teachers select texts that readers can process successfully with supportive teaching. • The teacher demonstrates effective strategies for comprehending text. • In the introduction to the text, the teacher explains words and concepts and assures that students activate their own prior knowledge. • Students have the opportunity to apply a range of strategies in response to the demands of texts.	"Comprehension is defined as 'intentional thinking during which meaning is constructed through interactions between text and reader' (Harris & Hodges, 1995). Thus, readers derive meaning from text when they engage in intentional, problem-solving thinking processes. The data suggest that text comprehension is enhanced when readers actively relate the ideas represented in print to their own knowledge and experiences and construct mental representations in memory." (1, p. 14) "In general, the evidence suggests that teaching a combination of reading comprehension techniques is the most effective. When students use them appropriately, they assist in recall, question answering, question generation, and summarization of texts. When used in combination, these techniques can improve results in standardized comprehension tests." (1, p. 15) "Text comprehension can be improved by instruction that helps readers use specific comprehension strategies." (2, p. 49)

• Students expand strategies by applying them, with teacher support, to texts that are more difficult than they could read independently. • Teachers help students extend their understandings through using oral language and writing. • Teachers help students extend their understanding through using graphic organizers to understand underlying text structures. • While teachers are working with students in small groups, other students read independently the books that they have previously read.	"Text comprehension can be improved by instruction that helps readers use specific comprehension strategies." (3, p. 9) "Graphic organizers illustrate concepts and interrelationships among concepts in a text, using diagrams or other pictorial devices. Regardless of the label, graphic organizers can help readers focus on concepts and how they are related to other concepts." "Comprehension strategies are not ends in themselves; they are means of helping your students understand what they are reading." (3, p. 6) "Help your students learn to use comprehension strategies in natural learning situations—for example, as they read in the content areas." (3, p. 65) "Readers must know what most of the words mean before they can understand what they are reading." (3, p. 45) "Children learn many new words by reading extensively on their own. The more children read on their own, the more words they encounter and the more word meanings they learn." (3, p. 35) "Teachers not only must have a firm grasp of the content presented in text, but also must have substantial knowledge of the strategies themselves, of which strategies are most effective for different students and types of content and of how best to teach and model strategy use." (1, p. 16)
Motivation Support in Guided Reading • Teachers select books that will be interesting to students. • Teachers introduce texts in a way that engages interest and motivation.	"Few if any studies have investigated the contribution of motivation to the effectiveness of phonics programs, not only the learner's motivation to learn but also the teacher's motivation to teach. The lack of attention to motivational factors by researchers in the design of phonics programs is potentially very serious … Future research should … be designed to determine which approaches teachers prefer to use and are most likely to use effectively in their classroom instruction." (2)
Motivation Support in Guided Reading • Teachers select books that will be interesting to students. • Teachers introduce texts in a way that engages interest and motivation.	"Interesting texts also provide mutual cognitive and motivational benefits (Schiefele, 1999). When students are interested in what they read, they process the material more deeply, gain richer conceptual understandings, and engage more fully with text." (4, p. 416)
Motivation Related to Reading Comprehension • Students who receive motivation support and strategy instruction improve their reading comprehension.	"Motivated students usually want to understand text content fully, and therefore, process information deeply. As they read frequently with these cognitive purposes, motivated students gain in reading proficiency. However, motivation and engagement have rarely been incorporated into experimental studies of instruction or interventions for reading comprehension." (4, p. 403) "(a) Engagement in reading refers to interaction with text that is simultaneously motivated and strategic, (b) engaged reading correlates with achievement in reading comprehension, (c) engaged reading and its constituents (motivation and cognitive strategies) can be increased by instruction practices directed toward them, and (d) an instructional framework that merges motivational and cognitive strategy support in reading will increase engaged reading and reading comprehension." (4, p. 403)

Effect of Engagement on Interest in Reading • Motivated readers are able to monitor their comprehension, recall what they read, and retain and organize the knowledge they gain. • Motivated readers are involved in their reading, often rereading and reflecting on their understanding. • Motivated readers know how reading is relevant to their lives. • Engaged readers find that reading is a meaningful, enjoyable activity.	"…the most highly interested students had positive affect toward books, favored certain authors, and enjoyed favorite topics. These high interest readers typically reread all or portions of books, pursued topics in and out of school, and connected reading to their personal experiences or feelings. Also salient was the students' deep comprehension and complex cognitive command of these texts that accompanied their enjoyment and enthusiasm. Students with high positive affect for a certain topic invariably had deep recollection of information or books about the topic, whereas students with low affect for reading on a topic displayed little recall and grasp of content. This suggests that high interest in reading is not limited to the strong, positive affect surrounding books, but also the high comprehension, recall, and organization of knowledge in memory typical of these readers." (5, p. 13)
Readers' Motivation to Be Responsible for Their Own Learning • Engaged readers are in control of their own learning and are able to express their opinions and their own understandings.	"A substantial proportion of students reported that knowledge and information was what they were seeking in books. We did not create this as a formal construct nor place it in our rubric, because we did not systematically ask all students about the extent that they read for knowledge. However, many students volunteered that they wanted to learn about their favorite topic, enjoyed gaining information, or liked being very well informed in certain domains. Being knowledgeable was an explicit goal mentioned by many, and while it is a commonsense purpose for reading, it has not been formalized quantitatively in prior research as a motivational construct. We believe that reading for the purpose of knowledge development is a vitally important motivational attribute for future investigation." (5, p. 26)
Readers' Engagement With Text • For engaged readers, reading is a highly visual experience as they imagine characters, settings, and events. • Readers who are emotionally engaged in text can often note and understand ideas the author does not explicitly state. • Readers engage in an interchange of ideas between themselves and the text.	"…reading narrative text is often affectively laden, and that readers adopt affective goals for narrative reading. They seek excitement, emotional relationship with characters, interpersonal drama, and a range of aesthetic experiences. Reading information books, in contrast, is energized by goals of reading for knowledge, seeking information, and the desire to explain our physical or cultural worlds. Thus, motivations for reading narrative and information books should be distinguished in studying how motivation develops or how it relates to other factors such as reading comprehension." (5, pp. 26-27)
Features of Engaging Classrooms • Engaging classrooms are observational, conceptual, self-directed, strategic, collaborative, coherent, and personalized.	"To increase motivational development, teachers should provide support for situated experiences that increase intrinsic motivation. For example, an exciting activity that may be entertaining, such as reader's theater for a specific book, may increase situated, intrinsic motivation. Likewise, hands-on activities with science materials (a terrarium with plants and animals, or a field trip to a park) or hands-on activities in history (a reenactment of a historical scene within the classroom) will increase situated, intrinsic motivation for texts related to these topics. However, these events will be insufficient to influence long-term motivation for reading. Experimental evidence suggests that increasing generalized intrinsic motivation requires the extended classroom practices of support for students' choices, collaborations, use of interesting texts, and real-world interactions related to literacy." (6, p. 21)

The ideas in this chart are referenced to the following documents:

(1) National Institute of Child Health and Human Development. (2001). *Report of the National Reading Panel: Teaching Children to Read: An Evidence-Based Assessment of the Scientific Research Literature on Reading and Its Implications for Reading Instruction.* Washington, DC: National Institutes of Health.

(2) National Institute of Child Health and Human Development. (2001). *Report of the National Reading Panel: Teaching Children to Read: An Evidence-Based Assessment of the Scientific Research Literature on Reading and Its Implications for Reading Instruction: Report of the Subgroups.* Washington, DC: National Institutes of Health.

(3) Armbruster, B. B., Lehr, F., & Osborn, J. (2001). *Put Reading First: The Research Building Blocks for Teaching Children to Read, Kindergarten through Grade 3.* Washington, DC: U.S. Department of Education.

[i] "Readers must know what most of the words mean before they can understand what they are reading." (*Put Reading First,* p. 45)

[ii] "Beginning readers use their oral vocabulary to make sense of the words they see in print ... Readers must know what most of the words mean before they can understand what they are reading." (*Put Reading First,* p. 45)

(4) Guthrie, John T.; Wigfield, Allan; Barbosa, Pedro, et al., "Increasing Reading Comprehension and Engagement Through Concept-Oriented Reading Instruction," *Journal of Education Psychology,* 2004, Vol. 96, No 3, 403–423.

(5) Guthrie, John T.; Hoa, Laurel W.; Wigfield, Allan; Tonks, Stephen M.; Humneick, Nicole M.; Littles, Erin, "Reading Motivation and Reading Comprehension Growth in the Later Elementary Years," *Contemporary Educational Psychology,* June 3, 2006.

(6) Guthrie, John T.; Hoa, Laurel W.; Wigfield, Allan; Tonks, Stephen M.; Perencevich, Kathleen C., "From Spark to Fire: Can Situational Reading Interest Lead to Long Term Reading Motivation?" *Reading Research and Instruction,* v45, n2, pp. 91–117, Winter 2006, College Reading Association, Brigham Young University, Provo, UT.

BIBLIOGRAPHY

Anderson, E., and Guthrie, J. T. (1999). *Motivating children to gain conceptual knowledge from text: The combination of science observation and interesting texts*. Paper presented at the annual meeting of the American Educational Research Association, Montreal, Canada.

Blevins, Wiley, and Boynton, Alice. "5 Keys to Reading Nonfiction." *The Art of Teaching*. Supplement to *Instructor Magazine*: 4–7.

Brown, H., and Cambourne, B. (1987). *Read and retell: A strategy for the whole-language/natural learning classroom*. Portsmouth, NH: Heinemann.

Chall, J. S. (1983). *Stages of reading development*. New York: McGraw-Hill.

Clay, M. M. (1993). *Reading Recovery: A Guidebook for Teachers in Training*. Portsmouth, NH: Heinemann.

Dreher, M. J. (2000). Fostering reading for learning. In L. Baker, M. J. Dreher & J. Guthrie (Eds.), *Engaging young readers: Promoting achievement and motivation* (pp. 94–118). New York: Guilford.

Duke, Nell K., and Bennett-Armistead, V. Susan (2003). *Reading & Writing Informational Text in the Primary Grades: Research-Based Practices*. New York, NY: Scholastic Inc.

Gibson, Akimi, Gold, Judith, and Sgouras, Charissa. (2003). "The Power of Story Retelling." *The Tutor*. Spring 2003.

Fountas, Irene, and Pinnell, G. S. (1996). *Guided Reading: Good First Teaching for All Children*. Portsmouth, NH: Heinemann.

Fountas, Irene, and Pinnell, G. S. (2001). *Guiding Readers and Writers, Grades 3–6*. Portsmouth, NH: Heinemann.

Fountas, Irene, and Pinnell, G. S., eds. (1999). *Voices on Word Matters*. Portsmouth, NH: Heinemann.

Jobe, R., & Dayton-Sakari, M. (2002). *Infokids: How to use nonfiction to turn reluctant readers into enthusiastic learners*. Markham, Ontario, Canada: Pembroke.

Kamil, M. L., & Lane, D. M. (1998). Researching the relation between technology and literacy: An agenda for the 21st century. In D. R. Reinking, L. D. Labbo, M. McKenna, & R. Kieffer (Eds.), *Literacy for the 21st century: Technological transformations in a post-typographic world* (pp. 235–251). Mahwah, NJ: Erlbaum.

Pinnell, Gay Su, and Fountas, I. C. (1999). *Matching Books to Readers: A Leveled Book List for Guided Reading, K–3*. Portsmouth, NH: Heinemann.

Pinnell, Gay Su, and Fountas, I. C. (1998). *Word Matters: Teaching Phonics and Spelling in the Reading/Writing Classroom*. Portsmouth, NH: Heinemann.

Pinnell, G. S., Pikulski, J. J., Wixson, K. K., Campbell, J. R., Gough, R. B., and Beatty, A. S. (1995). *Listening to Children Read Aloud: Data from NAEP's Integrated Reading Performance Record (IPRR) at Grade 4*. Report No. 23-FR-04 Prepared by Educational Testing Service under contract with the National Center for Education Statistics, Office of Educational Research and Improvement, U.S. Department of Education. (p. 15)

Venezky, R. L. (1982). The origins of the present-day chasm between adult literacy needs and school literacy instruction. *Visible Language, 16*, 112–127.

RESEARCH AND VALIDATION

A strong pattern of rising scores has been found in schools where daily guided reading has been combined with phonics and word study mini-lessons and daily writing workshops. For further information, see:

Williams, Jane. (2002). The power of data utilization in bringing about systemic school change. *Mid-Western Educational Researcher, 15*, 4–10.

Williams, E. J., Scharer, P., & Pinnell, G. S. (2000). *Literacy Collaborative 2002 Research Report*. Columbus, OH: The Ohio State University.

Scharer, P., Williams, E. J., & Pinnell, G. S. (2001). *Literacy Collaborative 2001 Research Report*. Columbus, OH: The Ohio State University.